Unbroken Soul

An Albanian girl's escape
from terror to freedom

YLLKA SINANI THOMPSON

Cover photo © Mario Bineri

Editing, design, typesetting and publishing by UK Book Publishing

www.ukbookpublishing.com

ISBN: 978-1-915338-99-0

To: Gill! xxx

"THE TRUE STORY OF
THE MOUNTAIN GIRL."

Love and Best Wishes

Yllka Thompson

CHAPTER 1

Escaping hell

The drive to the airport was eerie; the streets were dark and deserted. Not a soul stirred as we passed; no lights gleamed from the desolate shops and small cafes. Scarily silent, nothing moved, even the trees on the upper side of the road didn't rustle, as if they were paralysed with fear. They seemed to understand my sceptical feelings as if they read in my eyes my fear of the unknown, the truth or the lie. In the distance, dogs barked and a mournful howl split the night as the car slid away along the old dirt road, covered as it was in the grey dust that was scattered and lost in the half-light of early morning. Dawn sat on the horizon, and as the sun rose slowly it lit up the city, shining on the abandoned shops and ruined buildings. The country I loved had perished. The busy, bustling city of Tirana had ceased to exist, turning into a ghost town.

The more we moved away the more I felt this deep emptiness, the pain and sadness inside me grow. I drew my children, Enea and Hope, into my arms, holding them close, staring through the windows as outside, life as I knew it passed away before my eyes, while I thought nervously about the unknown future ahead. I felt a lump rise in my throat as I fought back the tears and tried to get rid of the rock that was gathered and hidden somewhere inside my wounded soul. I smiled down at my little ones and they looked back, frightened and confused. I could feel my smile fading away like the life I was leaving behind. I wanted to shout out so this knot of fear and uncertainty could escape from my body.

Was this craziness? Was I really leaving my country, my family and friends, my house that I had built with my bare hands from the ground up, or was it just a test of my ability? 'Wake up, woman.' The voice resounded in my head.

This was not a holiday trip somewhere on the beautiful coast, leaving home for one or two weeks and coming back to normality. This was an uncertain journey on the way to the unknown destiny that was going to affect our whole lives. Not sure how, where and when ... Not sure about the path we were taking, how long it was going to take, what was going to happen and when it was going to end. It was like taking a random chance in the middle of a rough sea not knowing which way the waves would drag us, somehow hoping that we wouldn't end up as lifeless bodies drifting onto the seashore.

After a short drive we arrived at the airport. The airport was crowded with armed soldiers everywhere. Loud voices frayed my already tense nerves. Every civilian face I glanced at was stamped with panic. Doing my best to hide my own fear from my terrified children, I steered us towards one of the long queues for passport control.

The queue moved unbelievably slowly and as the minutes ticked by my anxiety grew, churning like a hot ball in my stomach. I bent down to Hope and Enea and carefully whispered in their ear, 'Be careful not to forget, Enea, that your name on the new passport is Altin, and yours, Hope, is Anila.'

Finally, it was our turn and I handed over our passports with unsteady hands, trying to look as if there was nothing at all to be worried about. To my relief, the officer glanced at us and stamped the passports, handing them back as he waved us through, and we proceeded to Gate 3, where we waited to board an Alitalia plane. Behind the desk the flight attendant appeared, thin as a greyhound, with dark hair swept back from her face on a vertical roll, wearing a green uniform. She called through the twisted microphone for everyone to come forward to check in. It was our first time flying and as we stepped through the big glass doors, we could see on the tarmac the plane with a green horizontal stripe painted onto it, and Alitalia written in black letters and the red, white and green stripe of an Italian flag on the tail representing the Italian flag.

Once aboard we quickly settled into our seats. The plane started moving and after a few twists and turns, the noise of the engine grew louder as we lifted off, flying into cotton-like clouds which looked as if they were racing with each other. Suddenly, the orange light from the sun shone across the clouds straight into the window of the plane, like a searchlight reflecting along the river, and just for a moment I was seized with hope.

I felt Hope's red and white metal hairpins on her brown hair on my arm where she was laying her head, falling asleep, and I could see Enea staring out the little round window. Looking at them, I knew that the only reason I was on this plane was there in front of me: my children, their life, their future. But that didn't stop questions flooding into my mind. How could I be certain I was doing the right thing? I was trying to convince myself of the impossible. I was heading into a very different world and I really hoped that it would all be worth it.

The more the plane moved away into the sky, the more the stark truth hit me. This was going to be a very long journey and it hadn't started well. The anxiety was running high. Enea had been sick throughout the whole flight and looked really pale and weak. But I was soon to discover that this would be a small hitch compared with what was to follow.

Our first stop was Malpensa, Italy, where we had to change flights. As we made our way towards passport control, I was overtaken with a paralysing fear that this was as far as we would get. The end of our journey to freedom. My hands shook as I held out our passports to the officer, a smile pasted on my face, doing my best to disguise the fear twisting my gut. As he put the passports through the computer scanner to check them, his face screwed up. He twisted around in his chair towards his superior saying, in a voice like sandpaper, 'E falso.' My heart stopped as I heard the word 'False'.

His superior rose from his chair. He was a tall guy, of around 35 years of age, with deep green eyes, his hair parted in the middle and brushed to the side. He stared straight into my eyes and then looked at Hope who was clinging to me tightly as Enea gripped my hand, shaking with a fear that consumed his little face. Without saying a word to us, he lowered his head onto his left shoulder, in the direction his colleague was sitting and took the passports and started inspecting.

Behind us people were waiting impatiently but my gaze was locked on the officer's hand holding our passports. Those few minutes felt like hours. Our lives were going to be changed by the whim of one man. Without that stamp we had no future; our new life was in his hands.

The Italian Officer threw our passports across the table. 'Lascali andare,' he said, which means 'Let them go. They're just transit passengers.' He glanced at me briefly again and nodded his head affirmatively as if he wanted to assure me that I would go through. His colleague's face could not have been more shocked. He lifted his hand and gestured in disagreement. 'Sei pazzo? Lo non ci posso credere, lo non ci posso credere,' he ground out. (Are you crazy, I cannot believe this.) Then he took the entry stamp and stamped our passports, striking the table out of frustration.

I could not believe my eyes. One moment I had lost all hope, thinking we would be turned back, then something magical happened. The desperately-needed stamp was on our passports. He handed them back and I clutched them in my hand like I had been handed a million dollars as we ran happily through the airport to catch our next flight to Dusseldorf, Germany. Unfortunately, our flight from Albania to Italy had been delayed, so we missed the flight to Germany and were put up in an airport hotel for a flight scheduled the following morning. After a hot bath, Enea and Hope fell asleep straight away but I couldn't. I got up and moved the corner of the heavy curtains and looked through the large windows. There was no one outside but the old beggar who appeared with a trolley full of old clothes. Looking fragile, dressed in so many layers of fragmenting wool clothes that looked like rags. His hair was a perfect mop of silver and his old unshaven face showing signs of suffering. He sits on the wooden bench across the road and slowly gets an old sleeping bag out of the rusted trolley to make his bed for the night. Surprisingly he takes his shoes off, places them under the bench and clasps his hands and bows his head in prayer. Then he gets himself inside the sleeping bag with his face pointed into the sky. Sorrow shot through my body. I couldn't even get out of the airport to take a hot drink or something to him as we were in transit. I stared at the window into the dark sky. From the north a fine mist appeared and slowly was covering the horizon.

The triple large white lamp post from the corner of the hotel was reflecting through the path and entering into the old oak trees. It seemed like a welcoming sign of hopeful life in the darkness.

I felt a little cold. I closed the heavy green curtains and I slid into the bed with Hope and tried to sleep.

Around four in the morning I heard the creaking noise of a door opening somewhere down on the right, at the end of the corridor, quickly followed by another click click noise resembling the reloading of a gun. Panicked, I threw back the bedclothes and swiftly crossed to the door and peered through the peep hole. Silence. I couldn't see anyone. It seemed strange. If someone had come out of their hotel room they should have walked this way, passing our room to the lift that was on my left, but I heard nothing after that click. Shaking, I got the armchair that was next to the window and carried it over to the door, trying to wedge it under the handle. Then I sat on the floor with my back against the front of the chair. But I heard nothing; complete silence. I tried to lean my head against the armchair, not wanting to move from there. I closed my eyes, starting to drift, only to plunge into flashbacks of that dreadful April night. The click of the loading gun, the pull of the trigger and the sound of the gun firing resounded in my head, the long whistle of the bullets like tinnitus in my ears. A voice screamed, echoing and resounding until it slowly faded away. Another noise, a door opening down the corridor, startled me and brought me back to reality. I heard low voices and the clattering of suitcase wheels that echoed in the gloom of the corridor. And my paranoia climbed up a notch. The slightest noise or any suspicious action that triggered memories of the past gave me an overwhelming sense of insecurity and the horror of the life I so desperately wanted to leave behind. Even the smallest noises haunted me like a ghost and played with my mind. I shook my head as if I wanted to eradicate those images. I breathed a sigh of relief as silence once more blanketed the hotel. In the darkness of the room, I got up from the floor and opened the heavy green curtains, gazing out again. The tower block buildings were barely visible in the mist. It looked mysterious and unknown, just as the way my life felt at that moment. I stayed there, staring – I don't know for how long but I watched the fog clear slowly into the early hours, and the first light reflecting on the windows of the old white building opposite. I looked down. The wooden bench was empty. It seemed that the beggar had left before daybreak. I watched the first flight take off into the grey sky until it disappeared through the clouds. Down the road I saw the door of the little coffee shop open as the bald middle-aged proprietor in a white shirt came out with an A-board sign in his hands. Little by little the street came to life. Looking at my watch, I realised it was time to get my children up and get ready for our next flight.

I managed to get them up and take them for a quick breakfast, then we headed to the airport. Enea was trying to hide his nerves by talking and asking too many questions. It was clear that he was worried about our next journey after the experience we had had at Italian passport control. Hope looked anxious. She was very quiet as she tightly held onto my hand, not letting go. I put on a big smile, flung my arms around them and said, 'Another exciting day ahead for us, another plane.' With relief, I watched their faces relax. I was trying to make it one big adventure for them, trying to desperately shield them from the anxiety I was feeling.

The airport wasn't as busy as the night before. It seemed like a few passengers had spent the night there sleeping on the long rows of adjoining silver metal chairs. We made our way to the gate and once we got on the plane my anxiety finally eased a little and I dared hope the rest of the journey would be okay. Finally, the plane took off and we were flying through cotton wool clouds. I tried to relax and closed my eyes, desperate for a little rest as we had a long journey ahead. But the fear was always there, clogging my throat: would we make it through the next passport control? Or would we find ourselves turned back, forced once again to live in hell?

My nerves were stretched to breaking point and I was exhausted by the time we touched down at Dusseldorf. As I got my passport out, Enea nudged me on my left arm. 'Mum, look, there's no passport control.' I looked around in shock. No passport control! This couldn't be happening! Surely, it was too good to be true? Other passengers who were on the same plane were walking towards the exit doors. Enea's eyes met mine and we stared at each other in amazement. 'It seems like today is our lucky day, Mummy's sweetheart,' I said. 'Let's get out of here.'

Relief flooded my body as we walked outside to look for the car scheduled to pick us up. It was part of our journey as agreed with the man in charge back in Albania. We waited and waited, for more than an hour, the children so tired they could hardly stay on their feet, and anxiety like a poison surging through me, but no one arrived. I lost count of the times I tried to phone the guy who was picking us up, but there was no answer. We couldn't stay inside the airport and we couldn't stand outside either. I had to do something before the police recognised us. My panic was brought to an abrupt halt when I heard Enea say, 'I'm cold.'

The wind was harsh, and it was getting late. It was too risky to go back and wait inside the airport. I looked around, I had to do something. There was a hotel near the airport on the other side of the road that I could see in the distance. It was a large, tall building that stood out from the others. I looked at Enea and Hope's sorrowful faces. 'We're going somewhere warm and cosy,' I told them as I pointed towards the hotel. Without wasting any time, I grabbed their hands and we crossed the road together.

The grand entrance of the hotel looked far too extravagant and out of our league, but all I could think about at that moment was keeping my kids warm and staying inconspicuous. Booking in wasn't that easy due to the language barrier, but somehow the receptionist and I managed to understand each other through gestures, and finally, she took us to our room. I made a few phone calls to try and find out exactly what was going on. I sat on the bed exhausted and carefully took out the piece of paper with the name and number of Toni, the middleman, the one who was supposed to pick us up, written on it, and once more started to attempt to contact him. It took a good few hours, then, finally, I heard a deep voice on the other end of the phone. 'Who's this?'

'It's Yllka, the lady with two kids from Tirana that you were supposed to pick up early afternoon. What the hell is going on?' I asked him angrily.

'There was a misunderstanding as I was given the wrong time to pick you up. I'm waiting for you outside now,' he answered.

'Outside? Where?' I asked.

'The airport,' he said, cocky. 'Where else?'

'We're not there. We're at the hotel just across the road from the airport.'

'A hotel?'

'Yes, a hotel. My children and I were waiting in the cold for far too long,' I told him sharply.

'Get ready quickly, I'm on my way. I'll be there in five minutes,' he said.

Ten minutes later, the shrill of the phone echoed around the hotel room.

'Make your way downstairs,' he instructed.

We were waiting in the lobby of the hotel when a dark-haired guy, nearly six foot tall, wearing a black Gucci t-shirt and black jeans, pushed through the double doors of the entrance to the hotel. He looked to be in his early thirties, tanned and muscular, competent and hard. I could feel the tension in the air from the way he looked when he walked into the building. He stopped for a second at the entrance and opened his wallet (I guess he had my picture), raised his left eyebrow and stared at me inquisitively like the passport control officers who stare at you to make sure you are the person on the passport. He approached us slowly.

'Yllka?'

I nodded.

'I'm Toni,' he said as he shook my hand. 'Sorry about the misunderstanding. Bring your passport and follow me to reception. I'll pay the bill, we have to set off quickly.'

He finalised everything and led us out to the car, ready for the third part of our journey. To my surprise, waiting outside were four other people. A silver, short-haired lady named Mira with two grown-up children, a boy of twenty-two, and a girl of nineteen. There was also a tall Kosovan man of around thirty, called Artan.

'Right, come on, quick, get in everyone,' Toni said, his manner making it clear he was in a rush without having to raise his voice.

The car was a five-door black BMW—definitely not big enough for seven passengers and a driver.

'How are we all going to get in?' I asked. 'There are seven of us.'

'You get in the front seat and put your daughter on your lap, and the others in the back. It's not too far,' he explained. 'We'll be there before you know it.'

I looked at him in shock. 'What?' I exclaimed.

He stepped closer to me and said, 'We don't have time for this! Quick, get in the car! The police,' he whispered, nodding his head.

Although I had spotted the police car nearby, it was a waste of time arguing at this point. So, I grabbed Hope, opened the door and climbed in, placing her on my lap. The rest of them managed to crush into the back. Through the mirror I saw Enea looking worried as he sat next to a stranger. I gave him a quick smile to reassure him.

We started driving to our next destination, Belgium. Fear filled the car. No one uttered a word. Everyone looked apprehensive while staring out into that unknown, mysterious distance. After a few hours we stopped somewhere. Toni asked us to hand over our passports, telling us they were only valid to Belgium.

'How are we going to cross the border without a passport?' I questioned.

'Don't worry, I'm getting new ones at our next stop,' he said reassuringly. 'Everything is under control.' He glanced around our little group. 'If you need to use the toilet, do it now as quickly as you can before we set off. I can't stop anywhere.'

A short while later everyone piled back into the car and we set off again.

It was getting dark and cold, the harvest moon hung low in the distance, looking as if it was following us as the car sped away. Without warning, the headlights of a police vehicle appeared behind us and lit up our car.

'Shit! The police again, quick! All of you sitting on laps, put your heads down,' Toni shouted, alarmed.

I laid Hope in front of me and covered her with a thin scarf.

'Try not to show any sign of panic,' he muttered at me without turning his head.

Through the police car window, a policeman's face stared at me as they slowly drove parallel to us. My eyes met his as I desperately tried to hide my panic behind a smile, my heart racing like a gerbil on its wheel. The time we were followed was probably less than a minute but it seemed so much longer. I saw him picking up the radio as they passed us and sped away, and as I gulped air, I realized I hadn't dared to breathe. Relieved, everyone cheered.

At last, the car stopped, and I had to nudge Hope so she would wake up. I looked at my watch. It was nearly midnight. We had pulled off the road close to a forest. Toni told us all to get out. A bitterly cold north wind hit us the moment we were out of the car. I was only wearing a short sleeved cream suit and the children just a thin long sleeved shirt.

'Where are we going?' Mira asked.

'Follow me,' he instructed. No indication where he planned to take us.

We had no idea where we were, and no idea where we were going, and no idea what was going to happen to us. We had no other choice but to do what he asked.

CHAPTER 2

Stormy passage in the English Channel

Toni unbuttoned his jacket and pulled out a black plastic torch, switching it on. As he led us into the depths of the forest, the fear and darkness raged inside me. We didn't know what we were heading into and I was terrified for the safety of my children. We were moving through trees as if we were wading through a dense crowd, pushing left and pushing right. We squeezed ourselves through a narrow gap, dodging the twisted bare branches that interlocked with each other. After a while, we found ourselves amongst some ancient deciduous trees, stumbling over gnarled roots. I could smell the aroma of the old pine trees, mixed with the distinct earthy odour of damp soil, covered in golden-brown leaves that blanketed the forest floor.

A few minutes later and a little deeper into the forest, Toni stopped and said, 'Make yourselves comfortable here and wait for me. I'll be back in twenty minutes.'

After he had left, we tried to clear a space where we could sit down in the middle of the dark forest, haunted by the cold winter's air, whispering like witches' voices between the ancient trees. In the distance the eery hooting of owls could be heard. We shuffled around helplessly between the brittle fir trees, finally resigning ourselves to sitting on the damp leaves, huddled together, united in terror, silent. My children clung to me, scared and so vulnerable. I shivered as once more thoughts crowded my head that something bad might happen and that, if it did, it would be my fault. It was my decision to leave Albania. Yes, of course, I had made the choice out of desperation to ensure they would have a future. But still the guilt weighed heavy on me. The blackness surrounding us cultivated in me a feeling of claustrophobia. I looked up at the moonbeams shining through the arching branches.

How did we end up in here? On this awful night? I used to enjoy being in the forest near our school, with friends, after lessons, collecting chestnuts that had fallen to the ground. We used to wrap our jumper sleeves around our hands to protect them from the sharp chestnut burrs and to gather the ones where burrs had split, which meant they were ripe. Sometimes I would take long walks in the forest because its silent tranquillity was a relaxing balm. For a while, it would help to ease my sadness and pain, But now, in darkness, in an unknown place, it felt sinister, the silence of a graveyard—spooky and scary.

The deathly silence stretched as we waited and waited, for what seemed like forever. It was now the early hours of the morning And we were all beyond worry, wondering why he hadn't returned. Were we going to be abandoned in this forest? The children were miserable and shivering, and there was no sign of Toni yet. Artan could see Hope struggling to keep warm, so he took off his black jacket and wrapped it around her.

Eaten up with anxiety, between chattering teeth, I started humming the tune of an old song, and a seemingly crazy idea flew into my mind.

'Come on, everyone,' I said. 'We need to do something or we're going to freeze. Let's warm our souls by singing and our bodies by dancing.' I beckoned them to get up.

They looked at me with disbelief on their faces; a stranger with whom they had hardly exchanged two words was asking them to dance. I understood, but I persevered.

'Come on,' I said again. 'No one is going to bring you a fire or anything to keep you warm here. We need to help ourselves.'

'Are you for real? I don't think that will help us,' Mira said.

'Well, do you have a better idea?' I asked softly.

She looked at me hesitantly, smiled with quivering lips, and surprisingly she waved at her children to get up with her and then looked at Artan. He shook his head reluctantly, but stood up, and in a few minutes, while we were all holding hands and dancing in a circle, our voices erupted and echoed in the stillness of the night as Albanian traditional songs were sung. Everyone started laughing and our spirits truly lifted. Somehow my soul was getting warmer and the warmth was spreading through every limb of my body.

It was so hard to do when our morale was so low, but on so many occasions, I had learned to take whatever life threw at me and fight it with whatever strength was left in me. To this day I can't believe how I managed to come up with the idea of dancing and singing on a cold winter's night, in the middle of a forest where we thought our lives had nowhere to go. I can't believe myself, never mind expecting others to join in with me. I often ask myself how I found the strength to say and do what someone else would have called stupid. I know it's absurd to think it, but sometimes, when you don't have any other choice, and you have your children in front of you, you do crazy things in that instance because the only option left is to use the power of hope and I had to be the person to pass on that hope to others.

It was 3.30 am when Toni finally returned.

'Where have you been?' we chorused.

'I had a problem to deal with. Stop questioning, follow me and be quiet,' he growled.

Instantly, his attitude changed dramatically. He became a man whom you would not want to cross, especially in the middle of nowhere.

We arrived back at the roadside, where, through the dim moonlight, we saw a large lorry on the opposite side of the road. Quietly, we walked over to the shutters on the back of the lorry, already partly open.

'Quick, climb in one by one,' he whispered while he was waving his hand for us to get in, 'and be careful not to make any noise.'

'You first, with the little kids,' he said, pointing at me.

I hesitated, looking at him shocked and murmured angrily, 'Are you kidding me? Really? In the back of the lorry? I don't think so, if the agreement was for me and my children to jump in the back of a lorry, I would never have set off on this journey. That's why we chose the expensive option. We were promised safe passage! Where are our new passports?'

'Shhhhhhh,' he whispered through gritted teeth, tapping his finger against his lips. He leaned close to me and in the dim light I could see his cold, flat eyes in his stern-looking face. I felt his stale breath in my face and my stomach churned.

'Listen, lady, mademoiselle,' he said sarcastically. 'There are no other passports. I wouldn't ask you to jump in the back of the lorry otherwise. I don't have time for this right now, I don't care, and I don't give a damn even if you don't want to jump inside the lorry. This is the best option you get right now. You have less than a minute to get inside before the lorry driver wakes up. Stay in the forest if you want and let your kids be food for the animals, or you can jump in the lorry with everyone else and get to your destination.'

His words were so sinister. A gold tooth glistened on the right side of his mouth out of the dark while he was talking and somehow it was difficult to tear my attention away from it. I couldn't believe what was happening. Rage blasted through me. I could see the others looking at me, like unhappy ghosts, standing impatiently waiting for me to jump in and get out of their away. Enea and Hope grabbed hold of me, frightened, their faces masked by worry.

'Please, Mummy, let's get in, I'm cold,' Enea said, his voice trembling.

I looked at him, powerless to do anything because the decision had been made for us and our fate was in someone else's hands. There was no turning back now. I was in the middle of nowhere, thousands of miles away from home, my children totally dependent on me, so right there, at that moment, I had no other choice but to get inside the lorry. I had to do something I never thought I would do; something I had seen in the movies and thought it would never happen to me. I picked up Hope first and gently placed her inside the lorry before helping Enea to climb in. Finally, I pulled myself up and looked at my surroundings.

The lorry was full of empty pallets, just a one-metre space to the ceiling for us to sit in. We made our way to the very top, near the cabin, and tried to find a spot on top of the rough and scratchy pallets. I wasn't even appropriately dressed to sit in the back of the lorry. We had been told to wear smart clothes, to look efficient. So, I was wearing a cream suit with black kitten heel shoes. If I'd known that we were going to sit in the cold in the back of a lorry, I would have worn more suitable clothing for the journey. The others began climbing in one by one, and once we were all inside, Toni closed the shutters and I heard the ominous click of the padlock.

There was an eerie, scary silence in the dark inside the lorry where we exchanged a quick, frightened glance at each other without a word being said. At that moment the guarantor's face back in Albania appeared before me, when hands had been shaken and word had been given. Just one week before, a family friend had brought the dealer to the house; a tall man with dark messy hair and an unusual number of wrinkles on his face for a man so young, as if each one showed the trials and tribulations he had already been through in life. I sat there with my brother-in-law Goni. It was a very tense, serious meeting.

'Right,' Goni spoke sternly, 'what are the different deals you can offer to get my sister-in-law and her kids to London safely?'

He took a slow sip of coffee, looked directly into his eyes and replied in a very low voice, 'There are two ways of getting there. The first one is cheaper; half the journey to be done by dinghy boat followed by boarding the back of a lorry to get to England.

'The second option is more expensive, but safer and more comfortable. You go to Malpensa in Italy, then to Germany by air, with a car waiting to pick you up from the airport and drive you to Belgium. Then you get on the ferry over the Channel to England.'

I looked at him. It seemed too good to be true.

'I heard about people jumping on the back of lorries and I'm not setting off if that's going to be an option,' I said firmly.

'Trust me, that won't happen,' he replied confidently.

It was obvious that we would take the second option.

'I want them to arrive safely, above all else. So, if something happens to them, you are the one that will be responsible, and I *will* kill you,' Goni threatened, pointing his finger at the man.

Without an ounce of fear in his voice, he replied, 'You have my word that everything will be fine.'

After shaking hands, he handed him three passports and said, 'Good luck.'

So far it had all been just claptrap, lies and cheats. Everything that was happening was so different from what we were promised by our agreement about the journey.

That voice still rang in my ears, promising that we would not be put in the back of a lorry, and yet here we were, sitting inside of one, in the dark, on the top of rough wooden pallets. All the promises had been broken in front of my eyes. The anger I felt was gut-wrenching. Every step of the journey had been terrifying. I looked into the sad and frightened faces of Enea and Hope through the gloomy lights that flickered now and then from outside the lorry. Seeing my children this way felt like a knife to my heart. I tried to hide my fear, scooping them up into my arms and hugging them tight as I whispered, 'Hey, Mummy's sweethearts, it won't be too long now. We just have to get through this. Tomorrow we are going to be in London, and you are going to see your daddy.'

Enea lifted his head up near my ear and whispered, 'You are okay, aren't you, Mummy?'

'Of course I'm all right, my sweet boy,' I whispered back. 'Lay your head down on my lap and try to sleep.'

I felt a little kiss on my right arm and his frightened voice whispered, 'Love you, Mummy.' Right there, at that moment, my spirit soared and my soul was filled with love and agony at the same time.

After an hour of silence, the engine roared into life and we felt the vehicle start to move.

Hope, who was just four, put her head on the other side of my lap and tried to fall asleep, but the pallet she was sitting on was hurting her and she couldn't get comfortable. I lay down and put her on top of me to make a bed for her so she could sleep. Her exhausted body gave in immediately and she fell asleep in no time. Less than an hour later my body was aching and slowly a painful numbness crept over me. It seemed that I lay there for a lifetime, my body aching like it had never done before. For a long time afterwards, it bore the significant imprint of those dreadful pallets.

Less than two hours had passed when I heard a strange clanging sound. I got up quickly, still holding Hope in my arms, to try to find out what was making such an odd and worrying sound. Through a little gap in the corner of the vehicle, I saw people trying to chain the lorry to the ferry. A few seconds later, I heard a dog barking as it sat very close to us. Just around the corner from the green and white lorry next to us, I could see the border control police with their sniffer dogs. Level to the back doors of the lorry, one of the policemen asked the driver to open up. Huddled in the meagre protection of my vehicle, I saw someone being dragged out. He looked very young, around fourteen, malnourished and vulnerable. They dragged out five refugees altogether, clearly frightened and upset.

Panic surged through me like a wave; I did not want that to be us. I watched them unlock two other lorries. Turning my head, I quickly looked around. Everyone was getting up, afraid and hopeless.

'That's it,' Mira said, looking at me while shaking her head in despair. 'They're going to get us.' Her voice was flat, completely devoid of hope.

'Hey, don't give up just yet,' I answered quietly. 'Try to hold your breath for a few seconds if you can, everyone, when they come around our lorry.'

I covered my children's mouths with my hands, listening to the police faintly talking outside the lorry, only wood and material separating us. We looked at each other, silent fear twisting my gut. This moment could determine the rest of our lives, and we all knew it. Suddenly the dogs stopped barking and the only noise was the heavy footsteps of the policemen walking nearby. A strange silence surrounded the place. Footsteps were no longer heard. You could only hear the wagging of the dogs. It seemed as if they had stopped next to us, maybe they were observing if people were inside or not. I could hear my heart beating like a drum in my chest. Then I heard again the voices, the heavy footsteps of the policemen starting to move away, becoming fainter. We all raised our hands in silence with a sigh of joy, utter relief dancing through us. We couldn't believe our luck, congratulating each other on our good fortune. Our lorry was the only one that had not been checked by the police. We tried to sit back and settle down, feeling the ferry rocking and rolling as it crossed the English Channel.

My memory of that night floats into focus in my mind again and again. Seven of us, sitting on top of the wooden pallets in the darkness as the ferry ploughed across the channel, heading for England.

Hope fell asleep first, snuggled beside me on my left, with her head on my chest and her arms tucked under my armpits. On my right, Enea looked flat out with his head on my lap, next to his sister's, his arms around her shoulders. One by one everyone fell asleep around me and the strange eerie silence of the night filled the inside of the lorry. I was the only one awake, staring into the darkness whilst listening to the raging sea of the English Channel and the wind rustling lightly through the blue canvas.

Precisely one year before, at this very time, I was in a different place, surrounded by the love of my family at my niece Rudina's wedding, laughing, singing and dancing. I have a picture of that night. I'm wearing a dark green satin dress held in place by a thin gold belt that hung down on the left, matching my high heels. My hair is styled in a loose, classic French twist. I'm happier then than I could now imagine. A hint of a smile played around my lips at the memory of better days, but faded as quickly as it came. It seemed so long ago. That moment held little value for me now, only the future really mattered and *that* I couldn't see clearly; only a vague path where my instincts and my strength were leading me to an unknown and unseen destiny.

Suddenly, a loud clap of thunder sounded overhead. A bolt of lightning lit up the sky outside, and in that split second, I could see everyone around me resting, motionless, on top of the pallets. The wind gained in strength and the ferry began rocking from side to side. Anxiety took hold of me, flooding through me when I thought how many people had ended up on the bottom of this great stretch of turbid water. People with hopes just like us, unfortunately never to be realized, their lives ending beneath the dark waves.

Were we going to suffer the same fate?

I hoped to find the courage to answer the call of our destiny when it came. This journey, full of obstacles, full of dangers, had taken over my life like a pilgrimage. We had already faced the impossible and survived. Were we going to make it this time?

CHAPTER 3

Surviving the horrific ordeal

This endless, terrible journey dragged on and on. My eyelids weighed heavy and I drifted in and out of sleep, but the wind that flapped the blue canvas of the lorry woke me up each time I dozed off. I couldn't even move to have a look outside the lorry as Hope and her brother were lying over me and I didn't want to wake them up. There were so many thoughts fighting for space in my tired and confused mind. Lying inside the lorry, the uncertainty and fears of the journey added again to the dilemma of my life with my husband, the father of my children. Was I right in giving him a second chance after everything that had happened? As if it were not bad enough, along with the troubles, family blood feuds, crimes and insecurities of life in the country, my life too was in tatters. This was one of the maddest decisions I had ever made. Shivers shook me just at the thought of the past and I was frankly terrified about my future with him. I quickly gathered myself together, remembering again the real reason I was on this journey—the safety of my children, that was paramount and more precious than my own life right.

The silence inside the lorry was broken by a furious wind that announced its passage again, clashing into the blue canvas with powerful aggression. The noise of the waves was stirring up my emotions and bringing back horrific memories, the past once again flashing through my mind, washing over me again and again, never going away. That terrible night with a wild wind howling just like now, so fresh in my memory as if it was yesterday:

It was around 11.00 pm. The night had rolled over the city and the only streetlamps that worked flickered on and off intermittently at the junction that led to the main road. A strong wind was howling like crazy from all sides and seemed to torpedo the ancient trees where the branches bent as they were torn from the trunks. The children were in bed and my mother-in-law said her goodnights and went to her bedroom. I moved the vases full of lace fern asparagus plants that were hanging on the veranda and placed them on the floor, in the corner, before the mad wind threw them everywhere. I took my seat on the veranda behind the front boundary wall, placed the gun in my lap and peered through the branches of the orange tree.

My mother-in-law and I had devised a plan to take turns keeping watch on the veranda, guarding the house. Even though the state TV channels broadcast that the situation in the country had calmed down and was now safe, how safe was it really?

It didn't seem that long ago since the civil war broke out and the blood of the people smeared the pavements, the melody of songs turned to wailing and the loss to anger. People armed themselves by breaking into the army depots and taking what they could for their own safety and to protect their families. Even though communism had perished in Albania years ago, the history of war and bloodshed would repeat itself. Our house was a prime target for attempts of robbery or violence as it was a nice house with a big garden and large gates. It was also the very first house you would see when you entered the crossroads. To make it worse, people knew that we had owned a business before the troubles and therefore there was a good chance there would be money in the house. Our fear was exacerbated by the thought of the danger to my children. Now at least we had a Kalashnikov in the house, so the cloud of fear had slightly lifted.

I tried to create the idea that the house was home to menfolk by wearing my husband's dark leather jacket, drowning my tall thin frame, and a cap so I could tuck in all my long hair.

Suddenly the calm was broken by the sound of roaring engines filling my ears. In the distance, at the end of the road, I could see bright headlights approaching ever closer; two trucks filled with young men and boys. One of them was very young and was shouldering a rifle taller than himself. They started speeding up and down the hill, raising their guns into the air, shooting and loudly shouting expletives.

Hearing all the commotion, my mother-in-law rushed out, with Hope following behind. She whispered, 'Are you okay? What's...!' Before she had finished her sentence, her words were interrupted by the sound of continuous gunfire exploding into the air.

Bullets screamed past me as they thudded into the walls close to the shaking windows. I heard a scream from my daughter. I turned around and she was lying on the floor with her grandma, her face covered in fear. A tremor gripped my body as if it wanted to shake the whole night way. With a panicked shriek I ran towards her and as I held my baby, I realised she wasn't hurt. Relief washed over me, I nodded to them to get inside. My mother-in-law took my daughter and they both started to crawl into the house, towards safety. I quickly rushed back behind the veranda wall ready to fight. Fortunately, the trucks were speeding away from our house and the sounds of the gunshots faded slowly into the distance. Amazingly no one was hurt.

I was jolted from these memories by the jarring noise of loud thunder that startled the hell out of me as I was lying on the top of the pallets with Hope's body over mine, supporting Enea's head on my left arm. I was numb, and very doubtful as the ferry sailed into the English Channel.

We were lucky then but I asked myself, how lucky are we right now—inside this lorry? I trembled with fear as the whole ferry rocked from side to side. It felt like the English Channel's waves were rising and rocking with anger, reminding us who was in charge. One by one, the others had been roused from their sleep and I could see from their faces and hear in their voices how terrified they were.

'Mummy, what's happening? Where are we?' Enea squawked, his eyes wide with fear.

'We're on the ferry to England,' I said as I held them tightly against me. 'Don't worry, sweetheart, it's just a storm. Just hold on to me.'

The ferocious north wind pushed against the ferry with all its strength, whistling loudly, making scary noises between the lorry canvases. There was no mercy in the channel that night.

With one hand I firmly held onto the pallet, preventing myself from sliding, with the other I desperately grasped hold of Enea and Hope, pulling them close to my body. 'Hold tightly to me and don't let go,' I shouted. Quickly their little helpess hands, gripped around my waist and tried to hold with all their power. Their heads were joined together as if they wanted to give each other some strength and some love.

'Do you remember the tale of the little boy Ali with his father facing the storm while they were sailing in the middle of the Adriatic sea?' I asked, while feeling their little frightened bodies around me.

'Yes,' they replied almost at the same time.

'And what was the most important thing that got them through and survived?' I asked again.

'Hope and courage,' Enea replied quickly with a shaken voice.

'That's right, and we are going to do exactly the same,' I said. 'This storm, it will be over soon and will get there within no time.'

I felt their head affirming in a faint voice. Panic coursed through me, as I couldn't help but think about the worst-case scenario. What if something dire happened? Nobody knew that inside that lorry were seven humans that might need to be rescued—not even the lorry driver. Were we going to end up like the family of eight that was found dead on the back of a lorry earlier that year? The crossing seemed to be taking way too long. Where was land? Where exactly was the ferry going? If it had sailed towards England we would have arrived by now, surely?

Somehow, I felt that someone somewhere out there was giving me strength, telling me these crazy waves were just like a silly game, trying to scare, to make me believe that we would never get to the other side, never tread on English soil. Surely that someone, that invisible being, would not let us get lost now in the murky waters, after all our sacrifices and when we had passed so many obstacles. We were going to make it, I told myself, no matter what. It was our inescapable fate. We were going to survive. Another thunderbolt split the night, but this time its noise was further away.

Hope and Enea, relieved, sat down on the pallets and lined their bodies against me.

Inside the lorry everyone looked drained. I could see people's features lit up by a little light coming through a hole of ripped material in a corner of the lorry.

We were all hungry and dehydrated, especially the children. It had been more than 48 hours with neither food nor water. The journey felt endless, and the destination didn't seem to be getting any closer.

'Mummy,' Hope whispered, 'I'm thirsty.'

'I know, sweetheart,' I replied. 'We're nearly there. Be patient just a little bit longer.'

She put her head down on my arm, next to where Enea was lying, and as her brown eyes looked down at a corner of the lorry, tiredness overcame them. Her dry lips started whispering something I couldn't understand. I lowered my head, trying to wet her lips a little with my kisses. They were colder than an Eskimo's nose, and as I took her icy little hands between the palms of mine, a shiver rippled through me. She looked so pale and her whole body felt desperately cold.

Fear splintered my heart.

'Oh God, my baby!' I murmured. 'Please stay with me.'

I took her onto my lap, lifted my blouse and rested her head carefully on my chest. I pressed her body against my skin, hoping the heat from me would warm her. Her body lying on mine was like when I felt her presence, her existence, for the very first time on a beautiful March day in 1994. The lovely warm feeling of that March was nothing compared to that first connection with my child and what I felt right then. Now her body was cold. I had a terrible fear, a painful feeling of inability to help my child survive this moment. I kissed her all over, comforted her, desperate to keep her warm and give her all the love I had at that moment. I was trying to hold her tight and massage her shoulders, her little arms and small feet.

But despite all I could do, she was still so cold. I glanced over at Enea, trying not to show any sign of how worried I was. I prayed quietly, my voice trembling, and continued to massage her non-stop, even though I was exhausted and reaching the end of my strength. I took my top off and wrapped it around her. This caught Enea's attention. 'Is Hope okay, Mummy?' he asked.

'I'm just trying to warm her up, she feels a little cold.' I forced a smile to comfort him. 'You get back to sleep. She'll be fine.'

As he leant his head back on my arm next to Hope, the contrast in the colour of their faces made me tremble. Even though they looked so much alike, as if they were identical twins, at this very moment they couldn't have looked more different. Her face was as pale as a China doll and his, a healthy bronze colour. Terror consumed me. I got on my knees and wrapped her in my arms, rocking her like a little baby, and started singing her favourite song.

'Twinkle, twinkle little star...'

Every time we sang that song Hope would join in, but now she had no interest. Could she even hear my voice? I looked up while I was singing as if there was someone above who needed to hear or see me, someone who understood the heartfelt cry of a mother, desperate to save her child.

For a moment I stopped singing and whispered a little prayer which came from the depth of my soul.

'Do not abandon us, God,' I pleaded.

CHAPTER 4

The magical city (my origin)

The worst, it seemed, was over and the wind had eased to calm waves through the blue canvas. It looked as now it had discovered its direction was not against us, but with us, like it was helping us in the navigation to our destination. The more we moved away, the more I could sense the smell of the earth and the trees that penetrated through the blue canvas. The breeze, the smell, the fresh air was exactly the same that used to come from the Gjere mountain rattling gently through the window shutters in my house where I was born and grew up, in the city of stone, my town Gjirokastra. That's where my life began.

The magically historic city, in the south of Albania, created not only from nature but also from the hands of Gjirokastra masters, perched on the side of spectacular snow-glazed mountain ranges, which from the distance looked like they were touching the sky as they dominated the blue horizon in every part. The ancient lavish stone buildings embedded into them for centuries, seemed like they were stacked on top of each other like concertinas, where one corner of one roof overlapped the other and unexpectedly appeared after every alley. Within every one of those houses a verse or song could be heard, and from those houses was brought the hostess and the masters that created the city that we had been proud of for centuries, graceful and beautiful. The white houses with enormous gardens and cobbled streets were the foundation of my life. The glorious castle that sat at the heart of the city on a high hilltop towering over the town was my playground.

The city didn't look complete without the castle where from its top you could look over the whole city and stretching out around it the landscape of Drino valley and the architecture of the town that took your breath away as soon as you set eyes on it. The houses and the castle were connected, like the heart in the body, supplying its life blood. They shared together moments of sadness and happiness. The legends, songs, the victories, and the losses were held in the memories of the castle. Often it was called Argjiros Castle by the people, due to the famous legend of Gjirokastre's princess.

Princess Argjiro ruled the city in the fourteenth century. After the Turks' betrayal, they surrounded the castle. With no other path to escape, the princess with her little boy jumped out of the highest tower in the castle to avoid being captured by the Turks. Often when the mist descended on the city the castle looked like it was floating in the middle of the ocean.

The fresh air, the mountain, the castle and the colour of my city are embedded in my memory like a celebration of my childhood. To this day, in my eyes, it is the best city in the world. There's something unique about it – something that the other cities around the country didn't have. I have been in love with it since I was a little girl and it has always been close to my heart.

Every time I go back, the first thing I see when I enter the city is the big clock that stands in front of the castle like the helm of a giant ship coming out the water. The incredible cobblestone mosaic streets in the centre of the city had been laid by the golden hands of a well-known master craftsman of Gjirokastra, who had made them look like a hand-crafted carpet.

Driving through these brick roads which zigzagged like a serpent up the very steep hill, was a little old blue bus called 'Urbani Dunavatit' which would take passengers from the bottom of the town heading up to the top area of the neighbourhood called Dunavat 1, taking nearly an hour to get there. Due to the communist regime it was the only transport at the time as people weren't allowed to have a private car. Therefore, the little bus was always full of people and while it chugged noisily on the dangerous roads, a cloud of diesel smoke and fumes belched out after it as the engine laboured noisily.

As soon as you passed the castle, you could see a large nineteenth century stone building continuously caressed by the mountain breeze. It stood as a giant house surrounded by the greenery of a beautiful garden separated by terraces full of fruit trees and vines, which often looked like they were dancing as the wind blew down from Gjere mountain.

(This picture is taken from the bottom of the road and it shows only the top floor of the building. It's impossible to take a picture of all the houses in the high level)

There was my house, where I was born and raised, the house that heard my first cry and my laugh, my pain and my joy, our sorrows and weddings, our songs and verses of life. Inside the three-storey building there were two houses belonging to my father, Tasin, and his brother Nazmi. Although they had two different entrances, they were connected to each other by an inner door. The roof of the house was covered by grey slate tiles. The fine wooden brown-shuttered windows, dotted along the walls, had white curtains with lace borders made by my mother's precious hands. All the rooms in the house had beautiful high barrel-curved wooden ceilings. In a slightly lower level than the ground floor was a very large cistern to store and preserve the rainwater called 'Mustuk'. The fresh water meant that it would be cold in this part of the house. We would use this water during the dry summer periods, and would store lots of food, jars of vegetables and home-made jam, to keep it fresh and cold for the coming winter.

Because it was built in the nineteenth century, the house did not have a heating system. The main living room was dominated by a large open fire which we would gather around on cold winter nights to keep warm, roast the chestnuts or the corn, playing games related to our education to gain knowledge, especially in numbers and geography, which would allow us to get to know the countries and cities around the world.

The walls were lined by long-armed wooden ledges with upholstered seats, and their long wall cushions were covered by a white lace cotton material. On each of the remaining rooms we would place a large copper brazier in the middle filled with embers from the fire that filled the room with light and heat. On cold winter nights we would sit around the brazier to keep warm while we did our homework. It had a fantastic way of making me feel cosy and content. These two floors of the house were connected by a beautiful wooden spiral staircase.

The front of the house boasted a large terrace that overlooked the mountain, a quaint, beautiful area called Manalat, and the forest and Mount Gjere. The streets had rows of white houses that looked like a blanket of perfectly placed snow.

The front of the house also had a large patio that stretched into a large garden. Both were enclosed by a high dry-stone wall, with large grey iron double gates, Here also was a covered roof terrace, which was shaded by the branches of a huge almond tree. Twisting around the front walls and on the top of the patio were grape vines where, tied to wires, were bunches of grapes hanging down, creating lovely shade that was perfect in the summer. The back windows faced the city's castle, which was one of the many spectacular views that surrounded the house. On the other side you could see the mountains and the other houses, downhill and across the neighbourhood.

At the back of the house, dry stone walls formed a three-terraced garden full of fruit and nut trees, and as it connected with my Uncle Nazmi's plot, it surrounded the building like an enormous garden that, looking down the road, seemed to form a huge green orchard. The bottom garden tier was built onto the edge of a very steep hill where there was a little stone bench sheltered by the blossoming walnut tree that poured over the wall onto the stony path. It was like a green umbrella creating welcoming shade for people to rest on a hot summer's day as they climbed the hill. Often it was called Tasin's walnut station by many people who knew my father well. When you walked up the hill, the smell of fresh fruit would rush into your senses and make you feel the presence of Mother Nature. The striped grey and white cobbled path ran through the garden right up to the front door of the house.

However, my family roots didn't begin here; they were planted and started in an old stone house on the edge of beautiful mountains that had been destroyed over the years by the effect of time and war. That house had been surrounded by gardens filled with beautiful wildflowers and lusciously ripened grapes and fruits. At that time, the house was lit by oil lamps, as there was no electricity until 1951, when the power lines were erected in the area.

Rahman Sinani, grandfather on my father's side, was born in Gjirokastra in 1892. He had three sisters, Naxhije, Zurha, and Zebo, and one brother, Dino. My grandfather and his brother Dino emigrated to America in 1906. They both worked hard, and everything was going well, but my grandfather had a terrible accident that left him with one arm, so after years of work he came back to Albania. His brother Dino didn't return. He stayed in the States and got married to an Austrian woman. His son Edward became a pilot in America and went on to fight in the Vietnam War for which he received medals for his loyal service.

Back in Albania, my granddad married my grandma as part of an arranged marriage. They had never seen each other before. They only knew each other's names and that was it. My grandma, Muzejen, was born in Mecove, Greece, in 1905. She came to live in Albania when she was five or six years old. She had a brother who had died at a very young age and a sister called Safo. A tradition in Albania around those times was if you gave the hand of your daughter to get married, you were given money from the husband's family. So, this was a good opportunity for her parents and my grandma to have a secure life.

The day of the wedding my grandfather and family took my grandmother to his home. She had never set foot in the house before. Her beautiful, innocent face and her thick, dark hair were covered by a red coloured silk veil. Looking down to the floor, she was only able to see his shoes and hear his deep voice. She was a virgin, young, vulnerable and not free to choose her own future.

The day after the wedding, unhappy, my grandma stormed back to her parents' house after realising that they had married her to a man with one hand. With a sore look on her face, she asked, 'Was I so worthless that you would give me to anybody and especially a man with one hand?'

Her mother took her hand and dragged her to the window and said, 'You see the river over there? You either go back to your husband or you throw yourself in it. You can't leave shame on our family. You are not coming back in here.'

With no choice, she went back to my granddad. After a while she began to accept his disability and eventually fell in love with him. And on the fifth May 1928 the first cries of a baby were heard, the ninanat (lullaby) of the mother that was rocking the cradle of the first son of the house, my father Tasin. Time passed and two years later amid the pain and cold of a snowy winter on the first day of January 1930 the second son Nazmi was born. Then in the spring, on March 25, 1932 when the budding trees began to open and bloom, the third son and the last child Nevruz was born.

As the years passed, the sons grew up and got married. My father worked in the army and married my mum, Hamside. My uncle Nasmi worked as a wood manufacturer and married a girl called Ruho. The youngest brother, Nevruz, worked as a zootechnic and married a girl called Rabushe.

In 1954 all the family moved to what was to be our family home. While my father and uncle Nasmi stayed there, my uncle Nevruz moved away and settled in the city of Fier. He was promoted to head of Zootechnics and Agricultural Entrepreneurs. They were blessed with three daughters, Florentina, Adriana, and Bruna, and a son, Altin. My uncle Nasmi and his wife, Ruho, were blessed with a girl called

Lulezime and three boys, Bekim, Hektor, and Muzafer.

My father and my mother were blessed with five girls: Liljana, Lindita, Merita, Mimoza, me (Yllka), and two boys—my brothers Mero and Bushi.

Living in the same building, with the siblings and the cousins brought everybody very close together. They would communicate with each other from a small inner door between the houses. Even though it was two separate houses in one building, it was easy for us to go through the adjoining door to spend time with each other regularly – as if we lived in the same house. Uncle Nevruz and his family who were living in a different city, in Fier, never failed to come and visit with his family and have a special time together. One of his daughters, Adriana, was a very talented musician and often she used to gather us together around her firzamonika or piano that she used to play passionately, telling us to keep our harmonies while singing serenade songs, where the sound echoed through the gorge that separated the neighbourhood beyond. All the cousins were very close, and we had a sibling bond as a very tight-knit family. On official documents we existed as cousins, but in real life we were all sisters and brothers, together.

As a very trusted and knowledgeable man in the community, my granddad was named a *kryeplak* (councillor) in the area and everyone in the family used to call him Aga (the name usually implying a title of honour and respect to the eldest, the head of the family. And as for my grandmother we called her Mama while in the neigborhood she was called and known as Mama Muzo.

Ever since Grandfather returned from America, he would often go into the mountains and forests to spend time alone. They had barns full of lambs and sheep, and lots of beehives on the side of the valley that the shepherds who stayed on the mountain looked after. Unfortunately, I never met my granddad, as he passed away unexpectedly before I was born.

It was the morning of the 5th of December 1960, and my granddad was around 68 years old. He was sitting on the top of a rock on the edge of the mountain near the forest tending lambs and sheep with his friend. His friend went to get the bottle filled from the mountain stream and when he got back, he found my granddad motionless with his hand placed on his chest looking out into the valley. After calling his name once without a response, the friend came closer and realised that my granddad was dead.

During those days, the quickest (and only) way to pass messages to the house was by shouting through the valley to the nearest place and this echoing would continue until it was finally passed to the family.

His friend stood up at the edge of the valley, took in a deep breath, and put his hands up to his mouth and shouted, 'Ohhhheeeyyyyy.' Then he listened. 'Ohhhheeeeeyyyyyy, Rahman is deaaaaad ohheeeeeyyyy.'

The echo would bounce through the valley until it reached the closest house to the forest. Once they heard the message, they would then reply, 'Ohhhheeeeeey! I've heard you ohheeeey. Rahman is dead ohhhhhhhhhhey.' This would be repeated until the message arrived at the family home. When my grandma heard the news, she was in the house on her own with my brother Mero who was around six years old.

She pulled herself together quickly, got the horse and took Mero with her, plus a few blankets, and set off to bring my granddad's body home. The funeral was arranged for the next day. Grandma, then, became a widow at a very young age.

The tradition in Albania dictates that widows don't wear coloured clothes again. She covered her beautiful dark hair made into two plaits with a black scarf and wore black clothes that she used to wash by hand with cold water and a bar of soap, to stop the colour from fading, and on her feet she wore black shoes with gold buckles that she polished every day before she left the house. Out of respect for her dead husband, she never married again. She concentrated all her life on taking care of her children and focused on their future.

Usually, the bereaved parent had to live with one of their children. In my grandmother's case she lived with her youngest son, Nazmi. As we lived in the same building and had the same garden, I was fortunate enough to see her every day.

She was a very house-proud lady, extremely hard working and very loving. She would get up around 5:30 in the morning before the sun appeared from behind the mountain. After she had brushed her beautiful hair and put it in two long plaits, covered by the black scarf, she would start to water all the flowers, vegetables and grape vines in the garden. Then she would clean the outside of the house with a water hose, and then do the same to the large, metal gates. By the time we got up, the smell of freshly watered flowers and grass would greet us.

Every weekend, she would scurry to the top of the high step ladder to reach the top of the very high staircase to dust the ceiling. Often she would tumble down from the top onto the hard floor and she would get up, dust off her apron and carry on with her day like nothing had happened.

This particular time she had fallen quite badly. It was early Sunday morning when we heard the big bang through the adjoining walls. All the family and neighbours thought this time my Mama Muzo wouldn't recover as she was too old. She was taken unconscious to hospital under the red and white ambulance's flashing blue lights and loud siren.

The next morning when family and friends went to visit her in hospital, her bed was empty. As soon as she had recovered consciousness, 'the cat with nine lives' had decided to get herself back home, sneaking through the hospital's back fire doors and had taken the bus home. When people came to visit, expecting to see her laid out with maybe broken bones, they were surprised to see her shuffling actively around the garden, watering her red and yellow roses. That activity is something I inherited from her.

Often she would roast the coffee beans in a very traditional Albanian way. She would use a metal container with a long metal rod attached to it, which had a small hatch in the front. In Albania we would call this the 'coffee cupboard' to put the coffee in. She would then place it on top of an open fire and turn it around so that each coffee bean would be perfectly roasted. Next, she would put the warm coffee into a large, deep, white stone bowl that had been shaped by hand. She pressed the coffee beans into the side of the bowl with a heavy long iron rod until the coffee was ground into a very fine powder. The entire process would create a fantastic aroma of coffee that you could smell far away.

With her 'hands of gold' as you say in Albania, she was somebody who could put her hand to anything, and she would be skilful at whatever she chose. I watched her constantly in her spare time, knitting by hand with very fine needles and a thin white thread, making gorgeous white lace curtains, tablecloths, the collars for our dresses, the pillow borders, and lots of other things for around the house. I didn't have the patience like her, to try to do what she did, as some of the projects could take months.

She felt that it was important for her to pass her talent to her grandchildren, especially the girls of the family, as it would help us develop our future family home.

'Sit down and watch,' she used to demand. 'Don't hang around too much on the mountain like a boy. You are going to get married one day, so the good hostess wife should know everything about keeping a beautiful, clean home and how to make clothes for her children. Make me proud.' At the same time as giving me a lecture, in her hand she would be holding a needle with white cotton, offering it to me without asking if I wanted to do it or not. It was a tradition in Albania, that girls from a very young age had to learn how to embroider rugs, carpets, curtains, cushions, and lots of other things, and start to put them to one side for their dowry. So, on school holidays all the neighbouring girls in our community would gather together under the shade of the almond trees or terraces with something in their hands to embroider and my grandma would come around to check.

Although she was demanding in this respect, being protective, especially with the girls of the family, was another thing. Incorrectness and disregarding her word on the required time would have consequences and embarrassment. Sometimes in the hot month of July, the older siblings and cousins of our family were invited to an engagement party in the neighbourhood that was going to be held in their garden. I remember, before they left, my grandma would gather them together outside on the patio and order them all to be home by 10 pm.

'Don't worry, Grandma,' my older brother Mero would say, 'I'll take care of them and we will be home on time.'

Of course, being teenagers, curfew was not always kept, as the dancing and singing distracted them and the clock ticked merrily past 10 o'clock. My grandma became really annoyed and frustrated. Pacing up and down she made her way finally to the house where the party was, where everyone would be dancing in the garden.

To save face, she walked into the party with a very big smile on her face, waving at all of her acquaintances but at the same time scouring round the garden for the children. On one occasion, my sister Lindita was the first one to see my grandma. When their eyes locked, my sister knew that smile was for show and that she was going to be in big trouble. Grandma walked over to her and linked her arm and walked her over to the gates and then gathered the rest of the children one by one. They walked back, embarrassed, and after that they never dared to be back home late.

Above all, her fantastic sense of humour was known by everyone around the area and everyone loved being around her. At night when we all sat around the fire with our cousins, she used to get up and be the life and soul of the family. She created such a lot of laughter and fun times, telling jokes and impersonating different people. She was a character. She used to get us involved, giving us a role in a comedy act, for example. Most of the time, when we were all together, we would always have fun times. I used to laugh so much that my cheeks would hurt.

Was there anything that our grandma could not do? If we were ever struggling to do something in school, or to get a job, she wouldn't let anything stop her from sorting things out, even if she had to go to people in power with influence. As bureaucracy was inevitable in Albania, she was a woman without fear and she would even go straight to the mayor if she needed to until everything was sorted out. He and everyone else knew my grandma as a very respectful lady with a great sense of humour.

But that was nothing compared to the time when she went to see the Mayor about the authorisation for television. Living under a communist regime, very few people had a television in the city, as it was very difficult to get one and above all you needed an authorisation letter from the government which wasn't easy to obtain. As children we often used to walk nearly half an hour down and up the hill to go and watch TV when on the special movie night at the home of our Uncle Qazo (as we used to call him), a cousin of ours.

Being a proud woman and seeing us going and bothering our elderly cousins late in the evening to watch TV, she decided she had to do something about it. So, early Monday morning she set off to see the Mayor again, determined not to take no for an answer. Even though he had known her for a very long time, this time he thought that there was really something wrong after seeing her that early in the day, disregarding the security and demanding to see him immediately. He pulled out a chair for her to sit down, seeing her out of breath after walking up the long stairs. Without hesitation she got straight to the point.

'Last night I had a dream of my dear dead husband, and he said, "When are you coming to join me? What have you gained from staying alive longer in this world more than I did?"

'And I said to him, "I'm trying to get a television for my grandchildren, and as soon as authorisation is provided, I will come to your world immediately."

'So just in case he comes to my dreams again tonight, at least I can say that I did something. I secured the authorisation.'

The Mayor let out a chuckle. 'Oh, you had me really worried for a minute, Mama Muzo. I knew you were getting somewhere, well today is your lucky day,' and surprisingly without having another thought, he opened the drawer, took an authorisation letter from it and got his golden pen out to put his signature to it and passed it to Grandma cheerfully.

Grandma walked out of the mayor's office with the authorization letter, happy as a clam at high water.

The black and white television proudly purchased, I'll never forget watching endless Charlie Chaplin films. We couldn't have loved our grandma more.

She passed away at the age of 85, as she had wished all along. 'When my time's come, I want to die as quick as a flash, with my own legs and my own hands. I don't want to be a burden to anyone. And if I die like I wish, I don't want you crying, I want you singing and dancing.'

It was a cold winter day in early December when she got up early in the morning as usual, finished all the jobs and walked with her son Nazmi for one hour down to the bank and back, to get her pension. As soon she arrived home, she went upstairs to her bedroom to get changed and within minutes she was gone, with a massive brain haemorrhage. She passed away quickly, just as she had always wanted. She raised and educated many generations of our family and proudly I was the granddaughter of a resilient woman rarely found.

Unfortunately, I never had the chance to meet my granddad and grandma on my mother's side. Her father (my grandfather), called Hamit Bala, was very passionate about working with animals and passed away when he was almost 60. My grandmother, Afesa Bala, was a nice, quiet little lady of very few words. She couldn't have been any more different from my dad's mother, Mama Muzo. They were two different personalities, like chalk and cheese as we would say, but surprisingly they always got along together. She passed away in her seventies, way before Mama Muzo. She spent her last few months at our house, forging a very special bond with

Mama Muzo, ultimately becoming very close friends.

Often my grandma Mama Muzo used to say, 'Eh, you would have been so proud to have known your other grandma. You would have learnt some very valuable things from her, as *we* all did. Her soft caring manner would calm your soul as deep in the lake on a summer's night.'

I wished I could have met my grandma Afesa and granddad Hamit as they gave birth to my lovely mum, a very special lady who was well educated, hard-working and devoted to her family, putting them all before herself, and her brother, my uncle Nexhip, the man of unparalleled merit and intelligence. My mother was born on the 25th March 1935 and when she was just three years old her brother Nexhip was born in 1938. The brother and sister grew up in a very well-educated family. While my mother married my father Tasin, Nexhip finished training at a National Security Academy and worked in the city as chief of crime for the protection of the leaders of the country. He then married a young lady called Merjem, and they had three handsome boys, Maks, Ben, and Kastriot.

The three boys inherited from their father, my uncle Nexhip, ingenuity and wisdom and grew up with pride and integrity.

CHAPTER 5

The treasure of a moment embedded in my heart

The month of May, my father told me that often it reminded him of one of the most unforgettable days of his life – the day of his marriage to my mother, Hamside. She was the beautiful girl who was the dream of every boy in town. It was Sunday, when the smell of beautiful flowers and the freshness of trees created a feeling of contentment and peace of mind.

That day he was the happiest man in the world. In his arms he had a stunning princess. She was not princess Elizabeth or Victoria, she was *his* princess Hamside. For him she was the most beautiful woman his eyes had ever seen, and that would never change for anyone or anything in the world.

She was a slim, elegant lady, who stood out because of her elegant figure and her long, thick, dark brown hair that she used to pin by the side of her ears with two hair grips. The honest smile on her beautifully dimpled face said it all.

My father was a handsome man with olive-coloured eyes and dark hair. He was a jovial character with a great sense of humour, very charming and flirty with the ladies, which I guess to some extent I inherited from him.

They married one Sunday morning. Traditionally, in Albania, a bride stays at her parents' house until she marries. My father with his family made their way to my mother's family home and after my mother said her emotional goodbyes to her family, accompanied by my father and his family, she then left her family home wondering what her new family and husband would be like.

After a year of marriage, they were blessed with their first child, my sister Liljana. She was born in the spring, on 30th May 1953 when gorgeous daffodils stood out, swaying gently in the mountain breeze. She had dark hair and beautiful grey eyes. Grandma was delighted by the birth of my sister, as she herself had only given birth to boys so this was the first girl in the family.

Liljana was just over one year old when my older brother Ymer was born in the middle of a very cold winter on 10th December 1954. He was a very healthy child with dark brown hair and dark piercing eyes. You never could hear him crying. He was a quiet and contented baby.

Then three years later my sister Lindita was born on 10th of April 1957. She was a very chubby, beautiful child with chestnut hair and dark brown eyes which she inherited from my grandma Afo. Because she was born early in the morning, they decided to call her Lindita (in Albanian, 'lind' means born and 'dita' means day).

My other sister, Merita, was born late on the morning of the 12th of April 1959. She had beautiful chestnut eyes and chestnut hair. That morning when her birth pains started, my mother was scrubbing the wooden floor at the top of the house (the Oda).

This was a room that we used for special occasions so it was very important that the wooden floor was often scrubbed with a very hard brush to make it a bright colour as it reflected the cleanliness of the whole house. My father was working, and the children were at school. She didn't want to disturb anyone else from the family so she took the afternoon bus and made her way to the hospital on her own where she had a normal, quick birth.

My brother Rahman (Bushi) was born on the 30th of September 1961.

Before my mother had informed anybody of the pregnancy, according to my grandmother she had a dream in which her dead husband, my grandfather, came to her again. In the dream he said to my grandma that my mother was pregnant with a boy and he wanted him to be named after him, Rahman. So, my brother was called Rahman after my grandfather, but because the name was old fashioned, they called him Bushi, after *babush*, which would translate into dad/granddad.

My other sister, Moza, was born on the 2nd February 1964. She was born with dark olive skin and beautiful dark eyes. People always made jokes about her dark skin colour saying that she might have been swapped at the hospital for another child. She looked a very sweet child and beautiful. The day of her birth coincided with an incredible story that is unforgettable in our family. On the same day, our horse, Koli, gave birth to a foal. One of the sheep, Kruda, who every year used to give birth to one lamb, that day gave birth to two. Xikua the dog of the family also had a litter of puppies. Ever since, whenever we celebrate her birthday, we sit and laugh about that amazing day.

And I, Yllka, was born on the 30th of September 1967. I was born with greeny-blue eyes and dark hair. My mother named me after the first shooting star she had ever seen in her life. *Star* in

Albanian is Yll. So, to name a girl after a star, you just add the 'ka' on the end and that's why she called me Yllka. Also, I was the only one in the family who inherited the eye colour of my great-grandmother.

So, I was the youngest of seven: five sisters and two brothers.

My mother and father, Hamside and Tasin, were very well-respected members of the community and were honest and hardworking people. They provided a loving family atmosphere, and they made sure that they did not just give us the names, but they also instilled in each and every one of us the importance of honesty, love, and education.

For my father it was paramount that we grew up with integrity and principles, and he believed in the communist country. He always made sure that the household was disciplined, and we never could answer him or anyone else back in a bad way. It was fundamental that we were brought up to be well mannered and respectful to everyone, especially to people older than us. My father worked in the army and was a self-disciplined man with a strong sense of morality, and he was smart and intelligent. He was a well-respected man whose opinions people cared about and he was a character that everybody loved.

He was unique and extremely friendly, but when it came to money, he didn't trust anyone. Everything was sorted and recorded in a large black cloth notebook that was kept in a safe in the corner of his office where he had to write down all the money that he lent or gave to people with the exact date and year recorded by it.

Often, he was considered as being tight-fisted, and some people would ask him teasingly, 'Come on, Tasin, tell us how much money you have?' He used to shake his head and reply jokingly, 'Money and mistresses must never be revealed.' And that's why he never would be caught short of cash. Saving money was his security for bad or good days and for our future as he would often remind us, and he worked so hard to earn it.

Even when he used to shave, he would never use hot water. 'It's just a waste,' he used to say.

On the little wooden box where he used to keep his shaving stuff, there was only a little silver dish with green soap in it, a little wooden brush, and an old metal razor and a little wooden mirror.

It was fun to watch him shave in front of the little mirror in the bathroom. He used to splash his face with cold water to start with and some water on the soap. Then he would get hold of his little brush, rub it a few times to make a foam, then apply it to his face, then quickly switch to his old razor. Most of time he used to come out of the bathroom with little white pieces of newspaper covered in blood stuck on his face from little cuts made by his overused metal razor trying to shave quickly without giving it too much attention. To finish altogether, as an aftershave, he would put a little bit of raki – Albanian alcohol made from grapes – on the palm of his hand and massage it into his face again, making the excruciating noise of 'papapapa' from the tingling and burning sensation. This is the best he would say, and he was probably right, because his skin looked really good, except for two little ridges on the corner of his lips that used to show when he smiled.

He used to make a good raki and wine, but he had to work very hard to keep the vineyard healthy and watered with a good balance of nutrition to allow the grapes to ripen. Several times during the growing seasons as the vines grew, he would spray with pesticides against grapevine diseases and pests. It was very hard work, and as soon as he finished, he would come and lie on his stomach on the wooden floor and I would press my bare foot on his spine, moving my toes to try to massage between his shoulder blades. It was like a kind of neck and shoulder massage.

My mother was a very proud housewife and she also worked at the city wood factory. She was very bright and knowledgeable, and she was widely respected. She was the first one to get up in the morning and the last one to go to bed. My mother would always tie back my dark brown hair with glossy coloured ribbons. She was always very particular about the way we looked as children, and we always looked impeccable with gorgeous dresses and clothes that she used to design and make for us.

I was a very happy little girl who often enjoyed going to the mountains, to collect wildflowers and fruits. Being part of a big family, it was like having a built-in group of friends to play with every day. However, being the youngest did have its perks. I was often spoilt not only by my parents but also by my siblings. I was surrounded by loving crowds, which my dad believed accounted for my adroitness and confidence.

Even though we were brought up with discipline, it did not stop the fun and the enjoyment in our family. Our household was always filled with laughter and happiness. It was very important for our parents that we had healthy food. We always had a spoonful of mountain honey with walnuts followed by fresh eggs that had been collected from our little stone house at the end of our garden where the chickens used to roost before our breakfast.

My dad always wanted us to have the fresh raw egg, but not one of us children wanted it. As soon as he finished giving us the spoonful of honey, he also had one egg himself. He would tip back his head and swallowed it in one gulp. He used to smile while he watched us making faces.

He then used to say, 'You should have the egg raw; it is good for you.'

Following the honey and egg, he had his espresso. He then finished off with a little shot of raki.

So, his morning breakfast recipe was honey, raw eggs, espresso, and raki.

But in winter my mum always used to make a traditional Albanian breakfast called Trahana. She would prepare it way ahead of time, usually in the summer around August, so it would dry out for winter. It was a mixture of flour, soured yoghurt, butter and salt. I remember before she prepared it, she would leave the yoghurt for a few days to ferment, and when she opened the container the yoghurt would have curdled, it would have the smell of something that had gone off; however, that was meant to happen. Then she would mix it with flour and butter, making it into dough and leave it for a few days until the dough smelt sour. Then she would separate them into tablespoon-size balls and leave it till it was almost dry but not 100% quite dry. Once they were ready she would break them into tiny granules by hand and then let it dry on a white sheet that she laid on the terrace of the house under the shade of the grape vines. Once it was dry she would store the trahana in separate jars ready for winter. So, on cold winter mornings there would always be a large pan on the top of the wood burner stove. My mum would put a few wooden spoonfuls of trahana and water and stir them together until it formed a loose paste mixture. Then we had to separate the corn bread into very small pieces on the big tray and she would pour in the trahana, mixed together with bread and finish with olive oil and goat's cheese on the top. And that was our traditional winter breakfast in Albania.

While we all had the breakfast she would start to get everything ready for us for the school day. She would make sure that our uniforms were ironed, and all our shoes were polished. After she got us ready for school, she would hurry to get the bus to work. I always remember her rushing out of the door with her long checked grey dress with narrow waist cut in at the middle which flared out at the hem. My ears still remember the swishing and rustling of that dress like it was only yesterday.

During the summer, when masses of greenery covered the front of the house, we would gather under it and eat al fresco with beautiful summer flowers surrounding us. We would sit around a large walnut table covered with a heavy linen white tablecloth embroidered with flowers around the edges, with matching napkins which my mother had made.

She would serve by bringing the food and the drinks to us and take care of us, making us feel loved and wanted. The sunlight streamed through the branches of the almond trees, and the grape vines would shade us. The Monarch butterfly flitting amongst the rosemary and roses and the clicking of crickets would remind us of that hot summer. The breeze that drifted to us from the mountains brought the distinctive scent of rosemary which filled the air around us. It was just so serene.

September was always an unforgettable time of the year. It was the season of wine and raki celebrations when we would start picking the grapes. I was thrilled with joy, because I used to love it when grape gathering time arrived. It was so much fun, and we had more time to spend together as a family.

On Sunday mornings we all would gather together to make our way to the vines with crates and baskets. Then we would arrange ourselves in pairs and have a competition to see who could pick the most. Then all the collected grapes were put in a huge vat. But that wasn't the best part.

The best part was crushing the grapes, as we danced bare foot, splashing and getting dirty, singing along to Albanian music from our little yellow radio. Then we would put the crushed grapes into large tanks where they would stay for a few weeks until the grapes were ready to ferment and start to make raki and wine.

On these evenings of making the raki my dad would start an open fire outside and wait for the flames to die down. Then with Mum's help, he would put a large heavy copper cauldron into which they poured the crushed grapes and water, finally covering the mixture with a heavy thick lid. It was connected to a copper pipe to transfer the steam for distillation of the raki.

My mum would tirelessly progress to the next step of mixing together flour with water which she would use to seal any gaps between the cauldron and the lid to make sure that it was airtight. On the end of the pipe my dad would put the bottle with a funnel for the raki to drip into. The fire had to be constant and not too high as the distillation had to happen very slowly.

My memory of that night is still so vivid, when all of us sat around, drinking wine, singing traditional Albanian polyphonic songs under the orange light of the moon that streamed through the branches of the old almond trees that grew around us, towering over our heads, as we waited for the raki to emerge from the copper pipe.

The first dribbles of the clear liquid that had taken such precision to make, started rhythmically to dribble into the bottle, one drop at a time. My father lowered his gaze and excitedly said, 'Oooo here it comes! The beauty! Everybody, here it comes.'

As soon as the first bottle was filled, he placed a hygrometer inside it to measure the quality of the raki.

'Fantastic!' he shouted. 'Good gradation raki!'

We all knew that the higher the quality and alcoholic volume, the stronger the raki was getting, therefore, the better the quality of the drink. We all had a small empty glass into which our mother poured small amounts for us to try the first drops. Then my father stood up, raising his glass with pride. It was so predictable. We knew exactly what he was about to say and what game we were going to play. 'Cheers to my wonderful family, health and happiness.'

Then our old humorous game about the raki started. He asked us in order, starting with my older sister all the way to myself.

'Liljana,' he called to my older sister. 'What brings the first glass of raki?'

'Appetite,' my sister replied, laughing.

'Lindita, what brings the second?'

'Health' was her reply.

'Mero, the third?'

'Joy' was his answer.

'Merita, the fourth?'

'Happiness,' she sighed.

'Bushi, the fifth?'

'Excitement,' he shouted.

'Moza, the sixth?'

'Chatter' was the answer.

'Yllka, the seventh?'

'Love,' I replied, a huge smile on my face.

'Yeahhh, hop, hop,' we all cheered happily, and chinked our glasses together.

Dad sipped the last of the raki and waved to us to get our attention.

'Right, one more thing, everybody. Listen. Do not make any plans for next Sunday, because we are heading into the mountains.'

We all nodded in approval and excitement.

Those memories are still very much alive in my mind, of when we used to go and visit the old family house on the mountains, even though it was half in ruins. It was our family tradition to go there every last weekend of the month. And from there heading further towards the Gjere mountain, passing over the stone bridge of Ali Pashes and walking up on the very steep slope.

Early Sunday morning we very quietly grabbed our bags that we had packed the night before. We took Koli, the horse, and the dog Ziko, and headed up to the mountain.

The first stop was at our mountain house. We arrived at the house in the morning before the sunlight spilled over the mountain. I remember with nostalgia the tranquillity of nature, complete peace and joy, lost in the ocean of memories.

As children, we often used to run to a corner of the garden and poke our curious heads over the dry stone wall, fill our lungs with fresh air, and shout down towards the Bufanese creek, usually just 'helloooo', but when the loud and clear echo sang back we would laugh as if someone had told the funniest joke.

On the first day we would collect some fresh oregano, *Caj* (Albanian tea), and lots of different herbs that our father would use to cure different ailments and label them accordingly on separate jars. Our pastime would be to collect fresh figs and plums with which my mother and grandma made jam and marmalade for the winter.

The second day we started to harvest the tobacco that my dad had planted months before. The plants were grown in straight lines and would grow nearly two metres tall with big leaves that would be entwined within one another. My mum always made sure that we were wearing old clothes and covered our hair, as the leaves of tobacco were very sticky and dirty. Then our dad always would say, 'Don't forget, kids. Start removing the leaves from the bottom.'

After harvesting the tobacco leaves, they were strung together using a large needle with a string thread through them and put out to dry in a shed-like structure. They were left hanging under the shade until they finally dried.

When the tobacco was ready, my father used to go back with my brother to grate the tobacco into very thin pieces, and then would come back home with our two horses. Working all together as a family gave us a strong common bond.

Near the house also there was a large barn where our sheep and lambs were kept. They were taken care of by two shepherds, and two big dogs would also be used to guide and guard the flock. The sheep would often graze in the huge field surrounding us and would drink from a nearby river suplied by cold water coming from the gorge of the mountain.

On completion of our work at this time, we would refresh ourselves by taking our favourite Albanian drink called llall, which was yogurt-based, and which was prepared by the shepherds. Due to the lack of electricity, it was kept cool on the edge of the water running through the little white rocks.

Scooping fresh water with the palm of my hand, my toes being tickled by the ice-cold water, and watching as my brother tried to splash us all, I felt surrounded by unconditional love. I looked up at my mum, and her eyes radiated pride and love. While we were walking up towards the barn, my senses were aroused by the smell of the fresh cornbread made by the shepherds and the noise of the crackling fire that it was being baked on. As I walked, I ran my hands along the napes filled with mozzarella and feta cheese that were left there to drain, hanging from the trees' branches. We found a spot of shade created by a copse of enormous old trees, where we finished the rest of our cold llall as we looked over the valley and let the mountain breeze caress our sun-kissed face.

My mum would take the large wooden round tray (called sufa) that had three short legs to support it as it hung from the wall of the barn and the nine little wooden spoons with an eagle beautifully carved into the handle, and take out the steaming cornbread. She would place some cheese, tomatoes, olives, and some pastry with spinach and cheese that she had prepared at home, and we would sit down on the blanket of lambswool to eat.

My dad would go with the shepherds to get the lamb that they were going to slaughter for our dinner. They then would put the lamb on the spit ready to roast while my father prepared the fire. Everything then was ready.

As the sun set over the mountain and the night approached, we all settled around the fire, watching the lamb carcass turn around on the spit, roasting over the gloriously hot fire. The fresh red wine that had been made by my family was passed around by my father. We sang polyphonic songs on this warm night with a full moon shining down on us.

Everyone was happy and relaxed. Surrounded by my siblings and my mother's and father's love, I felt content and lucky to have such a wonderful family; the treasure of that moment embedded in my heart.

But the happiness, unbeknown to us, was about to vanish, without warning, like a black raven disappearing into the darkness of the night. Gone forever.

It had been just too good to be true. The family everyone wished for, would be destroyed in just a few days; like the cornerstone of a house crumbled and the roof fallen in, all would be lost forever.

In just a few days, those beautiful times would disappear, like a dream in the night. Everything would change forever.

CHAPTER 6

The black January

It was a late cold winter morning in January 1972 – a Saturday. The pale light of the winter sun brightened the day and slowly tried to melt the frost from the previous cold night that covered the pebbled street. My mother was taking me to the doctor's as I had not been well for the previous couple of weeks, and after the brief visit, we started our short 10-minute journey back home up the steep hill.

Suddenly my mother let go of my hand and stood still, she shut her eyes tight and only after feeling a light tug to her blue skirt she opened them to look down at me. She saw the worry in my eyes and forced a smile and said, 'Don't worry, I just got a little light-headed. Let's take a break and sit down.'

She took her scarf off and placed it on the icy stone bench under our walnut tree that had grown over our garden wall onto the grey stony path, displaying its lofty arms with naked branches. It looked like winter held this gaunt skeleton in its tight grasp, where twigs shivered from the bitter wind scything down from the snow-locked Gjere mountain. Then she picked me up, sat me there and wrapped my scarf around my neck, covering my lips, making sure that the chill was not seeping in, although my hands were freezing.

'Mammy,' I murmured. 'My hands are freezing.'

She took my red gloves from my hands, kissing them and blowing warmth from her breath. Unbuttoning her coat, she placed my hands inside next to her chest to warm them up.

'Is that better, Mammy's sweetheart?' she whispered. 'Yes?'

I shook my head as I looked up at her face which was as white as paper, and with her shoulders slightly slumped. She gazed up to our family home at the very top of the garden, let out a sigh, wiped her brow, and looked back over to me. After a few short minutes she held out her hand and said, 'Come on, we're nearly home. Let's go.'

After what seemed like a long time, we finally arrived at the front door. My mother slowly reached for the door handle, and as she put all of her effort into opening it, her legs crumbled beneath her, and she fell to the floor.

I screamed out, 'Mammy! Mammy!' but there was no answer. The urgency of my sudden shrieks meant that within a split second I saw my brother Mero leaving the axe where he was cutting wood at the end of the garden, running towards us, and my father appeared from the other side. Their faces were paralysed with fear when they saw Mum unconscious on the cold, stone floor. She was losing a lot of blood and getting worse. The ambulance arrived after what seemed an eternity. I could hear its sirens creeping closer when the flashing lights came into view.

The constant flashing of the lights reflecting across the gates and onto my face has stayed with me since that day. Although they were so bright and piercing they brought pain to my eyes, I couldn't keep my eyes off them. I was strangely entranced, probably because of the sheer shock.

The paramedics sprang into action, picked my mother up and took her to hospital. As the ambulance sped away, the high-pitched wail of the siren sent a shiver through my bones. I stood there and watched it disappearing around the corner and a great sadness washed over me. I sat on the stone bench next to the towering gates, wrapped my hands around my knees, bowed my head and prayed for my mother to return home soon and well.

I don't remember exactly for how long I was sitting there in the cold until our dog Xiko came to find me. I felt his head on my lap and his paw on my arm, trying to comfort me in his own way. From a distance I saw my sister Lindita rushing back from her concert, a distraught look disfiguring her face. She embraced me and said, 'Oh my sweetheart, it is too cold to stay out here. Let's go in.'

As we entered the hall, we could hear quiet sobbing in the corner. My other sister, Moza, had her face buried in a hand-embroidered handkerchief with white lace trimming that my mother had made. My sister Lindita rushed over to comfort her before we made our way into the living room where the atmosphere was so quiet and sad.

That night my worst nightmare grew out of the darkness. There was a fire at the end of our front garden. I shivered in the cold night air. When suddenly, I saw my mum in her chequered grey dress running across into the fire. I ran after her, stretching my arms out towards her to stop her going deeper into the fire, but she never turned her head back to respond to me. I was crying and calling her name, but my voice was swallowed by the crackling of the flames and the smoke where she faded away and appeared from time to time. A strong wind blew her thick dark hair around her body, almost blotting her out.

I tried to scream, but no voice crawled out of my mouth. The fire flickered alarmingly, and as she faded away into the flames, a flock of pigeons flew out past her, screeching loudly, and disappeared into the orange sky. I surfaced from that awful dream, my gaze locked onto the wooden ceiling as I gasped for air. Sleep escaped me for the rest of the night as I struggled with my emotions.

The news about my mother spread across the neighbourhood quickly. A constant stream of people flowed through the house in silence. A growing feeling that something wasn't right overcame me. I felt this sadness inside me, my eyes constantly filling with tears.

'When is my mammy coming from the hospital? I want my mammy!' I cried.

'She will be back soon,' my sister Lindita replied, trying to comfort me.

I turned around and saw my grandmother sitting on the white sofa near the window, sipping her espresso, a worried look swimming in her eyes.

The revving of a car engine destroyed the cloying silence. Everybody rushed to the front porch to see the door of the old, grey Jeep open slowly, to reveal a man with dark brown hair, dressed in a white buttoned-down shirt; my mother's only brother, Nexhip.

I was used to seeing my uncle with a beaming smile on his face and a brand-new toy for me to play with in his hands. But this time, his hands were empty, his famous smile had gone to be replaced by a blank expression and an unnatural glazed look that had no place in his once-friendly face.

My grandmother ran down the stone steps to the parked car. She whispered something inaudible, to which my uncle replied with a simple shake of his head. The frantic look in my grandmother's eyes and the gesture of shock and sadness told me that something really terrible had happened. I did not understand what this might mean as my ears were filled with the piercing shriek of my sister Merita's voice, 'Oh Mammyyyyyy!'

I turned my head to see my brothers and sisters weeping in each other's arms. My frightened eyes darted between my uncle and my siblings.

The unknown became too much. I ran over to my uncle, looked up at him and shrieked, 'What's going on? Where's my mammy?'

He crouched down, scooped me up in his arms and with a trembling sad voice he said, 'Oh, uncle's sweetheart. Your mammy has gone to heaven.'

Tears started to roll down my innocent cheeks. I shook my head and began to cry, 'No, she hasn't, you're lying, she would never leave me without kissing me goodbye.'

He struggled to talk, his voice shaking with emotion as his words seemed to stick in his throat. Sweeping me into his arms, he hugged me tightly while I wept into his shoulder.

The next day was the funeral, as is the tradition in Albania. The lifeless body of my mother was kept in an uncovered coffin overnight, on the top floor of the house, in the largest room – the oda.

Close friends and family had to stay awake and spend the last night together, sitting around crying. It was disturbing and horrendous to stare at a dead body all night. I and my siblings had been kept at our next-door neighbour's house and in the morning, they took us to say our goodbyes to our mum.

From outside the house I could hear women's voices crying aloud with words that terrified me, making me not want to go in. The big gates were wide open and lots of people were everywhere on the patio and in the corridor. A woman in black whom I didn't recognise, nor can remember to this day, came outside, took hold of my hand and led me inside the house. As I walked through the hallway, the sound of the crying started to fade away and from the bottom of the stairs, I could hear the low hum of people talking, trying to comfort my older sisters.

'Let's go up,' the woman said to me with a soft voice whilst holding my hand. I nodded and followed her. As we climbed the first few steps, the crying and wailing started again loudly. Panic knotted in the pit of my stomach.

'I don't want to go up there,' I cried, gripping the handrail of the stairs, not wanting to take another step.

She held my hand so tightly, insisting that I move on.

'Come on, you want to see your mummy for the last time, don't you?' she insisted.

I started to scream. I don't remember exactly what happened after that as the rest is just a blur; as if it has been erased from my memory. I do, however, remember myself on the terrace, sitting in my mother's rocking chair, wearing my best dress – a dark blue one with a white collar that my mum had made for me just a few weeks before – when my grandmother picked me up and took me away from the house to avoid upset as the coffin was brought out.

After what felt like hours sitting around at our next-door neighbour's house, I was finally allowed to walk out onto the front porch. I saw a long line of people walking down the hill following a large coffin covered in red satin with beautiful white flowers around it. I saw my oldest brother Bushi, with his head leaning against the stone wall, watching the funeral procession with tears streaming down his face. I walked over to him and tapped his shoulder; he quickly wiped the tears from his face to return to being the responsible brother that I was used to seeing. He gave me a hug and together we sat silently watching the long column of people in black, walking down the cobblestone path.

It had been just two days before that my mother and I had walked home together, and now she was following the same path but in the red coffin carried on people's shoulders. We sat there until the long line of people disappeared around the corner of the castle.

Sadness tore at my heart and plunged me into despair. The dearest, the most wonderful mum to seven children, taken away and gone forever – taken like the leaves stripped from the trees by a cyclone – at just 37 years old.

That was the saddest day in my entire life, and for all my sisters and brothers. We were left without the most loved person in our life: our dearest mother.

It was Monday, 24th January in the very cold winter of 1972.

At that time the only one of seven siblings who had left the house was the older sister Liljana. She was 19 and had married a lovely gentleman called Asllan, from an admired aristocratic family. Asllan was a wonderful man who loved my sister dearly. His self-respect shone through his words, gestures and the way he presented himself. They lived in a city called Fier, which was a three-hour drive from Gjirokastra and they were blessed with a beautiful baby daughter called Adela.

My next eldest sibling was my brother Mero, 17. He was an apprentice in mechanical engineering and continued the course at the industrial school of mechanics as my mother wanted him to do. He was a very shy and polite boy, loved by everyone. He was very hard-working and would always help in the house or go to the mountains to take food to our shepherd and stay there for few days helping them during the dairy season.

My sister Lindita was a good student in her last year of middle school. She was a very quiet, caring girl. Due to her being an exemplary student, she was offered a scholarship to carry on studying industrial chemistry at high school, but she chose not to. She decided to stay by our father's side and help him raise the other children. She knew her way around a sewing machine very well, so after she finished middle school, she found a job as a machinist at a very big tailoring company while still trying to finish her education at night school. She was efficient and thoughtful, and she always had with her a red net bag to go food shopping after finishing work. Even though she was only 14, she was trying to take my mother's place and did a good job of filling the void. After my mum's death, I used to sleep with Lindita and follow her everywhere. Sometimes my siblings used to tease me by describing me as the little lamb who followed the sheep.

My other sister Merita, 12, was in year six. My father used to call her 'Daddy's genius'. She was a very bright, clever, and a well-known student in the country through different competitions held nationwide. Just a few months after my mum's death, she received a condolence letter from the leader of Albania, Enver Hoxha.

In the letter, he also praised her for being a good student and at the same time expressing his deepest regrets about my mother's death to her and our family. However, the letter had a low tone of political propaganda; he did not forget to mention that from now on her acting mother would be the Communist Party, as she belonged to them as their daughter. It was a great honour that the leader of our country had taken his time to write to my sister and her family. For this, a big celebration at the school was held, where the Mayor of the city gave a speech.

My brother Bushi, ten, was in year four. He really did not enjoy school and as soon as lessons finished, he would run out playing with his friends, pretending to be driving the best cars. He didn't waste a lot of time trying to figure out a course of action. If he chose to do something, he would do it quickly; end of story – without having a second thought for the consequences or being scared of anybody. However, being the typical boy, he never failed to be that close to his sisters and brother.

My sister Moza, aged seven, had just started school. She was very studious in school and would often get picked to recite poems to big audiences. Her acting was incredible and she won awards for performances at such a young age. She never failed to remember her script and jokingly often she would get called the chatter box, as she never would stop talking. But sometimes she would get in trouble for not holding back her honest opinions to others without a second thought.

I had just turned four and was at kindergarten. I always remember the uniform – a little white pinafore with frills on the shoulders and my name embroidered on the front as a kindergarten uniform. My older sister Liliana and her husband, Asllan, took me to their home in the city of Fier for almost a year and took care of me together with her daughter Adela, a two-year-old. I don't remember a lot as I was only four myself at that time but I do remember her heavy posh white pram that I used to try and push with my sister Liljana on the evening around the beautiful parks full of daisy flowers and me proudly saying that she was my little sister. And I do recall that we not only shared a bedroom together but some of the clothes, too. Sometimes we used to fight over pink pyjamas or pink socks. To avoid all that, my sister embroidered our name on every piece of clothing and stuck it to our pyjamas.

Time was moving on, and finally I went back home to my city Gjirokastra and back to the mountain with my dad. The year away was like a medicine that had helped me to deal with her loss.

Since her death, nothing had been the same. My mind knew that she was gone, but my heart never accepted it. I tried to tell myself all of these years that her spirit was there when I needed her, and she was there next to my bed giving me a goodnight kiss. Every birthday before I blew out my candles, with my rosemary in my hands, my wish was not for a doll or bicycle like other children do, but it was to see my mother once more, feel her arms around me and hold her tight; though obviously that would never happen.

I wanted to believe that she was there taking care of me, following me like the breath in the air as they say on a cold winter's day and whispering through the leaves as I walked down the street, but deep down I always knew that I was never going to smell her scent and get to see and hug my mum again.

Her warmth, love and those little moments of affection and serenity, and her beautiful heart and sincerity, laid the foundation for my life, the person I am today.

CHAPTER 7

There is nothing like a mother's love (The Rosemary)

Walking hand in hand with my sister Lindita, we passed the ancient metal gate of the cemetery, looking at the rows of graves, as they sat silently. Once we had passed through the stark gates, a strange feeling pervaded my body, like dead people were watching us with their invisible eyes. Light wind seemed to whistle between the ancient trees like the ethereal voice of the owl. Apart from gravestones, the remaining ashes of those once living buried between the years and flowers that dominated the appearance of the cemetery nobody else was there – just my sister and I. Yet, I still felt like the soul of the dead presence following us; nonsensical in the extreme.

We walked quietly as if we didn't want to break the silence that hung over the graves. Halfway down the gravel path, on the left side, where three trees huddled together, we turned and as we passed other graves we stopped at the white marble grave and looked at the headstone that carried the picture of our mum, her thick wavy hair over framing her beautiful face seemed to be looking at us with compassion. I pressed my cold lips against the marble, my face touching the picture like I wanted to desperately feel her kiss and her hug. My heart heard the whispering of her voice, like she was next to me. The rosemary planted by my sister and brother had grown beautifully and the sprigs were spread around the marble stones as if they wanted to protect the grave, staying there like desperate guards. We filled the vase with water and put our bunch of lilies in it. After clearing the grave of debris, I plucked a stalk of rosemary and put it in my pocket to keep with me everywhere and anywhere I would go. It was so comforting that I could have the smell of my mother around me after helping me to drift off to sleep at night. Since my mum passed away, I was no longer the happy girl I once was. I felt lost. It felt like a part of my body had been ripped from me, and with it my mum's love and her embrace. Desperately I wanted this peace to return, but it never did. It disappeared into the empty air, never to return.

It had been several months since my mother had passed away and one late afternoon in spring my father picked me up from kindergarten, and as we were walking up the hill, my eyes settled on a lady walking in front of us. She had a bunch of rosemary in her hands, and she was wearing a similar checked dress to the one that my mum used to wear. Her long dark hair had been tied with two grips on each side, looking just like the way my mother wore her hair.

'Look, Daddy, look, Mammy is back from the sky,' I yelled. 'Mammyyyyyy!'

Without a second thought I started running towards her, calling her as I ran.

'Please stop, please, Mammyyyyyy, it's meeeeee!' I yelled again, but she never stopped or turned her head.

My dad caught up to me, lifted me and held me in his arms. While he was trying to comfort me, he whispered, 'That's not Mammy, sweetheart. That's somebody else.'

'No, no, that's my mammy. Look! The dress, the hair,' I gasped, as my voice shook, and my tears wouldn't stop running.

Yet, that woman never stopped; never even turned around to tell me that she wasn't my mammy, and that made me more suspicious and scream even more. My father hugged me tightly, raised his head towards the sky and told me to look up while pointing to the stars that had just begun to show as dusk began to fall. He said, 'Look at the star that shines the most, look your mummy is there.'

I cupped my hands around my mouth and shouted with all the power of my soul, 'Mammyyyyy, can you hear meeee, Mammyyyyyy.' But nothing. I kept calling her, waving at her, calling again and again, but nothing. Dissapointed, I turned my head, looking towards my dad and said quickly, 'She can't hear me, Daddy, she is not answering.'

He stroked my hair, kissed my forehead and replied, 'Mummy can hear you but we can't hear her as the atmosphere in the sky spreads the voice away.'

With tears streaming down my face, I wrapped my hand around his without saying another word.

That day, the pain in my father's tearful eyes appeared and reappeared constantly and *it* remained painfully embedded in my memory for a very long time.

Times were difficult for us all. Everyone tried to help. My grandma, my Auntie Ruho, with my uncle's wife, Merjemi, came for a few hours every day to shower us and clean the house. My siblings and my father tried to keep everything as normal as possible. Traditions needed to be maintained, to the extent that we still used to go to the mountain house to spend time together.

As the days passed, all my brothers and sisters took care of each other, and were especially considerate of me. They knew they had to keep my routine as similar as possible to when my mother was alive. So, everybody took turns to take me to school and back.

-o-

Growing up, I loved performing and singing on the school stage and still never stopped visiting my favourite place – the mountain Yet, my mum's absence created a gap that no one could fill. They realized that what had happened affected me deeply and because of it I developed a few strange behaviours as I have been told from my siblings. It was sometime in the summer that I started sleep walking through the house and even outside into the garden where I was surrounded by greenery. The only place I would head for directly was my tomato patch. As I walked between the stems, the sticky fur from the green branches would stick to my pyjamas, and once I had wandered around for a while, I would go back to my bed and wake up with green-yellow speckles on my pyjamas and my sheets. No one realised why until one Sunday morning my sister Lindita changed the white sheets and spotted the residue from the tomato plants and the smell from the tomato leaves which she found under the pillow.

From that day on they used to watch me at night and as soon as I got up they would follow me around without saying anything, being very cautions not to wake me in case they scared me. As well as this, I became a very emotional child, bursting into tears very quickly at the slightest things that seemed to hardly matter, and most of the times those tears would turn to anger. I would kick the other children in anger, and I wouldn't let them win any games we might be playing.

Getting into trouble and creating issues in school deliberately was another thing. It was unexpected for a girl of my age to behave in such a manner and I didn't appear to be listening to anyone.

Unlike other children I liked spiders and often I used to collect them, put them in a little jar and take them to school, where I released them in the table drawers, scaring the other children knowing how terrified they were of them, especially Rita the girl with ringlets in her hair. Her beautifully ironed red and white spotted dress and the shiny patent shoes with white daisy flowers that she always wore and her mum, who picked her up every day, called her out, 'Ritaaaa, Mami is here,' while shaking a square thin-shaped Chocolate Flora that was covered in a shiny red wrapping.

Somehow she would always walk in front of me, and always going on about how her mammy was the best mammy at doing hair.

I had had enough listening to her bragging about her mum and her hair. 'Shush,' I mimicked her voice. 'My mammy this and my mammy that.'

'Haha!' she laughed. 'You are so jealous because you don't have a mammy to do *your* hair.'

It didn't take me long to quickly fill my hand with a blue coloured powder from the cleaner's trolley that was standing by and throw it into the back of her ringlet hair without thinking of the damage that it might cause.

'There you go,' I said. 'Who has the best hair now that yours is about to turn blue, ha?'

Shocked, she ran towards the stairs, screaming. I got away with lots of things I shouldn't have, but this time it was a step too far. Within no time I was called to the headmistress's office. Disappointed but not surprised at what I had done this time, she asked me sternly, 'So what's your exuse this time?'

'I didn't do it,' I responded with defiance.

'Who did it then?' she asked crossly.

'I don't have a clue,' I replied, shaking my head as I stared at my knees. Only in that moment did I realise that the powder was all over my dark blue trousers too.

She frowned, looking down at my lap, shook her head in disbelief and said, 'How do you explain this?' pointing at my by-now blue trousers.

At this point I knew I had been found out and felt the tears spilling out of my eyes. I was upset, not because I was sorry for what I had done but because I was angry for having been caught out. I looked up and my eyes crossed with the head teacher's disappointed face waiting for my answer. I knew there and then that I wasn't getting away with it this time. I had to apologise and pretend that I meant it.

'Sorry,' I muttered, almost under my breath.

She got up from her chair and came towards me. She put her arm around my shoulders; her voice had softened. 'I just need to know why you did that. You can tell me.'

I lifted my head up and it all came out, I couldn't control myself.

'I hate her and her flat-faced mammy! It's not fair! Why does her mammy have to pick her up every day and wave at her with Chocolate Flora in her hand?' I snarled.

Her frown melted away as she gasped, 'Oh, little sweetheart.'

She looked at me sadly and took both of my little hands into hers and said, 'Because your mummy is not here, that doesn't mean that she is not with you. Although you can't see her or hear her voice, she walks beside you, she wraps her arms around you, and she'll be listening to your stories if you talk to her.'

Somehow for the first time since my mother had passed away, I felt my spirit lift, my eyes lit up from her heart-felt words, and I believed everything she said. To this day I recall those special words and the flora chocolate that she often used to bring for me at school on special days.

And that was the last warning.

By the time I left the headmistress's office, everyone else had gone home and I was the last person to leave the school. I took my blue jacket from the green painted wooden coat racks that were attached to the classroom wall and headed home.

Outside, the winter had wrapped around the city and there was a chill in the air. The windows were covered with frost and while I was walking, I discovered little frozen puddles. With my old brown boots, I started jumping onto the ice and let out the anger until the ice smashed. It was shattered into pieces and the water spilled out which made me feel triumphant and relieved. I didn't like the despairing face of the little girl who looked back at me in the reflection. Somehow for the first time since my mother had passed away at some point it dawned on me that nothing was going to bring my mother back; not hitting other kids, not destroying the books, not getting upset. I was only seven and I thought that I was being punished when my mum's life was taken away, but I didn't know that the worst was yet to come and *that* was to be just the start of my life's journey.

CHAPTER 8

Mountain House
(The TT Russian pistol)

O utside, the trees whispered from the early morning breeze while in the dark sky the last few stars were slowly disappearing. From the outside patio door light, I could see my father taking Koli, the horse, outside the large iron gate, hanging the bags full of food on both sides along with his rifle and an axe, and waving at me to come out.

'Are we ready to set off, mountain girl?' he said in a low voice.

'Yes, we are,' I replied cheerfully, jumping with excitement following Xiko our dog who was running towards the gates.

He picked me up and sat me on top of Koli, our horse, making sure that I was safe and comfortable.

'We have to leave before daybreak as on the way we have to stop at our old mountain house to pick up a few things and for 4-5 hours will be on our barns in Kracale (place name), on the Gjere Mountain,' he said in a low voice. 'Let's go.'

I shook my head in approval, rubbed Koli's head and carried on. Our family dog Xiko led the way as my father held the reins to guide the horse. He switched on the hand black torch to light the way on that quiet morning dawn where only the clip-clopping of a horse and the first chirping of a few birds could be heard nearby.

I didn't ride the horse all the way but would walk part of it, so the horse didn't become too tired, and it was also good exercise for me. As I became older and bigger, the horse wasn't an option anymore, as, according to my dad, I had to walk all the way up the mountain if I really wanted to become a strong mountain girl. Also, trotting up the mountain would have been too much for the horse, so we loaded him only with essentials to carry.

From being little, I had been drawn mystically to the mountain. I was amazed by its stunning beauty and became very passionate about it. Apart from playing with my friends, I spent most of my time as a child on the mountain with my father. He enjoyed this fact and often used to say, 'You have your father's blood running through your veins; you are Daddy's little mountain girl.' Which, as a little girl, made me push my shoulders back and strut about.

Occasionally I was scared and worried, wondering if he could remember the way before the daylight appeared, but he just knew with closed eyes how to get there. He knew where to take each path, every stream, every gorge, every mountain – he was better than a navigator. These mountains he grew up with were like his second home and much loved.

Of course, going to the mountain was enjoyable, but also it had its dangerous side. That's why my dad showed me how to shoot at a very young age, and he used to say, 'To become a strong mountain girl you need to protect yourself.' So, we often used to go shooting and from a very early age I learnt how to use a gun. I had no fear about this dangerous weapon; it became second nature to me. I took my first aim at the shooting board with a little revolver with no bullets when we were going to see my older brother Mero in the army.

The military base was situated near some green fields on the edge of a big hill full of olive trees and berry bushes. I could see lots of army barracks, where the young soldiers were training.

One of the officers was a commando called Muco who knew my father and came across to greet us. Behind his army green trousers, I saw a different coloured holster with a little pistol inside. Different from my father's pistol, it was a TT Russian model and had a gold handle that stood out. This made me curious and I wanted to have a go with it. And that's the revolver I shot with for the first time. While we were waiting for my brother Mero to come out of training, we walked fifty metres away from the main building into the open and stopped opposite the target board.

'Sit-down here for a minute,' my father said, pointing at the metal stands built on the top of the big rocks. And as he took the bullets out of the pistol he said, 'Now before you use this, I need to explain to you the danger of the revolver. This is not a plaything. If you don't use it properly, someone can get hurt, or even killed.'

Even knowing it was an empty gun he wanted to explain thoroughly in the simplest way possible, so I understood completely before I used the revolver. I nodded my head impatiently as I could not wait to get hold of it and shoot. He had to hoist me up by my waist and put me on the top of the stone bench where I could be on the same level as the shooting board. Finally, he handed me the pistol, and as I took aim, he put his hands around me, holding my arms, showing me how to shoot. When I pulled the trigger, I heard this dull click from the blank round, and in complete excitement I pressed the trigger several times.

Not long after that I used a gun with proper bullets and it wasn't as easy as I thought. To learn how to shoot with a gun with my father was beyond my imagination.

'You don't have time to stand in front of a target and shoot if the enemy is in front of you,' he would say.

He would stand me with my back towards the target, and then when he said 'Shoot!' I had to turn around quickly towards the target board and shoot quickly.

'You need only one shot, on the forehead between the brows, getting it right first time if you want to survive. That way you don't give your enemy time to kill you,' Dad used to say. It became like a little game that I used to love playing, and I was getting faster as I grew in confidence.

But this time my father and I were going to the Gjere Mountain to our barns built on the place called Kracale to help our shepherds Esat and Boco who were taking care of our cattle and helping them on the dairy-making. Often it was my brother Mero that used to go and help them, but he was still doing his army duty, so this time it was me and my father's turn.

After an hour we passed the old mountain house and ascended from the Ali Pash Tepelena Bridge built over the Bufanese creek and took the direction towards Gjere Mountain.

Five hours later we arrived, greeted Esat and Boco and dropped the bags full of food and essentials. We all freshened up with the cold water that was coming from the gorge of the mountain, then we had something to eat together.

The short break was done and without wasting any time my father and the shepherds went next door to the grey stone hut where they were making the cheese and storing other dairy products, while Xiko and I went to collect some Oregano, Caj (tea) and herbs together. I was intoxicated by the air filled with the scent of oregano and tea that grew among the wild grasses, and with the smell of the wild lilies that grew around the bottom of the trees. Sitting around by the open fire at night, roasting chestnuts and listening to the noise of the water gushing from the mountain stream was just wonderful.

The next morning we ascended to a cloudy sky followed by the light wind that was coming from the south. The clap of thunder rumbled somewhere over the horizon and a few clouds sparsely scattered in the sky. 'There's going to be a storm,' Esat said.

My dad looked around and replied, 'You got that right, Esat. We'd better hurry up. Finish what we left from last night and hopefully by afternoon we will be ready to move on before it catches up with us.'

And as my father said, we managed to finish and in few hours we got ready for another long journey back home. We said our goodbyes and set off. Another clap of thunder rumbled again but this time it was nearer to us. Suddenly the sky went dark and the clouds spread out so fast, they looked like they were chasing us. The wind started blowing stronger from the south as my father looked up in the sky. He shook his head anxiously and said, 'We are going to take a short cut over the little bridge, a different way from the one we took on our way here. There seems to be a bad storm coming, and so we must cross to the other side of the mountain before the rain starts as the bridge is too dangerous to cross in the rain.'

We reached the side of the mountain where we could see in the distance a narrow long bridge with no handrail that connected the two mountains.

'Wooooooow! There's no way I can go over that bridge. It's too narrow, and I won't be able to keep my balance,' I said to my father.

He came over to me, and, looking me straight in the eye, he took hold of my hand, and said, 'We don't have time to turn around. We need to get over that bridge now, Daddy's mountain girl.'

Before he could finish his sentence, I could feel Koli, my horse, starting to tremble. He pressed his tail down and his entire body tensed, which paralysed me with fear. My dad stared at me and without me saying anything he urged, 'He can feel your fear, so you need to remain calm and do not stress.' I nodded in agreement.

Knowing about the strong connection and understanding he had with all animals in our family and especially with Koli, somehow, I had faith in him. He took a minute to stroke Koli's fur softly, gave him a short-arm massage and rubbed the brown star on his forehead. He was taking time to calm him down and to make sure that Koli was steady and calm enough to take me over the bridge without throwing me down the abyss that was more than 1000 feet down.

Then I saw Koli draping his head right over my father's shoulder and rubbing his cheek against his face.

'He is happy and relaxed now and ready to go,' my dad said, trying to reassure me. 'Do not look down, close your eyes and hold on to Koli. Trust him and you will be on the other side of the mountain in no time.'

'All right,' I murmured.

I stroked Koli's withers softly and kissed the back of his head. He let out a loud breath through his nostrils and make a soft snorting sound.

'Let's go,' I whispered, staring into the distance, trying to control my worry. I trusted him. He had never let me down, and I felt that he loved and understood me, more than any human ever did sometime.

My little hands tried to hold tightly onto the horse as he started walking over the bridge. Xiko went first then after him came my dad, holding the rope that was tied to the horse's body to keep balanced. I shut my eyes and the only thing I could hear was his horseshoes clanging on the stones, marking time with the faint sound of my heartbeats as we passed over the bridge. Although my father was in front of me, it seemed to take forever. Within a minute the wind, blowing from the north, threw its torrent of rain at us, splashing into our faces. I heard Xiko barking tensely as Koli gently touched me with his muzzle, because he was scared, too. I lowered my head towards him and said, 'Nearly there, nearly there, big boy.'

'Stay still and do not look down,' I heard my father shouting. It was difficult to hear clearly because of the sound of the thunder and lightning which was getting louder.

Relieved we had made it to the other side of the mountain, but as the storm significantly worsened, it became impossible for me to remain seated on the horse. My father sat me on his shoulders and after a long tiring walk, we found a small, uninhabited wooden hut covered with green ivy and surrounded by ancient trees with roots that emerged from the earth and spread out as if they were long witches' fingernails. The doorway was covered with misty spider webs and clouded by branches.

Inside, it was almost empty apart from some dry logs for firewood and some old rusty tools left in the corner. He brought the horse Koli and our dog Xiko inside, took the rifle, the axe, and the bags off the horse, and stroked his mane. Xiko, drenched from the rain, shook his body and came towards me. I stroked him and placed some water in a little metal bowl for him and the horse to drink.

Cold and saturated from the rain, we got in and tried to make a little fire to get warm and dry. He got the axe and tried to cut some fine pieces of wood that luckily were dry. He taught me how to build a pirate fire by criss-crossing the wood into a pile that looked like the shape of a grand Lego. Then he took out his old-fashioned lighter which you switch on by using a small stone. Instead of fuel, when the switch was flicked the stone would twist and create the friction for the flame to appear.

He had a little fire stone wrapped in a white cloth inside a little metal box and asked me to hold it while he opened the lid of the lighter to get ready to put the stone in and said, 'The last stone, be careful, hold it tight, don't drop it.'

The little stone, smaller than a needle dropped from my freezing hands into the straw.

'Oh!' I shouted. 'I dropped it, Father, I dropped it'. He looked as my eyes filled with tears, grabbed my little hands, and said quietly, 'Mountain girls don't cry. Let's try something else.'

Then from the inside pocket of the bag he took out a small old wooden box. Inside the box were two little white shiny stones and dry grass, which he made into the shape of a little nest.

'Watch,' he said, striking the stones together very quickly for a few minutes until a little spark appeared. He drew the little nest close to his lips and blew through the sparks to the nest. The smoke started to come out of the nest, and after a few minutes fire climbed out like magic with sparks that were crackling up like they were dancing like Christmas lights.

He then placed the firewood on the top of the nest and the orange colour from the flames illuminated the room. In the corner I saw a thorny bush where a lot of spiders were scrambling. It was fascinating playing with those spiders, catching some of them and puting them on the palm of my hand, watching their thin little brown legs covered with fine hair climbing up like they were trying to stroke my arm.

My father started singing our old polyphonic song about Kapo, my mum's uncle, who was one of the first heroes to die in the war, gesturing with his hand for me to follow him singing in harmony. I put the spiders back on their web and carried on singing with him.

Kapo, man with no fear, fighting mountains.
Stood up on the front line, mountains
For the freedom of the people, he roared, mountains
Barrage of bullets took the hero down, mountains...

In every song he sang, there was a story and I could listen to him for hours and not get bored. He was an incredible storyteller. I was only little, but I was very curious about the war and fascinated by the family stories that Father used to often tell us.

'Dad,' I said inquisitively. 'We always sing this song about our hero, uncle Kapo, but you never told me the true story. What exactly happened?'

'Ah,' he nodded, smiling gently, 'it is a good thing that you want to know about the war and the heroes of our family.'

While I was waiting for his story to start, he lowered his head, took the cigarette that was already rolled from his silver box, lit it from the fire and after a few draws, he began to tell the story.

'Well, as you know,' he started, 'our old mountain house is full of different stories from years ago when the Italians and Germans invaded our country.

'We were occupied by Italian fascists on April 7, 1939. Albania was a primary base for Italian forces. With few weapons of their own, ordinary citizens and a military force of partisans that was created stood up fighting against heavy fascist artillery who intended to harm our country.

'Unfortunately, our old house was always in the middle of the Italian and German battles, and both sides of our family were involved with the partisans, fighting for our country's liberty. This would make our family and our home prime targets. Our families were always very patriotic, so any chance we could get we would help the partisans. We would give them food, clothes, a place to stay, and anything else that we could offer them.

'Your mum's uncle, Kapo Baco, was one of the first partisans to leave the city and go to the mountains to fight for the liberation of Albania against Italian fascists. He was a warrior dressed always in heavy shajak clothes (it's made of a processed black sheep wool elaborated into a very tight and heavy material with a rough finish). We rarely saw him in uniform. He was a battalion deputy commander from the summer of 1942 at the age of 22 and had participated in dozens of battles in the war and was known for his incredible bravery.

"Rruga e luftës është plot rreziqe e sakrifica, por ne jemi të vendosur që të ecim në këtë rrugë, sepse vetëm kjo do të na japë fitoren"!

'The road of war is dangerous and full of sacrifices, but we are determined to walk this way, because only this will give us victory.

Everyone knew Kapo for his bravery but the one story that surpassed all the rest and left anyone speechless was the battle of 8 April 1943. Kapo's garrison just arrived at the area of low Dropull. As soon as they approached the Dhivjani main road, the Italian convoy with an armed car accompanying their army wagons that was coming from Greece reached them. The vehicles kept coming and the number of soldiers seemed endless. There were far more than Kapo thought there would be; almost ten times as many as *his* battalion.

'He needed a quick plan. He needed to think on his feet to avoid the complete destruction of his own army. The armoured car was most dangerous. Somehow he had to defeat the Italian soldiers who were firing incessantly from inside and get hold of the armoured car.

'He turned to his team and yelled, 'Listen up.'

'The fight today is going to be tough,' he warned them. 'There are so many more of them than us, it looks like 100 so far. We need to split up. Half will take one side of the road, and the rest the other.

'My plan,' he continued, 'is to launch a grenade at them and then try to get myself to the armoured car first while you shoot at them continuously so that it might make a clear pathway for me and Themo to get there.'

'Surprised, one of the soldiers stepped forward, saying, "That is impossible!"

'Kapo looked at him and said sternly, "We have no choice, and we have no time. You will do what I say."

'Quickly, without an ounce of fear, Kapo was first to approach the armoured car, fighting the fascists, followed by Themo and some others, while the rest of the partisans covered them by constantly shooting and throwing the grenades towards the enemy. They got hold of the armoured car after overpowering the Italian soldiers that were in the car.

'Every day, every hour and minute Kapo was there in front line planning and fighting against the Italian invaders to the last day of his life.

'It was the 14th September 1943. After many battles against the Italian army, most of the garrisons were destroyed. Only one garrison remained. For one last time it was Kapo and his battalion's task to fight until their destruction and bring freedom for their country.

'Kapo and his friends were stationed at the top of the road in the place called Grohot, keeping a watchful eye. Through his binoculars he saw the last Italian garrison approaching the other side of the road. They had heavy artillery and the number of soldiers looked like a sea of black ants covering the earth.

'He stood up in plain view and carried on shooting continuously with no fear for his own safety.

'"Kapoooooo, get down," one of his friends Asllan shouted to him.

'But Kapo was not listening, while he kept firing his last words echoed through the dust raised by the gunfire.

'"For the freedom of the people!" he shouted, and his inspirational words stopped as the bullets hit him, and he fell with a smile on his face looking back at his soldiers on the bullet-covered road. He died for his country and his team, a true martyr. He was only 24 years old, and he was named one of the first heroes of our country.

'After the capitulation of the Italian forces, Germans invaded Albania. They committed murder and crimes against humanity; nearly 60,000 houses were either partially destroyed or completely knocked to the ground. They were supported by liberal nationalists called 'Balli' that had different motives and some of them eventually joined with the Nazi Germans. They fought as allies against partisans who fought for their country. They constantly had their people spying on families that supported partisans, so we always had to be careful in every movement. My cousin Bari was with the partisans in the mountains fighting the Germans and they would often visit our house, which would be watched by the Ballist spies, so we had to be careful.

'One cold, misty night, Bari came into the house to get washed and obtain some food for the partisans. As I looked out of the window, the head of the leading Ballist on the German front was directing them to our house. Obviously, the partisans understood Bari had been spotted. We didn't have much time, so my mother concealed him in the attic. The Ballists and Germans were banging on the gates with the bottom of their rifles, almost like they were going to knock it down. "Open the door!" they shouted loudly.

'They kicked the gates down before Mother could open it. They grabbed her by the shoulder and pushed her to the ground. They placed the pistol at her head and yelled, "Where is the partisan?" Their ballist translator was always with them. She was terrified. "I don't know. I haven't seen any partisan," she replied.

'Within a second the German commander ordered other Germans, "Get inside the house and check everything." Their behaviour was erratic; they started searching the house, shouting and rifling through everything with their bayonets. When they hadn't found anything, they came outside to the commander and shook their heads in disappointment. In his anger, the German commander grabbed my brother Nasmi and hit him on the back of the head with a rifle, knocking him unconscious.

'Mother rushed towards him and grabbed him to her chest. But the German commander took Nasmi from her and pushed him into the wall. The other German soldiers burst into other houses in the neighbourhood, dragging out five more young boys. They brought them outside our house, and they lined them up against the wall, and they pointed their rifles towards us, yelling, "You have five minutes to tell me where the partisan is or each one of you boys will die." A neighbour ran to get my father who was the kryeplak (councillor) in the area. As a kryeplak he had the right of speech to defend his people. He rushed back home and said in English to the German commander, "Leave the boys alone, there's no partisan in my house. I will be responsible if there is. You can kill me if I am lying."

'A German commander, much taller than my father, with a stern face approached him. He lowered his head and went nose to nose, his eyes narrowed with anger and with his louder voice said, "If you are lying, I will burn you alive."

'My father looked at him unflustered and nodded his head.

'Surprisingly, the Germans made their way out of the house as Mother quickly grabbed my brother and I and breathed a loud sigh of relief. To this day I cannot believe how lucky we were to be alive as just two weeks before that Germans barbarically killed 14 young boys (the youngest was only 12 years old) on the edge of the Manalat torrent.

'After a long war when hundreds of Albanians gave their life fighting the Germans, on the 29th of November 1944, Albania was finally liberated from the Germans.

'Eh, my mountain girl,' my father said, letting out a deep sigh. 'I could stay here forever and tell you lots of stories, but as it seems the rain has stopped so we must get ready to return home.'

Without saying a word, I smiled at him and nodded my head in approval.

We went out and the storm seemed to have stopped as quickly as it had started, and the clouds were moving from the south behind the mountain like they were trying to hide. I could smell the blissful air of the rain-soaked mountains and somewhere, the sound of pouring rainwater, overflowing from the little gorge and slithering down like serpents between the rocks. The clouds shrank away, and as it grew darker the stars appeared in the sky. Somewhere in the middle of the mountains we made our way back home, following the wet path that looked like a carpet covered by golden-brown rotten leaves and a few branches, scattered from the uprooted trees that had been attacked by the storm.

CHAPTER 9

The Wicked Stepmoms
(Salted tea)

That day, I saw only sorrow and worry in my father's eyes. No smile, no talk and certainly no jokes. He was sitting on the walnut table outside, gathering some dry tobacco leaves, and after squeezing them together he tied them with twine in a round shape. He took the knife that he had just sharpened a minute ago and began to slice the tobacco very thinly and place it on the cloth that he'd already laid under the shade of an almond tree before and let it dry and made his way to the living room. He sat by the window staring out at the large front gates in deep thought. I watched him out of the corner of my eye while he took out the silver box of tobacco and rolled a thin cigarette. Wondering why. Something wasn't right, as a pregnant silence filled the room. It had been nearly two and a half years since my mother's death, and it was still difficult for my father to come to terms with her passing, along with the fact that she had died at such a young age. He used to get up early before the sun peeked over the mountain and, before doing anything else, he would gather lilies from the garden to take to the cemetery. It took him one hour to walk down and more than an hour to come back uphill. Once there he would clean the white marble tombstones and water the rosemary around Mother's grave, and he would sit there for hours.

My father's aunts and my grandma became very concerned about him, deciding to find other women that he might marry and so to ease his pain. They thought, this would get his life back on track.

At that time divorce was seen as shameful, so there weren't many divorced women around. However, to our great surprise they managed to track one down, 3-4 hours' drive away from our city. She was twice divorced, with two daughters.

It was a Tuesday afternoon if my memory serves me right, towards the end of spring.

I ran upstairs to my sister's bedroom and just as I got there, the silence was broken by my father's aunt. Out of the blue, she arrived in our house with a big smile on her face. She gathered us all into the living room and said, 'We've found a wife for your dad. She is a very nice lady whose name is Lata, and don't let me down, I expect you to be good and respectful.'

'Oh, am I going to have a new mammy?' I shouted in excitement.

'Yes, you are, sweetheart,' she said reassuringly, drawing me into her arms.

'And will she pick me up from school like Rita's mummy, and bring me Flora chocolate?' I gasped, hardly able to contain my excitement.

'Of course she will,' she replied.

However, my excitement didn't last long as I turned around to look at my siblings. Within that one fleeting moment, everything had changed. The sad and tearful looks on their faces said it all.

'We don't want another woman replacing our mother,' my older sister said, her voice trembling with emotion.

'Your father is still so young and needs someone by his side and help to take care of you all,' my great-aunt replied softly. 'The decision is already made, and she is waiting outside in the car.'

From the window I saw my father open the big gates, and there she was – short hair, medium height, dressed in a yellow blouse and jacket. It was paired with a short, coffee-coloured skirt, with bright red lips.

'Not very good taste, perhaps?' my sister muttered. Then she turned around quickly and said, 'Don't run to your daddy and tell him what you heard.'

I looked at her, shaking my head, feeling so sad that I couldn't even speak up; if I spoke, I would cry. That was the last thing on my mind. Filled with confusion and fear, with disappointment etched on my face, I realised she was nothing like my mammy. Frowning deeply, we could see this woman was the exact opposite of our mother, and we couldn't have been more sad or disappointed.

I ran to my bedroom, took the branch of rosemary that I kept under my pillow, and, climbing to the terrace, I sat on the rocking chair that my mother would sit in, holding the rosemary to my chest. I gazed to the heavens in the sky, wishing that she would just come down and be there with me just for a few minutes. I needed her love. I desperately wanted her arms around me to tell me that everything would be all right.

I crossed my hands around my chest, closed my eyes, and imagined her embrace.

I felt her love whispering, 'My little star. Mammy is here, Mammy is here.'

I didn't want to open my eyes. I clasped my hands ever tighter around myself, wishing that she would always be there and not go away again. That was a special, irreplaceable moment that I wanted to last forever.

As the days went by, we all tried to accept the drastic changes in our family as our father's happiness was the most important thing to us. Everyone attended to their daily task and tried to return to normal. My father was working hard from the early morning to the late evenings.

Unfortunately, it didn't take long after the marriage for arguments between my father and her to begin, and as the days passed slowly, shouting and confrontation became more frequent. Their arguments were my first taste of martial dispute. The atmosphere in the house changed dramatically. No one in the family was happy anymore. My father didn't seem himself; he always looked sad and distressed. Often, in the late evening after finishing all his jobs, he would sit outside on the terrace drinking his raki with olives, eating goats' cheese and raw onion, along with smoking his cigarettes. Most nights he would sleep there on a portable sofa and cover himself with a heavy red velenza that had been made from lamb's wool.

I was too young to understand and work out exactly what was happening and whose fault it was but what I *do* remember is that I was terrified to be near my stepmum. My life was filled with silent fears. This made me miss my mum even more, and life couldn't get any worse for me. I felt trapped, but I never said a word. I was locked inside of myself, wishing that one day my mammy would come from heaven, take me in her wings and together we would fly into the sky away from everything.

This dreadful state of affairs began to affect our growing up. My brothers and sisters decided that it would be better for all of us to separate and take care of ourselves away from it all and leave Father to his married life. Fortunately, being a big house, it was decided by the family to divide the house into two separate paths. So, we opened a different entrance, just next door to my father's front door.

But how were we going to live with only two small salaries that came from Mero and Lindita? Had they really thought it through?

My older brother Mero, only 19, and sister Lindita, 17, become the head of our little family and took care of all of us. A lot of the time we didn't have basic food, decent clothes or other necessities. Mero had a gentle and caring nature and made sure we had what we needed. He would concoct something for us to eat and tried to cook with whatever food was left in the kitchen cupboards, and my sister Lindita tried to organize everything. She washed and ironed our clothes and put us all before herself, while Merita helped us with education. Bushi and Moza and myself were still in school.

Unforeseen, how everything changes so quickly. How ironic! Isn't it strange how life plays its part? How unpredictable it can be? Even though life can accompany sadness, as humans we have to face it and cope in one way or another and somehow make life as adequate as possible.

This was where life drastically changed for us all. One minute we were on top of the world growing up in a family that had everything and next minute we had nothing, except the love of our siblings. And it is not just any love, it's very special; it was love that kept us all afloat. The very first day of the month of May 1976 gave us all the first taste of penury life that we would face in continuous days. The reason I remember that day, it was because it was the 1st of May the International Workers Day, in Albania it is a known national public holiday – a day full of festivities throughout the country.

In the morning, on the long boulevard that ran through the main body of the capital of Tirana, the parade used to take place every year and march in front of Byro Politike. As they marched the people would clap hands, cheering Enver Hoxha. On the late morning a show would be held in the square of the other cities for people to watch and then families would come together for a celebratory meal or barbecue. Outside, in the parks, or around the Viroi lake in our city Gjirokaster, you could not avoid the beautiful smell of lamb from the spinning spit roast barbecue, as well as the sound of singing and dancing. We all went to watch the singing show, but afterwards, unlike everyone else who were having their feasts, we made our way home to have our dry spaghetti that our brother was making for dinner.

He put water and salt in the pan to boil ready for the spaghetti. We all sat there waiting impatiently for our dinner but unfortunately when my brother looked in the kitchen cabinet there was no spaghetti. To make it worse, there was nothing else to eat either. Realising our situation, my sister suggested that we have Caj (Albanian tea) with dry toast. So, my brother swiftly put the caj into the pan where the water was left boiling. In five minutes, the tea was beautiful boiled, the water turned a bronze colour and the dry toast was ready. We poured the tea into our cups, added a spoonful of sugar and finally sat down ready for our dinner. As soon as I took the first sip, the taste of the salt mixed with sugar made me baulk. I looked at my brother in horror and said, 'What have you put in the tea?'

He looked puzzled then after taking a quick sip himself he quickly realised what he had done. He had forgotten that he had put the tea to boil in the saltwater that he had got ready for the spaghetti. I will never forget his poor sorrowful face covered with guilt that he had spoiled the only chance of dinner we could have had that night. The spell was quickly broken when my sister started laughing.

'This is so funny,' she said as we all joined in laughing, trying to make our brother smile too. We knew that there was nothing else to eat so we just had dry toast topped with olive oil, salt and oregano. As we were laughing, my sister raised her cup and said, 'Happy 1st May and cheers to our unforgettable dinner.' That situation allowed us to develop our own motto which got us through – no matter what was happening – we were still surrounded by each other's love and care. Well, it happened, and we just had to accept the fact that certain things would never go back to the same as before.

My older brother Mero, old enough now, fell in love with a girl whom he used to sing on the stage with. She was a beautiful, blonde, blue-eyed girl called Firdes. They got married and we all lived together and became seven again.

Then my sister Lindita was sent to do volunteer work and that's when she met her husband, Petrit. Petrit had grown up near the capital city of Tirana. He was ever so quiet and such a nice man. She fell in love with him and got married. It was very upsetting for me when my sister Lindita left home. I used to sleep with her and no one else. She was like my second mum and as much as my other siblings tried to take care of me, it wasn't the same. My sister Merita went to a special electromechanical school in the city of Berat. So, my brother Bushi, my sister Moza and I were the only ones left living with my brother Mero's family.

Surprisingly, my stepmom became pregnant and they had a son called Edmond at the same time as my brother had a beautiful daughter called Gentjana. So, there was another sibling to add to our family, and we became eight.

He was a lovely child with dark hair and olive eyes. However, not very long after they had Edmond, their marriage broke down and it ended in a very nasty divorce, leaving my father on his own again.

Although his family continued to search to find him another woman to spend his life with, the horrible experience with his last wife took away any interest he might have shown for the time being. His priority at that moment was only working hard and taking care of us. So, we were sure he wouldn't get married again.

How wrong could we have been!

-o-

Not long after my father's divorce, his aunt, Naxho, took me to live with her in the capital city of Tirana to continue with my secondary school education. I was 12 years old, and she was around 70, living on her own and working for the minister of constructions, Rapo Dervishi. He was a single father with two kids after his wife passed away. My great-aunt Naxho took care of his family and dealt with everything that needed to be done. She was like a mother to him and grandmother to his children.

Late one Sunday afternoon, as the tea kettle whistled, we heard the knock on the door. We couldn't have been any more shocked when my great-aunty opened the apartment door. In front of us: my father with another woman.

'This is Dori,' my father said; 'your new mother.'

Stunned by this unexpected announcement that came out of the blue, for a moment I looked at my great-aunt with question in my face to find out if she knew about this or not. I put two and two together. She didn't need to say anything; her face said it all. She damn well knew. How could she not. She was the only one who always searched for my father's wives. My gaze turned to my father's future wife, my stepmother. I looked at her hesitantly. She looked way younger than my father. She was just over five feet tall, with brown hair, and wearing a long green flowery dress.

She gave me a hug with a smile and she moved to the living room. Despite trying to digest all that was happening, my eyes couldn't miss her laddered tights. Nervous, trying to make conversation, I said quietly and innocently, 'Do you know your tights are torn, do you want something to sew them?'

'Give me something to sew them with,' Dori replied.

I took my great-aunt's sewing box and passed it to her, still looking down at her legs. She threaded the white cotton into the eye of the needle, took her tights off, and placed them on her lap ready to sew them.

'My nana told me that you don't sew the tights with white cotton as it shows,' I said, quietly. 'You need to use the thread from these old tights, so it doesn't show a lot. Would you like me to sew them for you?' I smiled kindly.

She forced an embarrassed smile, and said, 'yes'.

I took the sewing box and fished out a pair of old tights that we used to get the thread to sew the new ones and I got a little cup to put inside the tights to stretch them while I was sewing.

In no time I handed them back to her while she went to the bedroom to put them on and returned with a happy face, showing how good they looked.

I saw my great-aunt's eyes fill with tears as she looked at me with pride and pity.

It was very important in Albania, and especially in our family, to be a proud wife; to be presentable, to be able to cook and manage the family life. But that was the last thing on our mind, as long as she was nice and had our father's best interests at heart; that was the main thing.

At that time my sister Merita graduated and moved back to the city. A family member played matchmaker and set her up with one of his friends called Vilson, and just after a year they were married. He came from a very well to do and respected family in the city which was fortunate for my sister.

My brother Bushi had been sent back to complete his army duty which wasn't too far away, just outside the city centre. I finished year seven and went back to my city Gjirokastra to live in the house with my sister, Moza, my father and stepmother. Back home I could not miss how people whispered on corners while I passed by, while others asked me with a pitying look on their face how I was and how my stepmum was treating me, which I found rather strange and uncomfortable.

Soon I found out about the previous life of our stepmum after the conversation I had one evening with my great-aunty. The new wife of our father was only in her early thirties, 20 years younger than my father. After two failed marriages she had four young children whom she had left behind. The youngest daughter whom she had with her second husband was only two years old. She left her village thrilled about her good fortune in marrying my father, believing him to be a rich man with a big house. Well, as they say, the news spread fast and the concern of our family and neighbours was understandable. They had their doubts as they used to say 'She left her own four young children', so there was great speculation how she would love and care for Hamside's children... And lots and lots more... but you can't stop people from talking so the only thing we could do was carry on as normal, hoping to prove people's opinions wrong and to try the best we could not to jeopardise the happiness between our stepmother and our father.

After everything he had gone through, we just wanted him to be happy.

But our wish wasn't to be granted as not long after she put her foot in the house different rules were made and our life became unbearable once again, but this time it was worse.

She put a lock on our food cupboard.

It was sometime in September, the start of the school year. Our father was away with his work. The next day, when my sister and I came back from school, we went to the kitchen, only to find that the cabinet had been locked with a heavy silver chain and a rusty lock, so we couldn't open it. We were shocked. We had never known such a thing could even be done to other human beings. My sister Moza turned around and asked our stepmother, 'Why are there padlocks on the kitchen cabinet? What century are we in? We have never had to have locks on the kitchen cabinet before.'

'Because I have to. I make the rules in this house from now on,' she scowled.

'Even the jam that our grandma made yesterday, you've locked that in?' I asked.

'Yep,' she snapped.

'So, what are we having for dinner?' my sister asked, changing the subject.

'Get some grapes from the garden and some bread; that will be your dinner,' she replied.

'We've been having that for days, and I have been having terrible tummy aches at school,' my sister replied, quite agitated.

'Can I have the bread with something else?'

She glared at my sister and said, 'Yes you can, with your teeth.'

We looked at each other in shock. We couldn't believe her cruelty. This wasn't even logical. We had so much food in the house that we used to help others, and to lock the food away for no reason just didn't make sense. She wasn't contributing anything to the household and yet she still deprived us of food. What was her real reason for doing this?

We would never have dared answer her back before, but it had got to the point where my sister could not hold back. She had the guts to turn to my stepmother and looking at her angrily said quietly, but firmly, 'My father needs to be told about this. This is not normal. Surely, you don't think you can come into our house and lock our food away?' Then she grabbed the padlock and said, 'Now, please open it.'

Our stepmother was now filled with rage from my sister's threat. With a knife in her hand she grabbed my sister Moza by her hair, pushed her head into the cabinets, and screamed, 'You'll do what I say or you're going to regret it, bad girl.'

I couldn't believe what was happening right there in front of me. I felt terrified. I ran to save my sister from her hands. My brother, who lived on the other side of the house, heard the commotion and jumped over the wall that separated our homes. Shocked at what he was seeing, he rushed quickly and grabbed hold of my stepmother, taking her away from my sister and glared, 'What the hell are you doing? You evil woman.'

It was a scene out of a horror movie. I could feel my body shaking from the trauma. I had never heard my brother raise his voice, never mind grab someone. Never, in our family, had there been such a thing. It was unbelievable what was happening. How could one person turn our family into something ugly? Having grown up in a very educated family, how can someone come to your home and not just take your mother's place but also turn your entire life upside down and everything that was built with love and integrity once again is ruined? With that question hanging over my head, I felt my brother's hand stroking my hair and embracing both me and my sister tightly and saying, 'Come with me.'

'No. I'm staying here at my house,' Moza insisted defiantly.

'Well, I can't leave you here, at least come and stay with me until Father comes back,' my brother Mero said softly to try to convince Moza and myself to go with him.

My father returned home, and everything was brushed under the carpet.

In order not to cause damage to their marriage, as well as not burden our brother's family once again, we parted and lived alone. Moza was at high school and I was in the year eight of secondary school and we were both in the year of exams, studying and surviving on a minimal amount of money that we had been given from a little pension following our mother's death, and from our father, and sometimes for working on the farm during school holidays. Life was tough. Our lives had changed just like that, from having everything, to having nothing. And along with that, after our mother's death Christmas presents somehow diminished. But the good thing was that the government supplied a few basic presents for Christmas for good students as incentives. Sometimes we would be lucky enough to be assigned by our school to be on the Christmas gift list. It would be something that would mean so much to us and brighten our lives just that little that we needed. We would go and pick them up at the city cinema building. We would pick up the surprise box, not knowing what was inside. The gifts would never get sorted in regards to gender, so the girls would find boys' toys in their box and vice-versa for the boys. If they were willing to exchange we would swop.

Because we had to take care of each other, we had to grow up quite quickly and somehow we made it work. We got on very well but as sisters do, we would have arguments now and then over silly things like games; our competitive spirit would always start something between us. I guess by now Moza and I had grown through the major crises together and had to deal with problems that no one should have to at our age. So that was the thing that kept us consistently together.

At the end of the month when we would run out of money, sometimes we would pick wild cabbages growing around the meadow and boil them for dinner or often have leftover dry bread, softened with boiling water and marinated with some olive oil, salt and oregano on top. I used to laugh with my sister Moza when she would say, 'Who is brave enough to eat boiled wild cabbage, but meat and potatoes anybody can eat.' She was so good at lifting anybody's spirits high.

In winter, to keep ourselves warm, we would sleep together in bed as we did not have any heating or fireplace. We bought a little kerosene stove that we used not only for cooking but also to dry our clothes that we'd hung up on chairs scattered all around. Sometimes while we were so focused on our studies the clothes would end up in flames and only the burning smell would make us realize that's what was happening. Often we would end up with one odd sock after singeing one, so we'd have to cut the other one that was left in two and make it a pair of socks again. Often our clothes were becoming worn out and the colour fading away, but we couldn't afford to get new ones. Thankfully having the sewing machine we used to unpick the seams, open them up and turn them inside out and sew them again. After a good ironing, people used to think that we had new pair of trousers. But more tremendous was the plastic bags that we had to wrap around my socks inside my school shoes, on rainy days to stop the rain getting through the holes. Otherwise, I would be wet and cold in school all day. Not only that, but the lack of the most important item of clothing for the winter – a reasonably warm jacket. That was essential, particularly on snowy days when the temperature fell below zero. Sometime around the end of 1980-81 I was lucky enough to have handmade woollen little grey coat. Call it coincidence or call it fate. As they say, someone was there, just at the right time and in the right place. It was a very cold winter. Snow covered the city like a plush feather cushion and the large snowflakes were prancing excitedly through the night sky onto the frosty cobbles. The branches of the naked trees were now wrapped in luxurious white winter coats, that were so heavy they caressed the floor.

I made my way to my sister Merita's house, which was a big house where she lived in with her mother-in-law and father-in-law. At the time she had a beautiful little girl Ornela that she used to dress in white handmade clothes. Every time she used to come to our house, somehow she had this tendency of going down to the cistern where she always fell on the stairs and ended up going back home with dirty clothes and cut knees.

Their house was usually around 30-40 minutes' walk away from our house but having to trek through the thick snow made it seem longer. The icy wind gripped my bare cheeks, turning them a scarlet red. To make it even worse, I was only wearing a jumper. I tried to walk faster to get warmer quicker.

When I finally arrived on their doorstep her mother-in-law Nezo's face said it all.

'Oh, my goodness,' she said, shocked, without even greeting me. 'Where is your coat?'

'I forgot to put it on,' I lied, embarrassed to tell her that I didn't actually have or own one.

'Oh dear, don't just stand there, get in quickly,' she ordered, ushering me inside.

As we climbed the large staircase into the living room, I noticed a large wardrobe at the top of the stairs fitted to the wall. She opened the white doors quickly, got a thick woollen handmade zipped grey jacket, and said, 'Wear this, I think it will fit you well.'

'I have a jacket,' lying blatantly again. 'Just forgot to...'

'Try it on,' she insisted, ignoring my protestations.

'See,' she said as I put it on, 'it fits you perfectly. It seems like it was made for you. Now let's have a hot tea to warm you right up.'

Kind gestures like this, that now sound like nothing, were colossal at the time. A new jacket, in the cold winter, in a communist country, was a treasure. I took such good care and pride of the jacket that I was able to wear it for a few years until the sleeves got shorter above my wrist, and never forgot that cold night in the freezing winter. Unlike us, thanks to the army, my brother Bushi had the biggest and warmest heavy khaki army coat, much bigger than his body, he looked like as if he had sunk in it. He was on army duty at that time, but it was going to be finished by the next year. In winter he used to bring back home chestnuts that he used to harvest from the orchard nearby and in the summer we used to take fruits from our garden. The only ones we didn't have were watermelons. We knew how much he liked them.

The minute watermelons filled the shops, we bought one, cut it through the middle and decided to take half of it to Bushi. Moza and I walked for nearly an hour on the hottest day in July to his barracks. We arrived at the big gate with the half of uncovered watermelon in our hands and asked for our brother. His embarrassed face said it all but his pain and his love at what we had done for him were plain to see. Together we walked a few minutes away from the barracks and sat down under a chestnut tree where the half of watermelon was sliced in three. And right there, you couldn't compare a brother's love with any other love in the world. He finished the army duty at the end of that year and we moved back on the other side of the house to live with him. This time there was no going back; too much damage had been done.

As long as our father was happy we were happy too. Of course, his wife's devious plan had worked well. She had it all worked out. It was her plan all along. She was trying to get us out of the house so she could bring her children to live there with her. As soon as we moved to the other side of the house with our brother, my stepmom took two of her own children (son and daughter) to live with them. Obviously, my father took care of them, educated them, and raised them as if they were his own. They grew up with a normal life and they had everything that we did not. But life goes on.

In this case, tragedy had formed a bond that was truly irreplaceable between us. Luckily, one by one, my brothers and sisters created their own family. Their homes were filled with the laugher of their children. My eldest sister Liljana and her husband Asllan by now had three beautiful daughters, Adela, Rozana, and Elisa. My brother Mero and his wife Firdes, had two wonderful daughters, Gentjana and Rudina, along with a son called Tasin – he was named after my father. My sister Lindita and her husband Petrit had a beautiful daughter, Enkelejda, and two sons, Ilir and Alban. My sister Merita and her husband Sone had two gorgeous daughters, Ornela and Nevila, and brother Bushi married a nice dark-haired girl Vjollca and they had two beautiful daughters, Silda and Ada. Moza, my other sister, married a nice lad Vladimir and had a daughter, Klara, and a son, Alex. And Edmond lived with his own mother in the different part of the house.

However, I was still quite young so they all took care of me until I too was old enough to marry (young girls at that time in Albania wouldn't be able to stay on their own, they had to stay with family until they got married). I had to travel from sibling to sibling like a ball rolling from one foot to another to live with them from year to year. My small, battered, wooden suitcase was my companion which I had to re-cover with a brownish material to make it look new.

As for my father, I would make a conscious effort to speak to him every day; even after the events that had gone on, my love for him was unbreakable. After a while, out of respect for our father, we tried to forgive and forget, to be civil, and to talk to his wife. Good or bad, she was our father's wife, and we had to try to live with it. We would visit them as often as we could, take presents for them both, and try to make life as normal as possible, as if nothing had happened in the past. It was obvious that my father wasn't a happily married man. He would cover his sadness by telling jokes and laughing, but there was no doubt that he missed us dearly. When I looked at him I knew what he was going through and suffered with him in silence. His guilt stayed with him for the rest of his life. My mother had always held a large place in his heart, and so he missed her greatly and would often go and lay her favourite lilies on her grave. Anytime her name entered a conversation, he would talk about her with pride tinged with more than a little sadness – a bittersweet memory. He would often state that there was no other woman on the planet like my mum and dredging a heart-felt sigh out of the depth of his soul, he would say, 'Ehhhh, her serene face could melt a monster's heart and her soft voice would calm your soul and warm the heart of people around her.'

As I could see his shattered heart through the despair in his eyes, I would run straight to hug him, to see if my love could help to ease his pain and sadness.

The only thing we all wanted for him was to be happy, but unfortunately, he wasn't. His happiness had faded forever, and his life had deteriorated, taking a tumble for the worse. The marriage was a disaster from start to finish and there were constant rows.

As the years went by, my father was getting older and she didn't care about his well-being anymore. Luckily he was still a strong, proud, and hardworking man, used to taking care of himself.

Many times they came to the point of divorce, but somehow, they would get together again after she would leave for months and then come back again. I never could understand why, because there was neither love, nor respect, nor care for each other left in the marriage. In that marriage, where words of love should be spoken, there remained only hate, anger, shouting and cursing. So, why did she come back to him? Why? What were her plans? Did she really love my father?

She had it all worked out, and the most shocking truth would be revealed thirty-three years after their marriage, when my father had passed away.

CHAPTER 10

Growing up under a communist regime

As I was growing up, the communist leader of Albania, Enver Hoxha, was my idol and inspiration. We were always told and made to believe that we were very lucky living in the best country in the world, having a very good life as children, and we should appreciate this. They used to tell us about African children and other children in the world who were starving and how lucky we were not to be one of them.

Despite the lies they feed you with, there comes a time when I started to process everything and wake up from the doctrines of communism. I began to think that so many things that were happening to us didn't make sense and didn't seem right. Those thoughts were reinforced when we managed to watch a programme from a foreign channel for the first time by creating a homemade aerial using a very thin aluminium pan lid. We cut it into very thin strips like the shape of an octopus to catch the intermittent signals. Before we were able to sit down to watch the foreign channel, we had to make sure that the aerial was hidden on the corner of the roof on the side of our garden where no outsider could see it. When I think how much time it used to take us to adjust the antenna in the right direction until it picked up Greek TV channels it makes me laugh. One of us had to be on the very top corner window and turn around the antenna while someone had to stay between the stairs shouting under their breath downstairs to the one that was trying desperately to find the channel: 'Turn from the north, turn from the south, noooooo, slowlyyy, stop it there', and so on and on until finally the channel was found and then quickly and quietly we were gathered around, desperate to find out what exactly was happening the other side of the world.

The door was locked, the curtains were drawn, and the sound of the TV was turned down low so that none of our neighbours could hear.

As we watched, the puzzlement became stamped on our faces. The life in these 'foreign' countries seemed like a different world to us. The documentaries with shops when people walked around with trolleys picking up any food, anything they like from the shelves of supermarkets, contrary to us queuing for hours very early in the morning for milk and eggs. Before the daylight, I used to walk with a little torch in my hands down the cobbled path to the shop that we called 'Hervos Shop'. First of all, I used to stay around one hour, then I used to replace my presence with a silver metal bottle tied to a heavy little stone so the wind didn't blow it away, placed behind the last one. The other people used to do the same, replacing themselves with an object, like a bag with a stone inside, or even a little vase, saving us from staying in the cold outside for a long time. About an hour before the milk wagon arrived, everybody would go back in the queue and replace the object with themselves from where it was left before. You could hear the glass empty bottles rattling in people's bags. They were milk bottles from the days before which we had to wash and bring back to the shop while we were buying other bottles full of milk. Sometimes there wasn't enough milk for all the people in the queue, so the last ones ended up going back home with their empty bottles they'd brought back.

But that wasn't all. Watching programmes about children playing with their beautiful bikes, wearing beautiful clothes, drinking coca-cola instead of collecting oregano, chamomile and molloho flowers like us to sell to medical herb shops helping to earn some money. By the time you dry them nicely on the big sheet on the terrace under the shade for one week they end up weighing nothing. We used to get the sacks over our shoulders and walk more than an hour to the medical herb shop and walk back home disappointed with a few pennies in our pockets. With the money we got we couldn't even buy enough books or notebooks for the start of the new semester.

We watched with envy, through the news, how ordinary people being interviewed on the street spoke their mind without fear. We watched people singing and dancing on the stage freely, without being caught or getting arrested, unlike like the great young singers at the famous 11 festival of December 1972 in our country. At the time the dictator Hoxha called the music too cheerful and western and declared the producers and participants of the show to be 'Enemies of the public' and ridiculously accused them of threatening the country's mental state by presenting an immoral aspect to the show and plotting against the government by influencing the Albanian youth. Shockingly, some of them were murdered and the rest spent their life in prison until democracy came to Albania in 1991. And all that for what? Dancing while singing on the stage.

We watched and watched constantly with our eyes transfixed on the TV for days and nights, and for the first time in my life, lots of different questions raced through my mind. We had always been told that the life we led in Albania was the best possible life we could have. But now, had all those 'truths' really been so? Was this the best way to live after all?

I began to believe that the country I lived in wasn't the best country in the world. I began to understand that what I had been told all along through books, through lessons and songs, wasn't at all real. After so many tragedies and bad things had happened to people around me, I had reached my tipping point. I began to hate the regime I lived under, and I didn't believe in the doctrine of communism anymore.

Albania was part of a communist regime, placed in self-imposed isolation from the rest of the world. Thousands of bunkers framed the countryside against foreign threats. And to make matters worse, in late 1948 we split up with our allies Yugoslavia, followed in 1961 with Russia. In 1949 we established a relationship with China but in the late seventies we abandoned our alliance with them too. The "FAMOUS WORDS" of Enver Hoxha on TV: 'We will eat grass and never lay our hands on the enemy, we are standing strong and unyielding.' It was impossible to forget as they always reminded us of his speech on TV programmes. We weren't allowed to be who we wanted to be, but rather the people had become brainwashed into believing the regime was all-powerful and omni-present, and seemed to be the only country in the world that crushed religious beliefs completely.

The ordinary people and politicians who dared to speak up were persecuted as traitors of the country and very often 'disappeared' or were killed. However, these murders were often explained by the leaders of the country as suicides or unfortunate accidents. We were told lots of different stories in school about those who went against the regime. Lots of the persecuted families were exiled far away from the city, isolated somewhere on the edge of the mountains or in lost villages. These people would have restricted freedom and had to do very hard labour under strict supervision. They used to work in the fields and were supposed to produce food and be able to survive without any aid from anyone else.

Life for them shouldn't have even been labelled as a life at all, it was just pure suffering. If people had the audacity to say or complain about anything, they would be taken to court in their local area and be humiliated in front of their whole community. This would be called an open appeal. This way no one would dare to do or say anything at all. You would say, how do you know, have you ever experienced any of it? Well, I haven't but my neighbour Taco has. A wise man of few words and Taco was a middle-aged family man, married with five children. One morning in early summer, he went shopping. On the way out, he greeted his next-door neighbour and made his way to the shops. He came back with an empty bag and the neighbour asked, 'Have you not been shopping, Taco?'

'Oh yeah,' Taco replied, 'but there was nothing.' He shook his empty brown bag around with a grin on his face.

The neighbour reported him to the police behind his back. Before he had had enough time to finish his coffee, the police came banging on his door. He came out of his house and before he could even ask what was going on the police said, 'In the name of the people and Communist Party, you are under arrest.'

The blood drained from his face in absolute shock. We were all shocked, as we had no idea what was happening. We looked on in horror at him as the policemen handcuffed him and pushed him into the police car. Neighbours were gazing with open-mouthed disbelief at each other. Frightened whispers were uttered almost silently by people who were scared that someone might hear them. Here and there questions could be caught in very low voices. What did he do? What did he say? As they were shaking their head in disappointment and shrugging their shoulders, they quickly disappeared inside their houses like ants quietly disappearing back inside their nests.

After a few weeks there was an open appeal which was held in a field and every family in the area had to be there. It was a very sad day. His wife and children were sitting at the front with their heads bowed in disbelief. The crowds were quiet and anxious. The atmosphere was very unpleasant, tense, and frightening. We couldn't believe what was happening. How could someone get arrested just because of the simple words he said?

There were lots of questions and answers that I don't exactly remember and understand. However, I remember the military judge, a medium-sized man with a hat that covered half of his hair, making him look self-important, standing up with a stern face and giving the verdict loudly.

'Today on the eleventh March 1978, T. M. is charged with agitation and distributing propaganda against the Party and the People and therefore he is sentenced to eleven years in prison.'

Everyone gasped and looked at each other with fear and disbelief in their incredulous eyes. I could see his children shedding silent, disbelieving tears, holding their mum's hands as frightened people tried to leave quietly. It was heart-breaking. Right there, at that moment, I felt as if I was suffocating. That was what communism had done to the people. No-one would ever dare to express an opinion about anything ever again.

But that was nothing compared to what they had done to my school friend Dona's parents. Dona's father was arrested as a political prisoner and her family were used as a means of control and punishment and called out as enemies of the people as a result of communist propaganda. The man who had spied on her father was their next-door neighbour; he worked as a spy in the secret service, and used a small device to intercept through their concrete walls, eavesdropping. He listened to their private conversations about the communist regime every day; one day he had enough information to arrest their father. But it doesn't end there... The night that he was arrested, they took their mother too. A few men believed to be working for the government barged into their house, shouting and swearing in front of the young children. They brutally took away their mother and father, leaving the three children bewildered, scared and alone in the house. Being only 13 years old at the time, Dona had taken the role of caring and comforting her two brothers, nine and six years old. She put them to sleep but she couldn't sleep herself, thinking constantly about never being able to see her parents again. In the early hours of the next morning, to Dona's surprise, her mother was dropped on the doorstep by a dark green jeep, bruised from being beaten and tortured. She was only wearing a t-shirt. It was clear what they had done but she remained strong and silent to protect her children. As if that wasn't enough of a punishment, her father had witnessed everything that happened that treacherous night to his own wife and mother of his children... Truly unspeakable. Their house was taken away and they were transferred to the back villages where they experienced awful things. Their life was destroyed forever.

Even schools became repressive in the extreme. Education was tightly controlled by the Communist Party. Political lessons were introduced in every school across the country. These lessons were based on the teachings of Russian Marxism-Leninism as more and more political instruction was introduced into school life. The books contained more propaganda and less classical literature. Most of the school activities became politicised. Every classroom was dominated by a huge portrait of the leader, Enver Hoxha.

I attended a secondary school which had a very strict regime like all other schools in Albania. Our uniform was a black buttoned through dress with a white collar and a red neckerchief. The day's lessons started at 8 am, but all children were expected to arrive at 7:30 am. The piercing sound of the school bell meant all gates would be closed, and all of us had to go to our assigned place in the playground.

The day would begin with an exercise routine delivered by the PE teacher for half an hour. After this, the head boy recited a very important message from the regime. His hand would be put into a tight fist and placed onto his temple. This young boy would then bark the words I have never forgotten:

'Pioneers. We swear on the name of the Communist Party and people that we will always be ready to fight for our country.'

We would then place our knuckles against our tiny temples and reply together at exactly the same time, 'We swear!'

Then the end of the day would end by cleaning the classroom. Not every day as we took turns between the students paired in twos. It had to be left spotless, as our form teacher used to say, 'Be careful when you mop, no lines left on the floor, change the water constantly.' The cleanliness was very important, not just in the school building but for us too. Every Monday our hair and nails had to be checked and our white collar had to be pure white.

Getting involved in singing contests every year, I was selected to sing in front of the political bureau coming from the capital city of Tirana to visit our town. It was a big event and there was high security all around the city. The song was about a little army soldier fighting against the enemies of our country, the revisionists and imperialists. It was very important that I perform well and do exactly as they asked me to, nothing more, nothing less.

28th of November. Liberation Day.

It was a big show, and I was to perform on the stage at the city's amphitheatre, dressed like a mini partisan. A khaki army uniform costume was made for me with a hat that bore a red star. It was important too, that I had to carry a rifle on my shoulder when I was singing. A long wooden rifle was made, but unfortunately it was bigger than me so that when I slung it over my shoulder, it dragged on the floor as I walked, and I sang the words that I never forget:

Because I'm a little soldier
With a star on my forehead,
I'm going to fight like a brave boy for my country,
Like a brave partisan.

Everything went well until I was leaving the stage, when the long wooden rifle hit the corner of the backstage and I ended up rolling down the stairs like a ball. As if that wasn't enough, as soon I got home, the loud alarm was sounding throughout the whole city. Due to the country being communist, it was a regulation that every year the whole city would have training on how to be safe just in case a war broke out. Every neighbourhood had already been told where to go when the alarm sounded. Our place of safety was to go and hide in the castle cellar, which was close to our neighbourhood.

Other people who lived further from the castle were expected to hide in tunnels that had been made for this purpose only. So, when the siren was heard, all the city lights were switched off and all the families would have to take some blankets, food, and drinks and run into the castle's cellars. Sometimes we were made to sit there all night and other times just for four to five hours and then we could return home.

Everything seemed to be happening at once. I ran with my siblings and cousins to the castle. As we arrived, through the darkness I could smell wild dill and barjlak that grew throughout the castle grounds in the shape of a white umbrella. We used to play there every day, climb on the rocks at the sides of the castle, and eat the wild dill while we were sitting on the top of the big grey rocks.

Finally, after five hours we were allowed to go home. Everyone rushed out. It had been a very long day. It was surprising how so many things could happen in one day. I was so tired I was asleep before my head hit the pillow.

As the high school approached the most important subjects in the eyes of the teachers and the leaders were lessons in politics and a military training class called Zbore. As part of the army, we had to develop strict discipline.

The school consisted of three floors which were all used for lessons. The cellar of the school was used to store army uniforms and weapons which included rifles, guns and ammunition. We used to have military lessons in the mountains and sometimes on the top of the castle or on the surrounding hills, full of olive trees. On the day of the army lessons we all lined up to collect the uniform and the arms which we were to use, which had to be signed out and in. We had to get dressed in an army khaki-coloured uniform, buttoned right up to the neck, and present ourselves on the regiment line. The officer standing at the front took the roll call to make sure everybody was there.

The officer, standing to attention, shouted his orders, 'Stand up straight. Eyes forward. Are we ready for the day?'

And we would reply by shouting, 'We are ready.'

Then he would say, 'I want you to dismantle and assemble your rifle in two minutes.' He would lift up his hand and, looking down to his watch, would growl, 'Start now.'

The silence was broken only by the clattering of the rifles.

Knowing that if someone didn't finish on time, we all would have to do it again, I would urgently pick up the rifle in front of me and start to dismantle the pieces and assemble them back together in time. After making sure that every student was ready, we started our long journey in single file up the mountain.

Once we arrived at a large field on the top of the mountain, I could see three other officers waiting for us. The officers stood in front of concrete barricades that were at knee height. Further into the distance I could see black and red target boards with the number 10 in the middle followed by the numbers 9, 8, 7, 6.

The objective of the lesson was to hit the target. This would then mean we would get a good grade. The place used to smell from the gunpowder and was covered by bullets flying everywhere.

After we had all finished, we got orders to take our place and clean the rifles.

I liked shooting. For me it was almost an everyday sport that I grew up with.

That was nothing compared with the gas mask training that we used to cover our face for hours. It was terrible and very uncomfortable. Running our way up and down the hills, the officers would then order all of us to lie down on the floor to take cover. They would always do this at a spot where muddy water had gathered in potholes in the ground which meant our uniforms would be drenched with dirty, cold water.

Most of the hills used to be covered with olives and lemon trees where we used to do voluntary work once a year away from home for a month.

As I spent alternate years living in my siblings' houses, I eventually had to move in with my sister Lindita in the capital, Tirana, to carry on my education and also help her with her children Enkelejda, Ilir, and Alban. She and her husband, Petrit, used to work out of the city, and they would leave the house very early and get back late at night.

Often, when I used to go to the school evening dancing as we used to call it back then, I would borrow Petrit's wedding shoes. They were one bigger size than mine. I used to put some cotton wool inside his shoes and wear wide trousers to cover it up. But not for so long as one of the evenings, the left side shoe slipped off and hit one of my friends' arm while I was dancing. I couldn't borrow my sister Lindita's shoes as she had feet like Cinderella's and she felt fortunate that none of us could wear her shoes.

Going out in the capital city, we often used to talk quietly about life in the West—the liberty of people, allowing them to have different views, the rights and the wrongs; the high living standards, the entertainment, and the modern music that we used to yearn for and listen to in hidden places. That was the kind of society that we wanted to live in. But unfortunately for us it was just a dream.

CHAPTER 11

The vote signed in blood

Western visitor

I was travelling back to my home city Gjirokastra to vote for the first time. Election day. It was meant to be a very important day and the people used to wear their best clothes. They used to leave the house early morning and join the queue very quietly, unlike the noisy queues for milk and eggs in the early morning hours. There were different groups and different beliefs. Some of them believed the Party deserved their loyalty and were proud to support the regime. The others were there against their wishes, pretending to be happy only because they knew they had no choice in this matter as their absence was unacceptable – they could not oppose the party as the consequences would have been fatal. Those who spoke openly and opposed, ended up in prison and they were called the enemy of the party and the people, and not just their life but their family's life was destroyed forever.

All over the city I could see only red, where lots of pre-election slogans and banners were everywhere saying 'One vote of the people is one bullet to the enemy. All the votes for popular assembly candidates'.

How could it turn out differently when that was the only candidate in the race? During the years of dictatorship, everybody had to vote and absolutely no abstaining was allowed even though there was only one party, which was the Communist Party. The people in charge of each city were responsible for making sure every single person voted, or else they were in big trouble.

As soon as I arrived back in Gjirokastra I went to look over my garden. I was at the top of the tree collecting some fruit when I heard the police shouting. It caught my attention, and I looked down the grey path. A few policemen were chasing a man called Kaco – one of the men from our area who was known to have severe depression. He was running like crazy on the top of the hill, shouting, 'Leave me alone. I don't want to vote.'

'You had better stop and be quiet,' they shouted back at him, 'as you are surrounded by the police. You can't escape.'

I climbed down and tried to hide behind the trunk, which extended from the back of the walnut tree. I could see Kaco clearly. He turned on the wall of the little stone bridge just 100 metres from my garden and shouted, 'If you don't leave me alone, I'm going to throw myself into the creek.'

But just as quickly as he said it, one of the policemen came out of the little bush and quickly grabbed him. All the other policemen dived in and attacked him. They threw him against the solid grey cobblestones, kicking him as if they were wild animals. Blood began to flow from his head and was covering his entire face. He was screaming from the pain, but they had no mercy. One of them, in army officer uniform, ordered them, 'Move back,' while he pushed the police out of the way. They stopped immediately and did as they were told. Obviously it seemed to be the man in charge. He looked with disgust down at Kaco who was crouched over in agony and covered in blood. He kicked him on his head and said, 'Move, donkey.' But he couldn't. Then he spat at him and growled, 'Get up.'

I could see Kaco's hand moving over his face as he wiped the blood from his eyes, trying hard to get up but he fell again. The officer got the revolver out of his holster and pointed it to his head and said, 'I won't tell you again.' As he started to count, one, two, three, I could see Kaco as he tried once again with his hand to crawl on the cobblestone but it seemed impossible for him to get up. Then I heard another voice. 'We can't kill him, we need his vote,' his colleague said.

'I know that, you idiot,' the officer snarled. 'Then you get him,' he ordered him. As they got him up, handcuffed him, and tried to pull him into the police jeep, I heard Kaco's agonising voice say, 'I will never sign, you bitches of communism.'

'Now I'll blow your brains out,' the officer said, holding the revolver to his head. 'Get in the jeep, crazy man.' Kaco knew, as I understand too, that they desperately needed his vote so they would never kill him.

I watched everything, totally shocked at what I was witnessing. I really wanted to go over there and do something, but I couldn't, because I didn't dare. Finally, they pulled him into the police jeep and started to drive away, fast. On the jeep window, through the steam, I could see the shadow of Kaco that was crawling and scratching the window, leaving clear lines screaming for help. The limbs of my body felt paralysed. I had no power even to get up and go into the house. I turned around and I saw my father coming towards me. He looked at me and asked, 'What was that about?'

I shook my head in disapproval without saying anything.

'Are you ok?' he asked. 'You look like you've seen a ghost.'

'Yes I have, Dad, I've just seen the ghost of communism,' I replied angrily.

'What? Where did that come from?'

'The police just took Kaco away,' I said.

My anger got the better of me, and I growled, 'It's not fair that people have to be forced to vote; it's not right to be treated like this, and I'm not voting myself either. I'm not voting for this government that takes away the freedom of the people, I'm not–' and abruptly my words were stopped, by his hand covering my mouth while he said through gritted teeth, 'Shuuuuush. Have you gone crazy like Kaco? Keep your voice down; someone may hear you. We are not having this conversation here. We are going to the house to talk, and until then, not another word. Even trees have ears. Do you understand me?'

His face had turned into a mask of irritation. He gestured for me to follow him up while walking and shaking his head in dismay and anger, his every muscle tensed.

When we reached the house we went upstairs on the top floor to one of the bedrooms that faced the back of the garden, where no one could hear us. He looked at me, fuming, and said, 'Sit down. I can't believe what I'm hearing. You are being selfish. Do you think of the consequences?'

'But, Father, if you'd witnessed what I have, of how they've brutally beaten Kaco for a single vote, you would feel the same,' I said angrily. 'I'm not voting. What are they going to do about it, eh?'

'I'll tell you what they will do, you little rebel,' he said with an angry voice. 'We are going to end up in prison, we are going to get chucked out of our family home and get transferred somewhere out into the lost villages, and live like wild animals. Have you forgotten what's happened to the Tahos family just for one word he said? Well, we are going to end up exactly the same. The Sinani family will be burdened and called enemies and traitors of the country, and there will be no future for any of you. Your life will be finished. So, before you do that, we will all climb to the top of the castle and throw ourselves from there like Argjiro. Shall we? At least we would be able to die with dignity and not with shame.'

He stalked around the room like a scalded cat while I sat, ready to break out in anger again.

'This is an injustice, Father. We can't live our life in fear of what we might do or say. Life without freedom is only half a life. Is that what you want for us? Slavery?' I said, trying to make my point for him to listen. But my father was not going to agree with me.

He shook his head disapprovingly, still looking furious.

'Listen to me closely now, as I won't repeat this,' he replied. 'This is very serious. We live in a communist country, and as long as the dictator is alive, the dictatorship will continue. When the dictator dies, dictatorship dies too. Till then we are going to try to live as normal a life as anyone else.'

He shook his head again in disappointment. I could see on his face the panic of something bad happening, and he was trying to stop that. I never forgot those words, as I had never seen my father raise his voice to me before as on that day.

'Now go and get everybody here including your cousins for an important family meeting. I want everyone here in less than

129

10 minutes,' he ordered.

'I'm going,' I said as I stood up, shaking my head.

I could see from his disappointed eyes that I had gone from hero to zero. But I understood that he was only trying to protect us from the punishment of the regime. Although deep down he knew that I was right, he could not agree because life under the power of communism was horrible and scary and one little mistake or one word out of place could cost us our lives. He was very protective to all his children but especially to me after the shocking death of my mother at such a young age. How I missed her and longed for her gentle wisdom at this moment. I wonder if she would have agreed with my father on this matter. That's the question.

I almost ran out of the door looking for my siblings and cousins and in a very short time we were all together in the room where my father was waiting.

He was sitting in his carved walnut chair, deep in thought, and had taken out the box of tobacco and rolled his thin cigarette. My father stubbed his last cigarette into the ashtray, and, turning around, he gestured to us with his hand to sit-down. He looked at each one of us, making sure that we were all concentrating and listening to what he had to say.

'I need you to listen to me carefully,' he said as the room went quiet. 'As my cousin Edward is going to be visiting us from the United States, I have just been to the meeting regarding his visit to our house for a few weeks on holiday. As much as I'm excited to see him, I can't hide that I am also very cautious at the same time. We have to be very careful what we say to avoid any slipups against the communist regime. We must not complain about the regime and not make any political comments. We must reassure him that it is not as they see on television and read in the newspapers over in America.'

I looked at him shocked and said, 'Is that telling the truth that you always told us to say?'

He turned to me and in a raised voice he grumbled, 'Don't start again. You know very well this is a very serious matter. This is not a joke. We all need to make sure that we are not showing any sign of unhappiness living in this country. We cannot say a word against the communists, or I could get put into prison forever. Do you understand?'

'Yes,' we muttered.

Staring at each other confused and disappointed at not saying another word, we made our way out to the veranda. Instead of looking forward to seeing Cousin Edward, we were too frightened, in case we might say something that we shouldn't, and get our father into great trouble. That was the last thing we wanted to happen to our father so without question we were going to do our best not to let him down.

It took a while for the application to visit Albania from the West to be accepted and lots of documents to go through. But that wasn't all. As the applications were carefully monitored, the chairman of the Communist Party knew of my cousin's planned visit.

So on the day that Edward arrived, a state car had been organized to take him, my father, and the translator to our home. Edward was extremely observant and was gazing out of the car window into this foreign country, asking questions that my father would answer carefully without forgetting what was discussed in the meeting beforehand, as each time he answered, the government driver would glare at him to see what he would reply to the inquisitive question.

He finally arrived at my father's house and after he had unpacked and settled in the guest bedroom, he was taken down to the dining room where the whole family had gathered. A long table full of food was laid out ready for our special guest. The celebrations had only just started. The first comment Edward made was, 'Oh, this is a tremendous amount of food. On the TV, over in the US, they just keep saying how poor Albania is.'

My father nodded while a little uncomfortable smile played on his lips and he said 'enjoy', pointing at the table. 'Have you tried byrek before?' he said, trying to change the subject, 'my mother bakes it under the embers.'

'I can't say that I have,' Edward replied, 'I'll try some now.' He took a piece of byrek and as he took a bite he said, 'Delicious.'

I could see the relief in my father's face. I felt so sorry for him because I knew that he didn't like not being truthful and especially in front of his family and he was struggling to give a proper answer. But that's what the communist regime did to you. You were made to do and say things that would be completely against your character, or you would have to face the consequences.

Next morning I was trying to hide our pan lid aerial in a box in the cellar, when Edward walked through, catching me off guard, and asked, 'What is that?'

I jumped at the sound of his voice. I was an awful liar and blurted out, 'Oh, emmmm, it's the little aerial that we made so we can watch programmes and listen to music from outside of the country.'

'So why you are trying to hide it?' he asked, confused.

'We hide it because we're only actually supposed to watch Albanian television; we're not allowed to watch other programmes from different countries,' I said, starting to panic.

'And if our father found out we had this he would not be happy. I have never been anywhere out of this country, and the only way I can understand a little bit about the way the West works is through this aerial. Please don't tell my father.'

'Oh do not worry about that. I won't,' he said while he put his finger to his lips. 'My lips are sealed. Let's just say that we never had this conversation.'

He winked at me with a smile. 'I understand why your father is trying to hide everything. I read about how life is here all the time. As much as they're trying to hide it, I know the rules of communism. My father used to tell me everything. I wish I could help and do something about it, but I know I can't. If I say something, I will never be allowed to visit here again, and all of your family will be in trouble and we don't want that, do we?'

I looked at him, saddened, and nodded in agreement.

'Come on, let's get out of here,' he suggested, waving me out. We walked on the grey stone path behind the house and took the cobblestone road on the right towards the castle.

We passed the giant front doors of the castle and walked in among the heavy artillery museum then went to the outer part where an old American airplane, a 'Lockheed T-33', was placed. According to the official version at the time the plane was called a 'SPY PLANE' and was forced to land by two Albanian Mig military planes at the Rinas airport in 1958 which at that time had not yet been built. After the collapse of communism, the political prisoners who worked in construction of the airport at that time and saw what had happened, opposed this version and testified that the plane had been landed in an emergency in the winter of 1958 and it had never got back to where it came from for some reason.

To my surprise Edward knew all about it as he was a pilot in America himself and had taken part in the war in Vietnam too, for which he was awarded medals for his bravery.

'What is life like out … there?' I asked as I waved my hand outwards.

'It is very different than here for sure. People have freedom and a good life. I wish I could take you with me one day and you could see for yourself,' he said.

During that month that Edward stayed with us, my cousin Kaku and I were left with the task of cleaning his bedroom and changing the sheets.

On the table he had a small box full of little green sweets that we had never seen before. Our curiosity got the better of us, and we each picked up a sweet and popped it in our mouth. A little while later, we both could not stop running to the toilet. Edward returned home only to find that we had taken some of his laxatives. However, when he found out, he erupted with laughter. We couldn't have been more embarrassed.

I listened to so many stories and learnt a lot about life in the United States and dreamed that one day the communists in Albania would be vanquished, and I would be able to visit my cousins in America and see what their life was like there.

Unfortunately, however, that was the last time I saw him. We always kept in contact by writing to each other, but our letters were very constricted as we had to be careful not to write anything to do with politics or anything that could tarnish the regime. Years later, he passed away and unfortunately we never had a chance to get in contact with his children and get to know them.

CHAPTER 12

Choosing the Wrong Path

I was living the teenage life, the life of dreams, surrounded by the happiness that life brings to reject negative feelings and not allow myself to be plunged into the poverty of fate. I was young, full of joy and hope as my future steps passed every morning over the stone bridge known as a Tabakeve bridge while carrying on with my studies in the capital city of Tirana. I was living with my sister Lindita's family again at this time. They used to live in a third floor apartment right in the centre of Tirana opposite the statue called 'The unknown partisan'. Just a few months after my arrival they moved back into a little village outside the capital called Yrshek. That's where I met the man who would become the father of my children, Dan.

It was the beginning of winter and the weather was deteriorating faster than expected. Window panes were covered with frost and the few water pipes that brought water to the village had frozen. The only one that had flowing water was the military department's supply at the top of the hill – five minutes' walk from my sister's house. Several times a day we would take large copper jugs to fill with water from an outside tap by the large doors where military guards stood on duty.

The barracks were full of soldiers from different parts of the country and in a small village every one of them became familiar with the locals. And there was Dan, my future husband at that time. He was a tall man with dark brown eyes and brown-copper hair. He carried himself with arrogance and self-pride. He was extremely persistent in trying to attract my attention and often he would wait at the roadside for my journey back home and would try to stop me. I categorically opposed it. Without a doubt he was not the man I would visualize my life with. There wasn't any connection or even a little bit of a spark that would have given me the desire to want to know more about him. I wanted love.

For my great aunt I couldn't be any more wrong. 'Such a thing called Love happens just in movies, not in the real world,' she used to say. 'Where are you going to live after your studies finish? With your wicked stepmother? Your siblings have their own families now and you need to create yours. You cannot live on your own until you get married. Don't let this good chance slip from your hands, he comes from a very good family.'

'How do you know?' my sister asked.

'A close family friend approached me yesterday, I had a conversation with G who told me very good things about Dan and his family. They live in a nice house and live a good life and Yllka would be one lucky girl and have the life of her dreams.' (Little did we know at the time that everything that so-called friend told to my great-aunt was lies, I came to recognise later, had been staged by my future husband. None of it was true.)

At that time if someone asked out the girl in your family, they would say that 'the girl's luck had come'. And according to my aunt, I was one of them. How absurd!

So, I was reminded over and over again, the time had come for me to get married, build my own family and have my own home. It wasn't just the fact that I was being a burden to my siblings, but I wanted to be the lady of my own house too. To be truthful, I eagerly and desperately desired it, I wanted that stability, my own permanent home where I didn't need to worry about where I would stay next month or next year. Whose house would I be in? Who would take care of me? For years I had been passed like a soccer ball from one stepmother to another, from a great-aunt to a sister or brother. I so wanted a home of my own.

And all my siblings were surrounded by the love and warmth of their own families except for me. So, I did like the feeling of being wanted.

I started seeing Dan, meeting him and going for walks together away from people's eyes. I had never had any experience of relationships and I had no idea what love really was, but I liked his attention, his hugs, his confidence. At that time in Albania it was shameful, especially for the girl, if a young man and woman were seen talking together in public as boyfriend and girlfriend without being engaged. So usually we would meet secretly out of the public eye to avoid any rumours circulating. However, even though we tried so hard to keep it under wraps, other people would talk and soon the word spread, and everyone heard about us. So, the families had to meet and have a coffee together, have a blessing as was tradition, and then the engagement would take place.

I returned to my city Gjirokastra, communicating with Dan through letters and phone calls. I was living with my brother Bushi, his lovely wife Vjollca and his two beautiful daughters, Silda and Ada, at this time. He lived on the other side of our family home where we grew up. Being a protective brother, unlike my aunt and sister, he was not happy about this relationship. Of course, for his sister he wanted the best man around. After the life they had had he wanted someone nice to make sure that his little sister would be treated properly, and in his opinion, Dan wasn't that man.

'There are lots of guys in our city that would love to be with you – why do you have to marry someone from the villages around Tirana, who may well be a fanatic and from a different background, with a different culture and traditions? You deserve better,' he explained, finally, without hiding his feelings about it. He spoke openly while sitting next to me at the breakfast table.

I couldn't argue with that. I looked at him while he was waiting for my answer, knowing very well that he was right but the only thing I could say was, 'Too late, you haven't forgotten that Dan and his family will be here later this afternoon.'

He shook his head, unhappy because that was not the response he wanted.

I was so entangled with Dan now that I would have been ashamed to refuse him after we had been seen together so often.

That March Day, after a long six-to-seven-hour journey from Tirana, Dan and his family arrived in the afternoon at our house, where both families would talk together, approve the engagement, to be followed by a grand dinner celebration. The hands had been shaken, the blessing was given and lots of songs had been sung and lots of jokes had been told. Everyone was happily laughing, but my brother was not. The disappointment and sadness that I saw in his eyes, and the words that he said to me the night of my engagement while tearfully holding me, plunged me into a deep despair I will never forget. 'Brother's sweetheart, one day you will regret this but it will be too late.'

'No, I won't,' I replied hastily but without conviction.

'Well, if you ever change your mind, just say so, and I will be here for you,' he reassured me.

I shook my head but inside I knew that was a promise that I could not give.

Once we were engaged the families spread the news around, and finally we were allowed to go out and be seen in public together. And cohabitation was out of question – couples didn't live together and have a relationship before committing to marriage. The important thing for a man was to know that the girl he was marrying was untouched. Therefore I always knew not to give away my virginity without getting engaged as I would be considered a dishonest and spoiled woman and no honourable man would ever want to be married to you, bringing shame on yourself and on your family. There was no sex education in Albania, and I was completely ignorant when it came to this subject. Therefore I wanted to take time but he imposed on me to discover the honest truth that I already knew.

That night I felt so self-conscious, I was afraid of intimacy, but he didn't seem to give a thought to my insecurities, feelings, and emotions. My virginity was stolen, by lies, like a thief in the night. That was it. I was his, and there was no way of going back. Along with my virginity went my dreams and hopes. He was convinced. That night he fell asleep, but I couldn't. Awake in the darkness of the room, I felt my body racked with all-consuming tears in silence until the early hours of the morning when I drifted off, feeling mentally and physically exhausted.

The noise of birds persistently tapping on the window woke me up. I dragged myself out of bed and opened the gold coloured curtains and started to make empty conversation with them to try to break what I felt was an awkward silence. My mouth was moving but my mind was drifting off with the birds. I was just thinking about how I would give anything to fly away with them, to open my wings and escape this feeling and regain my freedom. They were just staring at me, bobbing their heads up and down. I felt that they were the only souls in the world that could understand me, and truly look into *my* soul.

After a few weeks I found out that the inevitable had happened – I was pregnant. I was terrified of the unknown changes that were going to happen to my life. As Albania was still under the communist regime, and women who became pregnant out of wedlock were shunned, I had to get married before it began to show. So, without my even being there, without any consulation, the wedding date was set. It was put together as quickly as the Mexican free-tailed bat flying over the orange horizon.

-o-

It was a small wedding, not the type that you would dream of as a little girl. No fancy suits. No fancy dresses. It was just something that had to happen to avoid any social backlash. It felt like my life had been sealed like a deal to hide the downcast and avoid rumours. The obvious question would be, was this more important than my future? Living under a communist regime the answer to that question had to be a resounding *Yes*. The power to control my future had been taken out of my hands. The wedding day had been set towards the end of winter and beginning of spring. The buds on the trees were beginning to burst before the new leaves arrived, and the daffodils were starting to bloom. As a tradition, Saturday evening was the girl's wedding, then Sunday morning the husband and family picked the girl up and drove to their house which is their wedding Sunday. But Dan and his siblings came the night before as it was so far and also stayed at my wedding too.

That Saturday, the night of my wedding, the orchestra was playing outside on the terrace of my family home and everyone was dancing and laughing. I was dancing waltzes with my cousin Tore when out of the corner of my eye I caught Dan's angry face staring at me. A shiver of fear swept through my body. I pretended that I hadn't noticed and carried on dancing, not looking in his direction. But to my utter surprise he came outside, furious, and immediately told me to leave the dance floor and get inside. Without making a scene, embarrassed, I followed him and as we got inside he exploded. I was shocked to my bones after he demanded that I should not dance with another male, even with Tore who was my cousin. I could not disagree more and obviously this led to an argument. While his siblings and mine intervened, trying to lower the tension created out of his sick demands and jealousy, I walked out of the room in the dark outside into the garden looking towards the mountain. Shaken by what had just happened, I could not believe in the morning I was leaving my home, my city, to live with this man and never to return. It was an Albanian tradition that the day you got married you left your house and moved into your husband's house. And with what had just happened anxiety swirled around me. He was trying to control and humiliate me in front of my family, on my wedding day that was supposed to be the happiest day in my life. But that wasn't at all the point – what would happen the following days, the future of my life with him?

'Yllka, what are you doing here? Get inside,' my great-aunt's voice hit me.

I didn't reply.

She walked towards me and said, 'I just called you. Are you all right?'

'I'm scared,' I said. 'I don't feel that I want to go.'

Disappointment and shock were evident in the tone of her voice. 'Pu Pu Pu Pu, Shame shame shame,' she said while pinching her cheeks. 'Don't even think about it, there's no way you can go back from this now, sweetheart. You're pregnant with his baby, and if you don't go, you won't be able to walk the street again. Your life will be over before it's even started.'

Fear and sorrow gripped my throat as she put her arm around me, telling me not to worry as everything would be fine. Silence rolled across and enveloped us like a grey sea mist as we stared at the mountain.

I couldn't have wished for anything more than to change my circumstances at that moment in time. However, I convinced myself that I had to listen to my great-aunt. There was no solution, other than I had to go. Now I knew how my grandma felt the morning after *her* wedding in 1925, when she went back to her mum's, and she had the choice of ending it all in the river or going back to her husband. This mentality was still the same 63 years later. It felt like I had been sentenced to spend the rest of my life in purgatory, making me extremely frightened of and for my future.

In the morning I said farewell to my family and I got into the car with Dan and his siblings. The car slid quietly away over those cobblestone streets where I'd grown up and walked up and down my whole life towards the path of another life, disembarking into a new platform, wherever that was, along the road that cut between the green valley and the ancient trees which were swaying in the mountain breeze. Over the valley I caught sight of a grey strip of slated roof and the morning sunlight streaming through the branches of the trees, almost like a ray of hope.

Suddenly a flock of birds rose from the trees and, forming a V shape in flight, melted away into the blue sky. Tears streamed down my face, blurring my vision as Dan's arm slid around my shoulder, trying to comfort me and telling me that everything would be ok. As the car sped away, the city of Gjirokastra slid away behind us. Looking back one more time, all I was able to see was the big clock tower from the castle, shrinking into the far distance.

Leaving wasn't a choice, it was an obligation.

CHAPTER 13

The anguish of marriage

Collapse of communism – democracy prevails

From the beginning of our marriage, there was a fundamental difference between us. Growing up in his family was very different from mine, our culture and personalities sometimes clashed. Surprisingly the relationship between Dan and I was progressing much better than I had anticipated on the evening of my wedding and for a while life between us was as good as it could be.

However, our married life had to conform to the family rules and demands. It was a suppressed and apprehensive marriage, surrounded by the whole family's opinions and judgement, which consequently influenced our relationship. The first sign of a crack began to appear, and paved the way for abuse and control. And that was just the start.

Nevertheless we both worked hard while we were staying in a room that one of his siblings had vacated for us. We had to save every penny so we could buy a piece of land near the family houses, to build our own house and move in as soon as possible. Being pregnant didn't stop me helping with the construction and I worked alongside the builders. I laid the bricks, mixed the cement, and helped build the foundations of my new home.

While this was happening, unexpectedly, I gave birth to a premature (seven months) baby – my first child, Enea – early on the morning of 31st of October 1988. That night a heavy storm smashed into the city. While I was waiting on my own in the delivery room, through the pain, I could hear the hail lashing against the maternity room window's wooden shutters like someone throwing handfuls of pebbles. At some point, Eleni, the midwife, who was a small lady with long dark hair dragged into a bun with a pen stuck through it, walked in to check on me. Realising that I had a lot of time before baby joined us, she left me alone again like a piece of furniture staring at the dark windows. The labour dragged on for 12 hours, during which time I alternated my position from chair back to bed. Finally, after what seemed like an eternity, Eleni and a bald-headed doctor with big eyes, entered the delivery room. I can't remember his name.

'How's my baby doing?' I asked.

'It's you we are worried about at the moment, not your baby. Your life is in danger,' the doctor replied. 'It is too early to know whether the baby will survive.'

'I don't want a life without my baby, please!' I screamed, as sharp contractions again wracked my entire body. I desperately wanted my baby to survive – he was my love, my hope to make my life worth living.

'Nearly here,' I heard Eleni say.

'Breathe,' the nurse urged, 'and one last push, it's…'

'It's a boy,' I heard the doctor saying.

Then, quickly, he took him to one side to try to stimulate him, because there was no sound from the little boy – no crying, no whimpering, nothing. His little pink body looked so vulnerable as the doctor tried to stabilize him, rubbing his back vigorously while they were drying the baby, but still … nothing.

I caught the hopeless look in their faces, and my whole body shook with terror. Just when my hope was about to disappear altogether, a cry burst from his lungs and echoed around the room. The doctors were relieved. Everybody cheered. He weighed in at two kilos and 15 grams, with a full head of hair and looked more like a monkey. I didn't care and I wasn't going to change him for anything else in the world.

I couldn't stop looking at him; I felt such unexplicable love and joy. There in my hands was the most beautiful creature and I had never felt such delight in anything else before.

His hair fell out eventually and he wouldn't stop crying, night and day, so that I hardly got any sleep. He was so small in that incubator and I couldn't wait for him to grow so I could hold him. In the morning Dan came to see us, so happy and proud to have a son.

After forty days, when he had gained enough weight, we eventually went home. We were still living in the little bedroom at his sibling's house, trying desperately to finish our new home so we might move, joined by my mother-in-law (a tradition in Albania is that your parents move in with one of their sons, possibly the last one of the family).

It was December, the middle of winter, if memory serves me right, and severe cold had enveloped the town. Our new house was half-finished, and we had to move in and build it a bit at a time, as and when we had enough money. Still, I had a house to put my head in and a beautiful baby that filled my whole world with love and joy. For the time being, the rest didn't matter that much.

Early in the morning I lit the fire in the house and the first wisps of grey smoke curled out of our chimney, shifting like ghosts in the chilly wind. I was happier than I had been for some considerable time, cherishing that moment, while singing a lullaby to my boy and wishing that one day he would grow up to be a great man and have a better life than mine had turned out to be.

As Enea began to grow, we started to extend our house and make it more of a home – a project that would take my anxious mind from the unpredictable life that I was living.

Around this time, in 1990, when Enca was just two, four decades of communism in Albania finally collapsed. Revolution had erupted in many communist countries of the world, one after another, demanding democracy and freedom. If my memory serves me right, it was just after the collapse of the Berlin Wall, after Poland withdrew from the Warsaw Pact and got involved in the democracy movement. In Romania communism ended after 42 years and their dictator Ceausescu was executed along with his wife. Less than a year after that, the first revolution in Albania started. It started in Shkodra, which would be followed by many demonstrations led by students, the first ones who had started the hunger strike in Tirana. The statue of the dictator, once communist leader, Enver Hoxha, was knocked down by the brave young men in the middle of the Capital and the square around it was splattered by their blood. On the boulevard of Tirana where once people marched on parade, cheering and clapping for Enver Hoxha, they were now shouting for democracy with two fingers up and throwing his picture like a rubbish, the picture that once was so preciously displayed on the centre of the wall in their homes, now was worthless and despised. Tens of Albanians were climbing the walls and jumping unlawfully into foreign embassies in the capital. There were many fatalities and many injured.

In 1991, after a year of uncertainty, democracy finally prevailed. Consequently, people had the chance to build their own private businesses.

I started working at a design fashion company where I would make the clothes, and Dan continued to work as a truck driver. We both worked hard and continued to make more money as we were saving to buy a coach and develop a business that would take holidaymakers and travellers from the city of Tirana to the border with Greece, at Kakavi.

We bought our first coach and the business was going well, so we bought another coach and expanded the business further.

It was the end of autumn and the beginning of winter when all the trees were dressed in golden-bronze colours as they took the fresh breeze that wafted the scent along. On the last day of October it was Enea's birthday, when at a little party he blew out five candles.

'What's your wish?' a friend asked.

'I want a sister,' he replied quickly.

Speechless at his unusual wish for a five year old boy, I didn't say anything.

I knew that he needed a companion to spend those long winter nights with, as often he would go and play with his cousins Ana and Nat who lived across the road from our house. Then, after fighting with them, he would come home upset and would beg for a sister of his own to play with. At first, we thought it was just a phase and that he would grow out of it. But he did not stop; he threw tantrums and would shout, 'I want a sister! I want a sister to play with, like Ana and Nat.' To my eternal surprise, I became pregnant again.

After nine months, when the cold winter's footprints faded away and were left in the past, they were replaced by the new freshness of spring. It was March – the month of hope.

On a gloriously sunny afternoon – Thursday 24th, 1994, my beautiful daughter Hope was born. I had been admitted to hospital for a few weeks because my pregnancy was in a dangerous state. That afternoon, from across the road the smell of fresh cornbread cascaded through the hospital windows and tickled my senses. I was yearning to have some with my dinner. Slowly I got dressed and went to the bakery only to find that the last loaf had been sold.

'Oh, I'm sorry,' the baker said, looking down at my big swollen belly.

'Not even a little piece left?' I asked desperately.

'No.' He shook his head with sorrow.

Before he had finished the sentence, my waters broke. They stared at me in disbelief, and in no time I was lying on the bed in the delivery room where, after a few hours with the great help of my private doctor, Marika, I cradled in my arms my beautiful new-born baby girl, Hope.

So perfect, she was like a ray of sunshine lighting up my darkness. I felt an endless love like the deep clear water that runs through the eternal mountain; a love that was embedded within my soul that would never leave, never disappear. Joy danced through my heart. Carefully I drew her to my chest to feel the warmth and love that only mothers can give – her heart beating in unison with mine. She moved her tiny hands as if she was looking for something in this new unknown world, to reach out for something safe and comforting. I held her hand and then, unexpectedly, her eyes suddenly opened and gazed into mine. I kissed her little hand and whispered, 'Mammy's sweetheart. I'm here. I will love you unconditionally until the day I die.'

As if she had needed that reassurance, her eyes closed again, and she fell asleep.

-o-

Not long after the birth, I heard Enea's voice echoing in the hospital corridor, 'Where's my sister, Hope? I want to see my sister.'

He ran through the door and looked straight at Hope, next to me in bed. His eyes looked disappointed.

'Well, are you going to kiss your sister?' I asked.

'What's that?' He wrinkled his nose. 'She looks like a chicken.'

'This is your sister Hope,' I said joyfully.

'Nooo, I want a sister to play with,' he shouted as he ran out of the room and into the corridors, upset. The nurse had to catch him up and explain to him that his sister would grow up fast and that soon he would be able to play with her. She managed to calm him down and bring him back to the room.

After a few minutes there he was, holding his little baby sister and looking at her like nobody else mattered in the room. Sitting there by my side, I looked at them both and my heart filled with unconditional love.

Soon we returned home and every morning he would rush over to her cot, peek over and ask, 'Is she grown yet, Mammy? Is she going to play with me?'

It became routine that I would say, 'Not yet but soon she will be.'

He would then turn around with a long face and say, 'Maybe tomorrow she will grow inch by inch every day and then she will be big enough to play with her brother.'

I was so lucky to have these beautiful and healthy children to light up my life. Despite everything that was going on, we always kept a deep-felt hopefulness for their life and future. Everything else seemed so small and unimportant; my only focus was to make sure these children lived the happiest and best life that they possibly could.

Enea, only eight, was preparing himself for his first football match out of the country in Istanbul. The bunches of carrots full of mud that we had to clean and peel every day, to make him juice, and cows' fresh knee bones which we boiled to give him too. Drinking that his face looked like he was chewing a wasp. According to Enea's football coach, all this would only make him stronger and help him in his football training. While Hope, still little, was too obsessed with Buni, her best friend – a giant electric blue teddy bear that we used to put in her bed before she went to sleep to make her bed warm.

We tried to give them what we didn't have in life, hoping for the best.

CHAPTER 14

The Affair

Thrown like Kleenex

The branches of the fig tree were stretched over like a human's arms shadowing the window of the back bedroom and through the glass I could see the fruit showing its first crack. That meant they were fully ripe and were ready to be harvested. Usually I would make some into jam, and the rest I would thread with string and hang under the shade to dry for Christmas. It was the first tree that I had planted, to be followed by lemons, oranges, bay trees and grape vines that stretched around the house. In no time, the whole house was surrounded by greenery.

I went outside and put some food out for Lassie and Gina (our dogs) by the corner of the house. As I sat on one of the benches between the orange tree and the little palm tree, I closed my eyes, taking deep breaths and enjoying the fresh air and the smell of the garden that filled my lungs.

Before we had built this house, the land was covered by bushes and rubbish. Now I couldn't believe how much it had changed and how beautiful it had turned out to be. I was just in my 30s and despite the ups and downs we had managed to achieve almost everything we had planned. We had two beautiful children, our house had been built to our taste, and was surrounded by a beautiful garden that I had created. Our successful business seemed to be providing financial security for our daily life and everything else.

However, as the saying goes, money does not always buy you happiness. It seemed to be just a paper comfort blanket that would enable me to trudge through life slowly. Just when I was thinking that life might now be looking up, I heard on the grapevine that, now we had money and the business was going well, my husband Dan had been visiting bars, spending a large amount of cash and showing off in front of women.

The inevitable dawned on me. His attitude to me had changed for the worse, using offensive words, and most nights he crawled home very late. I was left to deal on my own with the house, kids, work and ... mother-in-law. He didn't seem that interested in his children anymore and definitely not in me. One of his nieces approached me and told me exactly what was going on – Dan had 'become "involved" with a married woman, one of the waitresses in the bar near the Qemal Stafa stadium, who had a well-known reputation in the capital'.

Suddenly, it all made sense. Of course, she would be attracted to him now that he had money. The business was going well, and he would show off his earnings in bars, giving out big tips. Of course, she would be the one to feed his ego.

Disturbed and anxious, I couldn't wait for him to return home that night.

Darkness had wrapped itself around the city and a little chill was evident in the air. I put the children to bed and said goodnight to my mother-in-law, who made her way to her bedroom. I was sitting on the veranda, watching the last rain drops after a long day and seeing a few stars starting to show through the dark sky. In the apartments across the street a few lights started to turn off, and the roads were becoming quiet. Lassie was sitting next to me half asleep with his head laid on my lap and Gina was lying down just a short distance away. Suddenly Lassie got up and barked loudly. Through the large wrought-iron gates the Mercedes' lights rolled over me, and there he was, looking so smug in that car as if he owned the world, with one arm out the window and a cigarette in-between his fingers. Strangely, that night he had come home earlier than other nights!

He didn't seem happy as he greeted me under his teeth and unlike other times he entered in the house without taking his shoes off.

'Where have *you* been?' I asked.

'Had a drink with friends,' he said.

His body language let him down. I knew there and then that he wasn't telling the truth. I needed to be blunt. So impatiently I asked, 'Are you having an affair?'

A dirty smirk appeared on his face; he either couldn't help showing it on his face or wore the expression purposefully, as if he was proud. 'No, I'm not,' he lied.

'Is that the truth?' I demanded.

'There's no truth to be told,' he said, 'and I'm tired. Where's my dinner?'

A part of me was screaming inside, 'Dinner? Don't give him his dinner until he sits down and tells you the truth.'

Yet, the other part of me, that was driven by fear and fear alone, couldn't refuse. I wouldn't dare not to. But that wasn't all – I didn't want to start any argument that late at night as the children were sleeping. My bravery was swallowed up by the anxiety that had swamped my body. It was as if I wasn't even in control, and before I knew it, I had gone into the kitchen and taken his dinner out of the oven. It was then I understood the power of fear; a feeling that could make you do anything without you even knowing. As soon as I placed it on the table in front of him, he lifted the fork, put some into his mouth, and slammed it down onto the plate.

'It's not hot enough,' he growled.

I was taken aback. 'I've just taken it out of the oven,' I replied.

'It is not hot enough!' he shouted again.

So, I went and re-heated it and brought it back to the table. A blind rage covered his face. Without even trying the food again, he lifted the plate and smashed it down onto the table with such force that the glistening glass table shattered into pieces. The shards of glass cascaded down onto the floor and the food splashed against the white walls as if the wall were an oily colour picture. He looked at himself covered in food too and rushed out of the living room towards the bathroom.

Just when I thought it couldn't have got any worse, suddenly the house phone rang.

I picked up the phone and on the other end a woman's voice was heard.

'Hello? Is Dan there?'

'Can I ask who's calling please?'

'Moka, his girlfriend,' she blurted out.

'Moka? His girlfriend? Ah, I'm Yllka, his wife, by the way,' I said, understanding that she was the woman my husband was cheating with. 'How dare you...'

Suddenly my words was brutally interrupted as Dan snatched the phone out of my hand with such force that it pulled me to my knees. The ringing tone had made him almost run from the bathroom to the living room. Without thinking twice he raised his foot and kicked me behind my head. I felt a sharp pain from his heavy cowboy boots; an excruciating pain that spread down my spine and down along my left arm. My face and hands went numb and my vision became blurred as I fell onto the sofa. I could just about make out his stern face, through my dazed eyes looking at me and saying, 'I talk to whom I want to talk to, and you can't stop me, you ugly face.'

I looked at him, the sad, pathetic man who was supposed to be my husband, but who had the audacity not just to be disloyal to me but also to talk in front of his wife, with his lover. I was thrown like Kleenex, my dignity and my rights had been stolen from me. Shocked and unable to speak or move for a minute, my stomach churned with disbelief. This was the most bizarre thing I had ever seen or heard. I mean, really? What was to be made of this? I wanted to yell with all the power of my soul, to tear out the pain that had engulfed me, allowing the force of my voice to push and banish this man from this world, never to return.

'Bastard,' I whispered helplessly, as my world came tumbling down around me. 'How could you?'

'Hmm.' He grinned down at me with contempt.

Shockingly I gasped, as my chest tightened and my head was grinding inside like crushed glass. 'I'm not wasting any more of my time or energy. I'm out of here.'

I managed to get up and I began to walk towards the front door. I could hardly breathe, and my vision had become blurred, but I could just about see the front gates which were nearly ten metres away as my weakened legs carried me towards them.

With every step I took my determination grew, and with every step, it felt like my invisible shackles were loosening. My hope was crushed by a sharp pain to the back of my head as it jolted backwards. He had come after me and grabbed a fistful of my hair and began to drag me viciously backwards into the house, like a predator that had just caught its prey.

'Where do you think you're going?' he slurred.

The pain was unbearable and as much as the screams wanted to escape my body, my mouth opened but no sound came out as I was being pulled back into my inescapable prison.

My trance was broken by the voice that I least expected to hear. His mum had come out, shouting at him to leave me alone. I saw pity in her eyes; I felt worthless.

He kicked me into the living room and said to his mum with a sarcastic smile splitting his face, 'Oh, feeling sorry for *her* now are you, what changed?' he said. 'Weren't you always telling me to hit her hard as in this house the only one who sings is the cockerel not the chicken?'

Her face dropped, she looked up at him angrly and said, 'Not for that Moka whore, no,' she said, while waving her hand in the air.

Well, it was true, she had been the one telling her son that the answer to everything regarding his wife, was violence as it has always been, but now things had changed. Her ice-cold mask melting before my eyes. The reality of what had been going on in the house had suddenly hit her. Dan turned away, shaking his head, unhappy. He finally broke the gaze, quickly grabbed the keys to his Mercedes, rushed out and drove away.

I didn't move until I heard the screech of the tyres that I was able at last to go. I staggered to my bedroom and let out a series of gasps and cries. I clutched my chest, finding it very hard to catch my breath. The effect he had had on me had been so momentous. Suddenly I felt like I was stuck in dense black smoke without a way of escape. My breathing started to quicken like someone was trying to strangle me and I felt like I was gasping under water. My hands began to tremble, and my fingers started to distort. I tried to stand up, but my legs froze, and they couldn't hold my body. I panicked, feeling that the ground beneath me was about to open and I was going to die. Powerless, I lay in bed and tried to normalize my breath. Tormented and shattered, I tried to close my eyes and get a few hours' sleep. But I couldn't. My eyes were swollen from insomnia. I got up and looked through the window facing north. Outside the only light in the lamppost was flickering to ignite the dark. Just like my thoughts right now. Questions jostled for attention. What am I going to do? Where can I go?

How could I possibly stay even for one day, listening to my husband talking to his lover on the phone in front of my own eyes in my own house? I could not stand his infidelity, humiliation and abuse anymore. He had taken away the most beautiful years of my life, my happiness, and my dignity. Even my soul cried out 'Enough!'.

It was somewhere around midnight I heard the car engine approaching the house and the door open. I heard Dan's footsteps going into the living room and the creaking noise of the sofa bed open, then silence. I guessed he had gone to sleep.

-o-

In the morning I took my children to school and nursery for the time being and I returned home to gather up some kids' clothes and some of mine ready for when I picked them up. I knew I lived in a country where leaving your husband's house wasn't easy, was shameful and you would be called a lot of names, even when it wasn't your fault. People would look down on you and you would never have a proper life again. What sort of a life was this anyway?

A strong determination was still running through my veins. I was heading to my sister's house for the time being and never intended to return.

I went to collect Enea and Hope and then we all took a taxi to my sister's home.

'Where are we going, Mami?' Enea asked.

'To your auntie's house; just for few days,' I replied.

'Is Dad coming?' he said innocently.

'No, he's at work, sweetheart,' I said quickly.

Less than half an hour later the taxi pulled into my sister's drive in her village. She came out onto the veranda, narrowing her eyes, and held up her hand to her forehead to guard her eyes against the sun. A smile spread across her face once she saw us get out of the car. She ran down the path to greet us. My great-auntie happened to be at her house at that moment watching from the veranda.

'What a surprise!' my sister shouted.

I smiled at her as I hugged her and asked her older daughter to play with Enea and Hope outside.

'What's going on?' she asked.

Reluctantly I looked at her and said, 'I have left Dan and I'm never going back.'

'What?' my great-auntie said, a look of shock crossing her face. 'You can't leave your husband's house! You will bring shame. Have you thought about where you are going to go?'

I stood in front of her, unable to either move or to say a word.

With hindsight, I regretted turning up on her doorstep after what had been said. What was I was thinking? I knew my sister loved me and would have done anything to help, but there was nothing she could do about it, and that reality was staring me in the face.

Somehow, I had a glimmer of hope that maybe, just maybe, something could be done, to save me and take me away from that miserable life, but in just a second, that hope was extinguished just like water on hot coals.

'Oh sweetheart,' my sister said softly, as she embraced me quickly. 'Don't worry, l will make us a strong espresso and we will talk.'

I tried to quickly wipe my tears away as I saw Hope walk in the front door. She took my hand and led me over to the couch, where she sat on my lap. She hugged me tightly, wiped the rest of the tears from my face, and smiled. She was only three years old and still wanted to cheer me up. Although I saw sadness on her face, and the guilt grew inside me, I felt an incredible responsibility for their happiness.

'Ah, there is not enough coffee, I'm just going to the Spar around the corner; I won't be long,' my sister said.

My great-auntie said goodbye and went with her. I was glad that she was gone. I was sick of her interfering, sticking her nose into everything and demanding. All she cared was other people's opininon rather that her niece's happiness.

My sister had only been gone for five minutes when I heard a car engine coming to a halt outside her house.

'Daddy is here,' Enea said.

My heart began to tremble. Enea ran out and I followed him. Hope was holding on to me tightly and wouldn't let go, so I carried her on my hip.

'Come to Daddy,' Dan said sharply, with a false smile etched on his face.

'No, I want to stay with my mammy,' she replied.

His smile disappeared into a frown full of anger, shaking his head in frustration that he couldn't do anything. His tone changed, and he growled through gritted teeth, 'Get the kids; we are going home.'

I should have said no, I'm not coming, but I didn't. I had to go with him and think what to do and how, but not in my sister's house. It was the wrong move. Somehow, I needed to sort myself out and get out of this marriage. And the only one that could save me, was ... me.

I got in the car without saying a word. I was paralysed with terror.

As he was driving away, he was laughing with Enea and Hope, like nothing bothered him. My skin crawled. I didn't want to look at him or hear his voice.

As if it wasn't bad enough back home I was "welcomed" by the reprimands of my mother-in-law, standing on the doorstep, pointing towards me, telling me exactly the same words as my great aunt had done. Instead of empathy came anger. Instead of a kind word came insults and shame. I was made to feel nothing, worthless.

Ironically, a saying in my country is: *'It is bad enough that the donkey died but, the flies don't leave you alone either.'*

I didn't even acknowledge her. I said nothing even though I was boiling with anger inside. I didn't have the energy to even comment on the nonsense pouring out of her mouth. Instead, I went to my room. I closed my bedroom door and felt drained. I felt completely lifeless. In my bedroom where, although the decor, the colours, the pictures create a cosy ambience, I felt like the walls as if by magic were closing in on each other, giving my chest an almost unbearable pressure. Hearing the noise of the car engine driving away from the house, I finally felt a degree of relief and could relax. Lying on the bed looking blankly at the magnolia-painted walls, I felt that they heard my despair, felt my pain and somehow would defend and support my needs. My body sank into the bed because I felt so heavy and tired. It was as if the events of the day were anchoring me there.

Questions raced through my mind. What am I going to do? Where can I go? How can I escape this world with my children? There were no social services in Albania, no benefits and no groups or outside help for women like me. I couldn't just go to my sisters' and brothers' houses and expect them to take care of me and my kids again. They had done their duty, by raising me and taking care of me. Without hope and with no answers to my questions, I felt like a bird that wanted to escape from its cage and fly away, never to return.

I got up, and as I was wandering around, out of the corner of my eye, I noticed that the bottom of my drawer was half open. I took out my little box which contained my school diary. While I was opening it, a little black and white photograph fell out onto the wooden floor. With my trembling hand, I managed to pick up the photo. There I was with my high school best friends Eva, Izolt and Ada, on a school trip to Dajti mountain, playing and laughing in the snow. Other friends Pranvera and Moza N were throwing snowballs towards Moza C and Arjan. What a beautiful picture!

We looked so innocent and happy. In front of my eyes they appeared as moments of care-free adolescent life surrounded by wonderful and kind friends, euphoric and trouble-free. Then, for a few minutes I immersed myself in the memories of those years – climbing the steep mountain Dajt; stopping halfway to have a break before arriving at the top. Suddenly the trees and natural surroundings flashed into my mind, bringing fresh aromas to my senses to uplift me spiritually and providing me with peace and tranquillity. Sitting on the rock with Izolt and Eva, he took out a bag with packed lunches that had been prepared and nicely wrapped by his mother which he shared with us.

Izolt had been lucky enough to grow up in a regular family with both parents where the education that had been carved into his character was undoubtedly evident in his demeanour and knowledge of life. There was a benevolence in his smile, a sincerity in his blue eyes that showed you could live life without falsehood, without deceit. He looked at me as if he knew my inner heart; even so I was full of self-doubt. He would not hesitate to raise my spirits and make me feel valued without judgment, without condition, without hypocrisy saying, 'You have wealth in your heart, Yllka. Never change that for anyone.' And Eva that always had only smiles and love for everyone. Her mum used to make the best beans ever and we were always invited to dip some. Then I looked at Ada, so innocent and beautiful. Her hair was covered with snow, with her hand up covering her face to protect herself from the snowballs some boy was throwing at her.

Then my memory moved to Moza, remembering when she took out the spinach and cheese pastry that had accidentally fallen into the snow. We tried not to waste any of it by eating them with the snow on, trying not to be too cautious about who was looking at us and laughing out loud as we ate them.

That was nothing compared with the laughter we shared on the historic party to Peza village. We went by bus and returned walking the nineteen kilometres the next morning until we reached Tirana. It was the place that celebrated on the 16th September every year remembering the Peza Conference that was held in 1942. This was where the decision was made to open a new and secure National Liberation Front of Albania's Resistance that led the way for the liberation from the Nazis' occupation during World War Two.

It was a traditional celebration organised by our school. Even the bus was jam packed, and we were having fun singing out loud without a care in the world. That night around the fire, someone played the guitar as we sang a serenade and shared the little food we had brought from home. The warmth of the fire that night slowly faded along with the melody of the song that became lost, farther and farther away, like a distant sound. Then I was back in that cold room in the reality of the truth and the present. For a few minutes I had disappeared into the most beautiful memories of my life. I so wished that they weren't just memories. I so wished that I was free and happy like then.

Through my sadness my lips curved into a little smile. I doubted that one day I would be able to laugh from the bottom of my heart again like in that picture, to sing with my heart and soul and hear the sound of my voice as it echoed through the mountain's gorges. To dance and turn around with no care in the world just like then. Now, I would have given anything to bring that time back. I missed the friends that I hadn't seen since the day I got married, as I had been forbidden to see them.

I felt that I was breaking down. I didn't feel that the happy girl in the picture was me, and I didn't know myself anymore. Those years with suffering and pain had changed me altogether. I wasn't interested in how I looked anymore, how I styled my hair, how I did my make up or what I wore. I was lost. I felt like a candle wick that had slowly burned down the candle until it melted in the darkness, extinguished and unseen. Sadly, I put the box back in the drawer and closed the heavy curtains to shut out the outside, as I lay down in the dark.

Suddenly, I heard a faint knocking at the front door, and I heard my mother-in-law greeting my sister. I couldn't get up and face her, as I regretted going to her house in the first place. What a stupid thing to have done! What was I thinking? What could she possibly do? A few seconds later, the bedroom door opened, and I heard her soft voice saying, 'Sis, are you ok?'

'I'm fine,' I sighed. 'Sorry to bother you before. I was being silly. It was something and nothing.'

She sat at the bottom of the bed looking down at me as if she didn't recognise the woman I had become. She gently took my arm and pulled me into a warm hug. There was so much I wanted to say. Like the old times when I was little and I couldn't wait for her to come home from work so I could complain about Moza arguing over the coloured pencils or Bushi who had stolen my last roasted chestnut that I had been hiding in my bedroom. Now I wasn't little anymore. I was married with children and wasn't her responsibility anymore. She had done her duty – she had helped me to grow up and took care of me until the day she went to her husband's house.

My emotions had completely frozen, and I felt like an icicle that was stuck in between two boulders craving warmth that would finally melt it and return it to the pure water it once was. It felt like she had held me for an age, in deafening silence. When she let go, she held onto my shoulders and looked deep into my soul and demanded that if I ever needed her for anything that I would ask her. I nodded unwillingly.

-o-

My anxiety got so bad that panic attacks became part of my daily routine and it was obvious that my body was completely and utterly exhausted from the stress and anxiety. For the time being I was trying to instil an element of normality for my children, while at the same time thinking about how we might get out of this misery.

For a few days, the house was as quiet as a graveyard. The silence was broken by the arrival of G and his wife N, the older son of Dan's sister. So even though he was Dan's nephew, G was older than him. They were blessed with two beautiful children. Luckily they only lived a 20-minute car journey away from us. They entered the house with smiles on their faces that soon faded when they realized that something must have happened. I was so happy to see them as their presence always transformed any unhappiness into a glimpse of joy. They always brought light into the situation, just like the rainbows would spread across the sky after the storm. They were a very genuine couple who lived how people should live, with hard work and honestly. Regardless of what others thought or said, they would stand up for what was right and bring nothing less than love and comfort to every circumstance. Without a doubt, I would hold them close to my heart, as close as my siblings, due to the extra mile they would go for me at any time. Despite their presence, though, I couldn't bear to look at Dan, never mind talk to him.

As if it wasn't enough what was happening in our household, to make things worse a civil war had broken out. Even though Communism had perished in Albania, the history of war and bloodshed would repeat itself. This was due to the government pushing pyramid schemes, promising the citizens of Albania money if they invested. This caused violent protests to break out all over the country, and this then turned into a battle between the citizens and the government.

The country had entered a state of emergency. Buildings were getting burned, things were being stolen, armed hooligans were parading the streets, and people were being killed for no reason every day. Thousands of protestors gathered in Tirana and once again clashed with police. By this time the violent protesting had spread throughout the entire country. It became clear that counter-revolution was supported by most of the population in Albania. The situation was like we were going back to 1990-91 when people got up in revolution for freedom, for democracy in the hope of a better future. But this time there was no hope for the future. In people's eyes you could see only sadness, loss and disappointment. Most people lost their money that they had saved for years through hard work, some of them lost their homes, and others lost their lives. Their sacrifice and effort in 1991 now seems to be for nothing, worthless. If before then, they had lost their freedom, now it was their life, their future, everything they had. Absolutely chaotic.

The ability of the government and military to maintain order began to collapse, especially in the southern half of Albania, which fell under the control of rebels and criminal gangs. People were frightened daily that these violent acts would affect their family members or friends. They decided to take action and arm themselves by breaking into the army depots and taking what they could for their own safety and to protect their families. Like everyone else, we managed to secure a Kalashnikov that we took from the army depot located on top of a steep hill, twenty to thirty minutes from our house.

Hooligans and criminals took advantage of the situation and built barricades in the middle of roads and especially in the south from where people used to travel to Greece to steal *their* money, jewellery, and anything else valuable, like latter-day highway men. They even killed people on the buses if they didn't hand over what they had. Hearing about the situation, and of course having our own buses travelling from Tirana to the border with Greece at Kakavije, the bus drivers were told not to stop anywhere on the journey until they arrived at their destination.

It was scary that cold night in December when Dan drove back home with the bus full of holes bombarded with bullets from highway men. He was lucky to be alive as he did not stop the bus. One noble thing about him was that when it came to passengers that were travelling on his bus he would protect them with his life. He couldn't believe how they had managed to pass through the barricades that were often full of bombs and grenades. It was very dangerous and they were very lucky to survive. It was at that point that the business had to be sold.

'Now that you have sold the business, come and work with us in England,' his brothers suggested to Dan, thinking of taking him away from the temptation, the bloodfeud and the trouble he had got himself into. After days of talking, they finally managed to persuade Dan to go with them.

At this point even though we lived separately but in the same house, the dangerous situation in Albania forced us to put our problems behind us for the time being and dedicate ourselves to concentrating on protecting our children. So this serious situation kept us communicating and being civil to each other.

Over the next few weeks they arranged everything for their journey, with Dan and two of his older brothers trying to get their documents to escape to England. On the news it said that the government was getting the situation under control all over the country and that things would soon improve. So, the three brothers were ready to set off the very next day.

I was sitting on the veranda and knitting a blue coloured winter jumper for Enea. I could feel Dan's presence around me and finally he sat down across from me. He looked at me in silence for a minute, stubbed out the butt of his cigarette, grinding it into the ashtray.

'The jumper looks good,' he said, grinning at me.

Suddenly, he was trying to be charming. I gestured with my head without looking at him and carried on knitting, trying to control my shaking hands.

'We are leaving in ten minutes,' he added. 'Take care of the kids, and yourself, too. I'm going to call you as soon as we arrive in London.'

I shook my head in disbelief and an ironic smile crept into my face.

'Just so you know, I'm not taking anyone with me,' he answered. 'I left her. It's just us three brothers. No one else.'

'Is that you asking for a medal?' I said sarcastically.

'I do care. You are my wife and they are my children,' he replied slowly.

'Ha!' I sneered. 'Lost your memory?'

The conversation was interrupted by his brothers coming through the door.

'Come on. We are going to be late,' they said. They all said their goodbyes and the children waved as the car faded into the dark at the end of the road.

I was left in my mundane little life in the house with my mother-in-law and my children.

-o-

In my mind I ruled him out, never to be with him again. Dan and his brothers had settled in London. His brothers told the family that Dan didn't take her with him to England over there because he regretted what he had done and wanted to mend things with his wife and children.

'Everyone deserves a second chance,' they would say!

Dan stayed in regular contact with me and the children, asking if the situation in Albania was still unsafe. It was hard for me to forgive and forget. His persistence in asking for forgiveness and for a second chance to start again continued. His voice over the phone sounded like it was remorseful.

Was that really genuine? Had he changed? Could he change?

CHAPTER 15

The survivors

Friday morning dawned after a sleepless night filled with the frightening noise of gunfire. I was up at 5 am, thinking this would be the safest time of day. Outside was a deathly silence that early in the morning. It was so quiet I could hear my own steady rhythm from within. I felt a chill in my blood; it was such a fragile peace and I knew from experience it wouldn't be long before it was once more shattered. I made a long journey to the flour mill; the supermarkets were shut and lack of food was becoming an issue. Arriving at the mill, like lots of people there, I quickly grabbed a large sack of flour and threw it over my shoulder before turning for home.

Halfway back, I suddenly heard gunfire again. The sound of the shot cracked out, rising and echoing through the air. I had heard the sound before, the signature tune of two gangs attacking each other. I looked around at my surroundings and saw a half wall of a burning house leaning like a skeleton. As silently and quickly as I could I hunkered down behind the wall, hiding myself from view. I heard shouting; an aggressive exchange of threats and profanities. It seemed to be a family blood feud, lately these were becoming more and more frequent. Suddenly the voice of a man who seemed to be very close to me on my right, yelling at the other side made me tremble. 'Get out of there, you fucking arsehole, if you're a brave man.'

The piercing sound of machine gun fire was the only answer he received.

'My brother's blood won't be forgotten,' he shouted again. 'I'm going to drag you out and gut you like the dog you are.'

'He brought it up himself,' came the reply.

'Fuck your sister...' The rest of the words were lost under the violent sound of gunfire that was rapidly growing more intense. I slowly moved to the skeletal remains of a window, frame half destroyed, and the panes long gone, smashed by the blasts of random bombs. Suddenly, I saw one of the guys emerge out of the ginnel, crouching low, moving as fast as a rat, from behind the wall, along the narrow path connecting both sides of the road.

Now it's safe to carry on with my journey, I thought. I came out and began running, the sack over my head. To my horror, I had only gone a few paces when the shooting started again. Birds flew up in the sky. This time I had nowhere to hide as I was out in the middle of the road. Left without any alternative, I carried on running, crouching down and covering my head with the sack, hoping that somehow it would keep me safe. Fear constricted my chest and my mouth was as dry as a bone. But oddly, I could feel the weight of the bag getting lighter. Perhaps the adrenaline had given me extra strength? Finally, I reached home and deposited the sack on the floor. As I put it down, I realized it was half-empty. How strange, I thought. It was definitely full when I picked it up. It wasn't until my mother-in-law squinted at me, and shrieked, 'You've been shot!' that I noticed a bullet hole in the corner of the sack.

'God must love you. I guess it wasn't your time to die yet,' she muttered. A tremor seized me; a mix of fear and relief. Fear from the realisation that I was almost shot, and relief that they caught only the corner of the sack and not me! I was very, very lucky for once. But was I going to be lucky next time? What about if it was outside in the garden where my children play?

The unstable situation in the country made most of people who had money chose to pay to get out of the country. They paid for very expensive fake passports to either fly, travel by boat, or in a lorry to get to their destination.

Dan suggested that I take Hope and Enea and go and live with him in England. A chance to start all over again and to give the children the best possible life they could have, but somehow I was reluctant. I knew it would be foolish to take a big risk to trust him again, after everything that had happened, but the safety of my children's life was more important.

This was a massive decision that could make or break us as a family and the scariest part was that I did not have a clue whether I would do it. One side of me was thinking I should go and give him a second chance. The other side of me was saying that I would be crazy to even give it a thought. Ironically, believe it or not, I gave it some thought and I made the worst possible decision: I decided to go to England.

Was I a fool for making that decision?

Absolutely, yes; damn right I was! Once again I found myself trapped in an abusive life and much worse than before.

To this day I cannot believe how or why I launched myself towards the hell I endured, and I'm sure no-one else in their right mind would either.

I thought there would be a better future and greater safety for my children, and maybe even for me too.

When the children found out they shrieked with excitement – so small and fragile – and I could see in their frightened faces how desperate they were to get out of there,

Dan's good friend Lani knew the people who dealt with transporting families and individuals to different countries. They had arranged for us to be taken out of the country to London so we could be reunited with Dan. The passports were done and everything else was ready to go. Lani came to the house that night together with the guy in charge. He took the passport out of his inside pocket and handed it to me. 'Good luck,' he said.

'I'm telling you again, you are responsible for their life.' My brother-in-law pointed at the guy.

'Stop worrying,' he said. 'They will travel like Royals, as soon as they get out of Dusseldorf airport the car is outside to pick them up and take them to England.'

That night the hands were shaken as a promise and we were convinced that everything would be just fine.

Even as I was holding the passports in my hand, it didn't seem real. I had never flown out of the country before, never mind flying with fake passports. Apprehensive, worried and responsible for my children's life I had to be really certain that nothing would happen to them.

'Trust me,' Lani said. 'You're not the first and won't be the last. Lots of people have been doing the same and their life is much safer in London than here. It's a secure country and your children will grow up safely.'

There and then I decided. There wasn't time to waste. We were scheduled to leave the following morning.

Around 5am, I got the children up and put the silver kettle with mountain tea on and went to the garden to get a lemon. The scent of lemons hanging in the branches and golden orange trees which were overflowing with young fruits filled my surroundings.

I looked at the house and sighed. How quickly my passion and devotion had brought the garden to life as it became full of greenery, full of fruits and flowers that surrounded the house like a beautiful scarf.

Mixed emotions played in my mind as I was sad to leave, but then happy to go. I picked one lemon and took in its beautiful fresh scent, knowing that I might not smell that again for quite some time. On the veranda Hope and Enea were hugging their dogs, Lassie and Gina, their faces filled with sadness. Lassie was Enea's hero and best friend; he was his buddy. They had that special bond together. Just seeing their faces made everything seem so real. I felt the anxiety of the unknown future had overtaken my body, but I was quickly distracted on hearing the loud beeping of a car horn.

'Come on, children, the car is here. Let's go,' I said, holding back my tears and putting on a brave face as I spoke.

We said our goodbyes to everyone as quickly as possible.

'Good luck,' my mother-in-law said. 'Be careful with Hope and Enea.'

'I will,' I managed to whisper.

As we drove away, I couldn't help but look back at my house. I stared from the car window until the amber light spilling onto the veranda faded away, and the tip of the grey roof disappeared completely.

-o-

I was jolted from these memories by the jarring noise of more thunder that startled the hell out of me, as I was lying on the top of the pallets with Hope's body over mine and supporting Enea's head on my left arm. Thinking and going on about the past, that now held very little value. It seemed very distant, foreign. It seemed as if it had been months since we started this journey even though it had only been two days since we said our goodbyes and left home, and yet it was not over. It seemed like it had grown to become a thread but spinning through the days like a flash. How many disappointments and betrayals, how much fear and pain, how many things had happened in such a short time! That's long gone. The question is what does life hold for us right now? I felt numb and very doubtful as the ferry sailed into the English Channel. This is a wilder nightmare, more than anything I could have expected. I want to use all my senses but the cold has frozen my body and affected my brain power too. This cold is trying to steal the warmth of my soul but the limbs of my body do their best to withstand this pain and survive.

I'm holding my baby girl tight and trying to keep her warmth from dissipating as much as I can. The ferry slowing down and the noise of gears shifting make me think that we are near the land. Slowly I tried to get up while holding Hope, but my leg seemed to have given way to gravity, numbed and unstable. I tried again with all my strength and as I stood up, a little swing of the ferry made me lose my balance and flap into the blue canvas. Not hurt. Finally the ferry stopped. I got up again and through a little hole in the canvas, I saw the land. The land that I thought I would never see again. Everyone was up, exchanging glances with each other. Artan, the Kosovan, looked outside too. 'We've arrived. We're in England,' he exclaimed. Everyone was relieved and cheering quietly. 'Stay quiet till we get on the road.

Not too long to go now,' Artan said with a low voice.

I looked down and two guys in luminous orange jackets unchained the lorry from the ferry and finally the lorry started moving, driving its way on the road. I lay down again, I lifted my blouse and brought Hope closer to my body again and covered her around me. I gasped from the cold touch and a shiver ran through my body. I tried to massage her body again and again constantly. Then the noise of the engine stopped, the lorry pulled up. We looked outside again. There were lots of other lorries on the opposite side. It was a truck stop.

Relief surged through my body. We all stood up. Hope was in my arms, almost unconscious. Then together with Enea and the others we ran to the back of the lorry cabin and started thumping and banging on it.

'Help, help! Open the doors!' we shouted. No answer.

'Come on, everyone, knock harder, we need to get out of this lorry nowwww, my daughter looks like she is not breathing, come on.'

Without a word everyone quickly starting knocking again on the back of the cabin again shouting, 'Heeeelp, heeeeelp, open the doooor', but still nothing, no reply. There was a pain behind that shout, a pain mixed with despair, a desperation to get out of that lorry at last, the lorry that was occupied by strangers, holding and protecting seven humans in it, the lorry that had taken us all through the Channel and landed us safely on the land, the lorry that was once quiet now was polluted by shouting to be abandoned.

Suddenly we heard the door slam. The exclamations immediately stopped and the silence prevailed. It looked like everyone was holding their breath and looking at each impatiently for what they thought was going to happen next.

Surprisingly, the back large doors of the lorry were being opened and strong sunlight rushed into the darkness we had endured for so long. Standing before us, the lorry driver – a tall young man of around 30, with dark hair and glasses and a friendly face, looked at us with shock in his eyes, glancing at all of us, then at Hope, who was cradled in my arms with her eyes closed. Without wasting any time he gestured for me to come and sit on the front of the lorry. He took a hot blanket from the metal bunk bed that was on the top of the cabin and quickly wrapped Hope in it, and while he gave me a bottle of water immediately called the ambulance.

I tried to give Hope some water while Enea was stroking his sister's hair with concern and frightened eyes. I could soon hear the sirens of the ambulance and police as they approached.

Everybody was so quiet and their attention was drawn in Hope's direction. I could only hear the paramedic's voice talking in a language that I could not understand and I didn't know what was happening to my daughter. I questioned Artan, 'What are they saying? Tell me.' But before he could say anything I heard the cheering of the paramedics. She blinked and opened her beautiful tired eyes, looked around, puzzled, and whispered, 'Mami.' It was the same feeling of that beautiful afternoon in the March of 1994 when she opened her eyes for the very first time, looking at me. It was as if she had been born again. That was the most incredible feeling ever. She had survived. We all had. The lorry driver took out a loaf of bread, cut it into very thin slices and with a little jar of strawberry jam started to spread it on the bread and handed it out to all of us.

The police cars took us away to the station.

The translators came to help us answer the questions the police had for us. The next morning, we all boarded a train to

London where our loved ones were waiting for us.

I was happy that we had survived, but once the fear of the journey and the elation of our safe arrival had passed, I was aware of another dilemma awaiting me at our destination. As the train raced towards London, my feelings were a mixture of fear and worry about my life with him again. Everyone was so happy, but within me, the closer I got to seeing him, the more fearful I became.

Was the road of destiny painted in black or white? Reversal or fulfilment?

CHAPTER 16

Too late to repent

The unbearable London life

The train was heading into the unknown, toward the path that would urge me to use every tiny bit of power remaining in my wounded soul so that we might survive the impossible, the merciless. I looked at the people sitting around me who had shared those terrible 48 hours with me. All of them seemed happy. But why not me? Why did I not share that emotion? I should be happy too, shouldn't I? We survived. Yet, this weird feeling had invaded my body and soul.

The closer the train got to London the more I felt lost and scared, my intuition telling me I was entering a gloomy path with no light, without an ounce of hope. Why? What really was there to make me feel this way? It was me who had made the decision in the first place to take this journey; no one had forced me.

Hope and Enea were sitting next to me, happy; they couldn't wait to see their daddy. My face tried to smile, but my heart was churning, evoking something not good. I shook my head, shivering as if to remove those bad thoughts from my mind and looked out of the window. The train was travelling fast and would soon be in London and I'd be there face to face with him, to see the truth or hear the lies. In no time, we had arrived. There we were, right there, and he was standing at the top of the grey stairs, waiting.

'There's Daddy!' Enea shouted, pointing at him.

There he was, a grin splitting his face that said it all. I knew that damnable smile. His motives were painted in black and white; uncovered, plastered all over him. Doubts shot through me like a hot knife going through butter. Had this terrifying journey been worth it?

My instinct told me that I had made the wrong decision. I had been foolish. What had I done? Or maybe I was just being paranoid, trying to convince myself. Shivers ran down my spine as Enea and Hope ran towards him, both of them squealing 'Daddy!' as they flung their arms around his neck.

We greeted each other, as a far too familiar anxiety rushed into every part of my body. Our interaction was stranger than normal – he was talking to me, but he couldn't look me in the eye.

The station was very busy with people rushing in and out of the bustling streets. Going through London was amazing, a place we had never seen before. It was so different from Albania, with its unknown seventeenth- and eighteenth-century buildings, Georgian houses, gorgeous stone arched bridges and the double decker red buses. We finally arrived at the house situated in an area called Forest Gate which he shared with the siblings, for the time being, until we could find our own place to live.

Trying to settle down somehow and explore the surroundings in the days ahead with the children. It was late morning. The streets were filled with lots of orange-brown leaves, damp from the rain of the day before. Suddenly in the distance walking in front of us, my cousin Tani appeared with a few friends. I couldn't believe my eyes! Really? Is that Tani? If he was in England I would have known! We hadn't seen each other for a very long time. In fact, the last time I saw him, Tani was a young boy. I was at my uncle's Nevruz's (Tani's grandparents) family home in the city of Fier in Albania having dinner when he spilled red wine all over the white tablecloth whilst trying to be a gentleman by filling our glasses. And now there he was, unexpectedly in front of me in a foreign country. Quickly we found ourselves embracing each other. Fate had brought us together at the right time and place, for whatever reason. How do you even begin to explain something like this? Even better, Tani offered for us to stay in one of his empty houses. At last, we had found somewhere to live! Dan and I agreed without question, and in no time, we moved to the house with two floors, plenty of room for the kids and opposite a park. It was perfect.

We stayed there for a couple of months until they provided accommodation for us in one of the hostels. We were given three rooms, one for us and one for each child. I managed to find a school for Hope and Enea and tried to find a job for myself.

Things were moving slowly and calmly, and it seemed that hopefully it was going to be a good new start for our family as promised by Dan. A very normal routine for a stable family, or so I thought. But it didn't last long, as I found out that Moka was in London with *her* son.

I felt as if my world was crashing down again and a boulder had lodged in my throat. My woman's instinct was right.

All this time everything was going too well, it was just too good to be true. All the things he had said on the phone were lies; the lies that I feared the most were the ones closest to the truth. They were the root of my fear. How could I fall for his lies and deceit again? Had I not learned from all the other times that a leopard never changes his spots?

Dan was out with the children in the park nearby. I was strutting around in the hostel room unable to relax, waiting impatiently for them to come back. In the corridor I heard their voices running after each other towards the room. I opened the door quickly and before I knew it I was covered by their hugs. Hope's hands were covered in daisy flowers that she had collected for me and she was telling me that she had made a new Kosovan friend called Debora, while Enea, unlike other times, was very quiet.

'Where's your father?' I asked.

'Dad just went to get some tobacco,' Enea said shiftily with a disheartened look on his face.

'What's the matter?' I asked.

He looked hesitantly at first; scared almost, so I encouraged him.

'It's okay, you can tell me anything,' I said.

He looked down at the floor and said sheepishly, 'Mum, that bad woman Moka is here, I saw her at the park with her son.'

'I know, sweetheart,' I replied. 'Don't you worry about anything. I promise you it will all be sorted out.'

They both embraced my body that at that moment was frozen, as cold as stone.

Trying not to show it in front of the kids, I was trying to hold it in, but internally my body was raging with anger and disappointment. He came in later after the children were asleep.

'How could you do this to us?' I raged. 'You swore to me that you were no longer with her.'

'I'm not.' He turned away to shield his face. 'It's a free country, I can't stop her being here.'

'Don't tell me that is just coincidence her being here.'

'It is,' he replied.

'I would rather you were honest with me,' I said. 'If you love her, then leave me alone. I'll understand. Don't put us through this again.'

'I don't love her,' he insisted. 'She is here with her son, and her husband has just arrived in the UK.'

I stood there in front of him, hurt and disappointed. For a moment I wanted to believe him. I wished I had a single glimmer of hope that what he said was true, but I couldn't. But for the time being I had to wait and see. As the days passed it became clear that the lies he tried to feed me finally came out, just like the snake's head coming out from behind a hidden stone trying to poison you. What I feared would happen, had happened in a deceitful and dirty way.

His siblings told me the truth. Not only had he paid for Moka and her son to come to England, but also he had been living with them till her husband arrived a few days ago. It didn't make sense. Why on earth had he wanted me to come to England in the first place? Shockingly, my questions were answered by her, the woman who had destroyed my family, when I sat face to face with her and heard the first words dropping out of her mouth; it couldn't have been any more absurd. According to her she didn't love Dan. She was trying to leave him and to reunite the family that she broke up once by playing the part of a good woman who had already regretted her mistake. Really? Would you believe that? The truth of the matter was she wasn't doing this because she felt guilty and wanted my family to get together again; after she had cleaned him out she wanted to fob him off, just like the catfish sneaker that changes its look by changing its colouration. I mean, who was going to believe such a fairy tale?

Her game was as filthy as it was diabolical. And she was trying to include me in her game. By the children and I being there, it would give her lots of excuses and give her better underhand tactics, just like a plan organized on the football pitch. But it was too late. Dan had fallen madly in love with her. He was blinded by a love that smelt foul, like a dead fish. From the beginning, a love of devilish interest so vile but he could not see.

Ironically, all along, not surprisingly, I knew she never loved him, but she was prepared to destroy my family for money. I believe that *my* family wasn't the first to be destroyed by her, nor would it be the last, I was convinced. The idiotic thing was that, just like the fool he was, he thought the money he had, made him think he was the most good-looking fella on the planet – to become seduced by this horrible woman.

Of course, she didn't want him anymore. She had spent all his money, especially after he'd paid thousands of pounds for her and her son to come to England with fake documents and settling them down in London. He was left with nothing, nothing left, not enough even to support his own kids; nor did he have a house and a business anymore. After all those years working hard and saving the pennies, managing to have what he'd never had before, he threw it away as simple as that, as if he had never had it in the first place. It disappeared just like the salt in water. He had nothing left.

While she was talking, trying to tell me the 'truth', in her voice of mock despair, my mind darted back to the night when she'd phoned our house. I heard her voice, telling my husband how much she loved him, knowing I was right there next to him, intentionally to cause trouble and destroy our marriage. Even when I was covered in blood, feeling humiliated and degraded mentally and physically for trying not to allow that flirtatious conversation between my husband and her to continue in my own house.

But that was nothing compared to the morning after. On my way to work. On the back road, a car had approached fast and unsuspectingly from nowhere and on purpose had quickly driven towards me from behind. If I hadn't jumped over a nearby garden wall the car would have hit me and it may have been a different story and I wouldn't be able to tell the story today. Shockingly now she admitted that these were her orders and vicious plans.

And when I asked her why, her ridiculous answer was 'to warn you off'.

'What for?'

Well, a question like that she could not possibly answer. She stood in front of me, shrugging her shoulders and claimed to be so innocent. Her smile was stained with filthy intrigue that had caused so much pain and tears, so much drama and destruction.

Did the facts match her words? Certainly not. But let's be truthful. This game was not played by her alone but also by Dan. As they say it takes two to tango. It was a waste of time even giving her the time of the day and listening to the proclamations by this woman. The one I had to talk to and end this marriage once and for all was the father of my children, Dan.

Back at the hostel without restraint I angrily confronted him.

'You've been lying to me. I gave you a second chance that you didn't deserve. I'm taking the kids and flying back to Albania.'

'You're can't go anywhere,' he replied sharply, grinning as he did so. 'You don't have any passports.'

'I'll find a way somehow,' I hissed through clenched teeth.

'Try if you dare,' he answered aggressively.

His scepticism and indifference made my blood boil from his vileness. At these moments words were superfluous.

The reality hit me even harder. What had I done? How had I got myself into this situation again? Alone, with nowhere to go, no money, and no support. It was like I had crawled out of the frying pan and jumped into the fire.

Unfortunately, I had no option but to stay in London; however, I needed to get as far away from this man as possible before he destroyed me completely. Maybe I could set up my own life with the kids. Yet, with little resource, how was I going to do that, in a strange country with no money and where we couldn't even speak the language properly? Dan had spent all the money on Moka so there was nothing left for us.

The next morning, I took my children to school and returned to the hostel only to see through the patio doors that led to the hostel garden, my husband kissing Moka without a care in the world. She had started working there. I felt desecrated. I did not even want to *try* to intervene.

I walked through the door and rushed into my room. My breathing had become laboured, and I felt like someone had put their hand around my throat and wanted to strangle me. My hands started to tingle, making it feel like I was having a panic attack. I opened the window and I tried to encourage myself to breathe slowly. A ray of sun came out of the sky between the clouds and I felt its warmth. I breathed in deeply, as if I wanted to absorb that ray of sunshine and get some strength finally for once, to make the decision that I should have made a long time ago. I walked out of the bedroom and went downstairs to the hall. He was sitting relaxed at the tables outside, puffing at his cigarette.

I sat down facing him and said, 'We're finished. I'm applying for a divorce. That's it. We are done.'

Angrily he replied, 'No you are not. I am the only one that can tell you what you are allowed to do.'

'Not anymore, you're not,' I replied. 'It's over, you don't own me. I'm not your possession.'

He came so close to my face that I could smell the stench of his breath and he whispered angrily, 'I'm going to twist your head like a chicken,' gesturing as if my head was in his hands.

'We are in England, and it takes only one phone call to the police,' I replied confidently.

'You think I give a damn about the police?' he smirked, pretending that he didn't care.

'Hmm,' I added sarcastically. 'Of course you don't, but I'm taking the double room with my children, so you can get all your clothes and keep out.'

As I got up to make my way to the bedroom, he followed me, but I shut the bedroom door in his face, and locked it.

'Open the door now, or your ugly face will regret it!' he shouted, hammering on the door like an animal that wanted to grab its prey and tear it apart.

I was scared. I couldn't even get out of that door to run to the phone box to ring the police. Then somewhere, at the end of the corridor, I heard the hostel manager shouting, 'What the hell is that noise?'

I was so relieved to hear the cowardly steps of Dan's cowboy shoes slapping away to his bedroom, making my body shake with every step, hoping that he wouldn't bother me again, allowing me to live my own life. A huge sigh of relief flooded through my body and I realised how frightening it had all been.

Once again we were living separate lives, although he didn't want to remove the chain that was trying to keep me tied, he had become more confident, more arrogant, and would even flaunt it before me. Unfortunately, however, he was still in the room next door.

Every day, especially at night, I became fearful of him forcing his way into our bedroom.

That night, around midnight, I could hear sexual noises as loud as laughing hyenas coming from their bedroom, wakening Hope. She got up, rubbed her eyes, and asked me, 'What is that noise, Mammy?'

'Oh sweetheart,' I replied, 'maybe it's a film on TV. Why don't we go out for a little walk, until the film's finished?'

Enea was sleeping soundly, so quietly we got up, got dressed and made our way out into the dark. Outside the cold air made me shiver like guitar strings, and through the light of the red phone box I saw the first raindrops splashing on the glass.

'It's so cold, Mammy.' Hope shivered, shrugging her shoulders. I scooped her up in my arms and together we stood under the hostel porch for a while, staring at the rain falling, as it bounced off the grey stone pavement. The thunder grumbled somewhere in the distance and startled us. Laughing at the noise it made, we made our way back into the room. The noises had stopped, so I tucked Hope back into bed and tried to get some sleep myself.

-o-

In the morning as I opened the green curtains through the large wooden windows I saw Dan leaving the hostel wearing his best leather jacket, walking all merry after an enjoyable night.

As I stood there watching him walk away into the distance, their erotic voices from the night before resounded in my head. From the depths of my soul I felt an aversion mixed with hurt. I needed peace of mind even just for a little while. I had to get myself out of there, out from this filthy affair or I would sink and never be able to rise again. For so long he had caused me so much excruciating pain, that inside my heart his existence had vanished.

My thoughts were disturbed by the knocking on the room door. It was a lovely Muslim African lady called Hatixha. Her eyes were wide open, she raised her hands up in despair and said, 'Allah, Allah protect us from the evil.'

'What is wrong, Hatixha?' I asked her impatiently. 'You are scaring me.'

She was breathing heavily and finally managed to let out the words: 'That slag, your husband's woman, is in the kitchen. She started working here as a cleaner.'.

'I know,' I replied, sadly.

'How can you be so calm?' she said angrily. 'What are you waiting for? Let's go and kick the shit out of her.'

'What's the point, Hatixha?' I said, shrugging my shoulders, resigned.

She looked at me in surprise and said, 'In the country I come from, you have to fight for your man.'

I shook my head in despair. 'Not for a man like him, Hatixha, not for a man like him.' I sighed with sadness.

Without saying another word, she hugged me tightly, and then made her way back to her room, shaking her head in disappointment.

I often used to see Moka now that she was working at the hostel. To make her feel good, Dan tried everything to get at me from the constant emotional blackmail involving our children to threatening me at every given opportunity; he tried to intimidate me and scare me at the same time.

Even though we were leading separate lives, we couldn't avoid seeing each other as we were living under the same roof. Since Moka's plans were not going as she had anticipated, she kept trying hard to convince me that she didn't love Dan and I should get back with him to save the marriage...

Throughout this garbled story, I was becoming more and more irritated and annoyed and could contain my impatience no longer, and asked, 'So why are you here? Why you leave your husband and son and come and sleep with another man next door to his wife and his kids' bedroom if you are genuine?'

'Because he wants me to,' she said, as the lies poured out of her mouth. 'I'm telling you the truth.'

Her response was crass and unbelievable. 'You and I are the same,' she said. 'We are both victims.'

I drew my face close to her face and, looking her in the eye, I said, 'I don't think so. I just wanted to be happy, needing my husband to treat me right, to be loyal and honest, and to give my children a good life. You wanted him for the wrong reason. *You* were after his money.'

She had no answer.

I knew the truth all along, both in my head and in my heart. I wouldn't trust that woman as far as I could throw her. I had reached that point in my life where I didn't care anymore about him or her. He wasn't worth fighting for.

An unexpected phone call from Hope's school made me worry and rush to get her as quickly as possible.

She was burning up from a high temperature that had crept up slowly due to a severe earache. I had to make my way to the hospital as soon as I could where the doctors took care of her immediately. It was a nasty ear infection and consequently antibiotics were prescribed.

Back at the hostel, Hope's temperature started to fall with painkillers and the antibiotics allowing her eventually to fall asleep.

As I was getting ready to go to the kitchen, out of the blue Dan pushed our bedroom door open without knocking and yelled, 'I want you to get out of this hostel now.'

'What?' I shushed him. 'Get out of my room. Even animals take care of their babies. Your daughter is ill, and your stupid antics are the last thing she needs right now.'

'I don't care,' he said with a stupid and inane grin growing. 'I want you out of this hostel by the morning. Moka is not happy with you living in the room next to me.'

Sternly but quietly I said, 'Well, fortunately, it is not your hostel or hers, and we are not sleeping on the street to suit you. I don't give a tick what *she* thinks, she shouldn't be here, so sling your hook.'

I tried to shut the door in his face, but he kicked the door like a mule a few times and shouted, 'You had better leave, or I'm going to slaughter you.'

The door next to our left opened and I heard Hatixha coming out of her bedroom door and saying to him, 'If you don't go away, I am going to call the police. You horrible man!'

'Haha! You can kiss my ass, you stupid woman,' he sneered as he made his way back to his room.

Clearly, it wasn't enough what she had done, this two-faced, double-dealing, back-stabbing treacherous bitch was playing one against the other, and he was so stupid he couldn't see it. On the one hand she was telling me that she was sorry and was trying to bring the family together, and on the other, she was encouraging him to cause more suffering and destruction with his wife and children. Would this evil woman ever stop being vindictive? Clearly not. Once again it showed her non-existent morals.

I checked Hope's temperature, relieved that it was going down. While she fell asleep I made my way to the kitchen to start cooking the tea. Since Hope was on antibiotics she needed some proteins and vegetables which I prepared quickly and in no time the pot was on the stove.

The heavy footsteps coming from the hallway towards the kitchen made me wary. As Dan stormed into the kitchen my anxiety took a hold of me.

'Get out of this kitchen now!' he demanded aggressively.

'Excuse me?' I replied in shock.

'Well, I told you once and I won't tell you again, Moka is getting jealous of you being around and she's told me she will leave me if you don't go,' he ranted again.

'You are out of your mind?' I said. 'I can't believe what I'm hearing.' My hands were shaking with the adrenaline pumping through my veins.

'Bugger off now or I'm going to kill you.' He approached aggressively.

'I'm not going anywhere, I'm cooking for our children,' I replied. 'She is the one who shouldn't be here.'

He turned into a raging bull. He grabbed me by my shoulders, turned me round, and with his steel-capped cowboy shoes kicked me in the stomach. Then he grabbed the pan full of food that was cooking on the stove and threw it all in the bin. At this point, I was hunched down on the floor, my hands holding my stomach. I looked up at him with tears in my eyes and snarled, 'You bastard. How could you throw your children's food away?'

Staring down at me and stabbing his finger aggressively at me, he brought his face close to mine, and sneered, 'This is nothing compared to what I'm going to do to you if you don't go. Do you understand me?'

I had lost. The adrenaline had diminished, and the fear had well and truly returned.

'That's it, I'm going to ring the police,' I said, as I made my way out of the kitchen door. Suddenly Enea's face appeared. He had heard everything.

'What? Oh no!' He started screaming. 'Please Mammy, don't do that. They will arrest and take my daddy away. Please don't.'

I looked at my boy's frightened face, and my heart sank. I stopped and held him tight.

'I won't, I won't,' I said quickly. 'Stop screaming please.'

'Please, Mammy,' he sobbed, 'promise me you won't ring the police. If you do, I'll run away, and you'll never see me again.'

'I promise,' I said, trying to comfort him.

From the other side of the corridor his Russian friend was coming with a ball in his hands, asking Enea to play football with him. Unsure what I was going to do, he looked at me again as if he wanted to be sure that I wasn't going to ring the police.

'Don't worry,' I said. 'You go and play with your friend.' And as he gave me a little kiss I made my way back to the bedroom.

I fumbled in my purse for some money, I went out to the phone box. So many times I had come so close to ringing the police but I couldn't. I had never had to deal with them in my whole life and the idea of ringing them terrified and shamed me. And most importantly, Enea was deeply affected by all this turmoil and watching the cops handcuff his father would destroy him even more. But I had to speak to my sister Lindita in Albania and tell her about the situation and let her know that I was going to get out of this place and until I got a new address, she was not to be worried just in case she tried to contact me through the hostel. As soon as I heard her voice on the end of the phone I spoke faster.

'Sis,' I urged, 'I need to get away from Dan. I have to get away from here.'

Before she could even ask what was wrong, Dan appeared at the telephone box, obviously not finished with his rampage. He thought I was ringing the police. He started banging on the glass door with his fists and his feet, yelling expletives, along with 'I'm going to kill you'.

Startled by the noise my sister asked, 'What is that banging noise?'

'He is here,' I said, my voice trembling with fear. 'I have to go. I'll ring you later.'

As I was trying to hold the phone box door closed to stop him getting in, the phone slipped out of my trembling hands and hung by its flex just above the floor.

I could hear the distant echo of her voice shouting with worry. 'Yllka, Yllkaaaaa? Are you there? What's going on?'

I managed to grab the phone and tell her, 'I'm ok. I have to go. I'll talk to you later.'

'Please ring the police, sis!'

'I will ring the police now,' I repeated to him.

He managed to get into the booth and grabbed the phone out of my hands, yelling, 'Come on then, let's see. Do you have the balls to ring the police? I'm going to slay you,' he hissed, while he drew his finger across his neck.

I managed to get out of the phone box while dodging his kicks. I ran back to the hostel and rushed into the room in fear of my life, with not an ounce of hope, feeling degraded and violated. I had lost the will to live and all reason to continue. My heart was burning and there was nothing left – just like the ashes and charcoal left when the fire has been extinguished, black and lifeless.

I saw my children waiting at the top of the stairs, frightened. Enea had returned from playing football and was trying to comfort Hope. I looked at them with a pain that surged through every limb. Taking a deep breath, I gathered all my strength to speak.

'Get your jackets, children,' I urged them. 'We're going for a McDonald's.'

They looked at me strangely.

'Really, Mum?' Enea asked.

'Of course,' I said, trying to keep myself together.

On the way out, I put my arms around their little shoulders and starting walking towards the busy main road where fast-moving cars were speeding almost nose to tail. We stopped at the crossroads. My soul was invaded by the unknown, dangerous darkness. Through this darkness I couldn't see the pathway. There was no light, no hope, only the end.

I took the first step, but deep inside me I felt I heard the voice of my mother calling, 'Hold on, hold on', then I felt Enea's hand pulling me back by the corner of my grey jacket. I looked at his sad brown eyes staring at me.

'Where are you going, Mammy? That's not the way to McDonald's. It's this way,' he said, pointing on the left side of the road where the big yellow M sign beckoned. I looked at the innocent and frightened faces of my children, as I felt a lump forming in my throat and numbness infusing my body.

'Are you okay, Mammy?' The expression on his face showed concern.

My words wouldn't even come out, so I nodded in agreement. I looked into his sad and uncertain eyes. There in front of me were two beautiful open faces who were my responsibility. 'Get yourself together, woman, and face this present reality,' a shrill voice screamed in my head. 'This is your chance to prove yourself. It's now or never. You have to pass this trial; your children's lives are in your hands. Maybe now is the time for you to show how strong you really are, mountain girl. Being strong is not just walking and climbing the treacherous mountains or shooting perfectly towards a target board. It is in fact dealing with barriers and obstacles throughout life.'

I wanted to scream out so this knot of horror could escape my body. With every ounce of my being I gathered all of the remaining strength in me, I inhaled and let out a heart-felt sigh. With this deep breath, it felt as if my body had let go of the pain I had felt previously and instead imbued me with a sincere sense of determination to see this through. It coursed through every part of my body and I felt as if I was unbreakably cleansed. I scooped up my children and squeezed them tight and kissed their foreheads. My body had grappled with the thoughts of fight or flight, but my forces were by my side, and once I realised that, the only option was fight. My mind reassessed its position in the midst of that intersection between the paths of life and death. It was then that I felt I had turned the wheel of life.

I smiled and their faces smiled back at me. 'Oh, silly Mammy, sorry, of course the McDonald's is that way, let's go.' Walking towards the building with the big yellow sign M. We ordered and sat down to eat at the table by the window in front of a busy park full of people. I was envious watching a couple play with their son and my heart sank. How much I wanted the same for my children. To have two parents, to offer warmth and love, just like them. How much I wanted it, but right now I had to live with the present reality and transcend this deep gap to emerge on the other side, the legitimate side.

Back at the hostel, I felt sick and ran to the bathroom. As I washed my face I looked at myself in the mirror. My eyes spoke more than a thousand words. They spoke of the intense suffering and my battered soul. My face told the story of the anguish and the wounded heart of a rejected wife. I looked like a wounded bird with damaged wings falling on the side of the road crawling to look for something to survive. The only difference? The birds are often rescued from or by humans; I had to rescue myself as there was no one else around to rescue me. I had to rebuild those wings and move on from the wasted years of cruelty and with time the wounds would heal again; their marks remaining painless, just like a hole left after a nail has been removed from the wall. But I'd fly again and I would not allow them to break my soul.

That night I made my decision to leave in the morning and find a suitable place away from Dan and all his demons and never to look back. I knew it was going to be a hard road. The only way out of this muck, Tani suggested, was social services, just until we got our life back on track.

We were seated in the waiting area. After half an hour our names were called and we went into the smaller interview room that had a glass screen separating us from the interviewer's office. She was a thin blonde lady with a parchment-pale face and hazel eyes. She sat behind a white desk strewn with papers and large folders.

She beckoned to us to sit-down and started to ask us for a few documents. It took more than two hours of questioning and answering, all of which was translated by my cousin Tani as my English wasn't good enough to understand. The decision was made. We were going to be transferred to Bournemouth into a small flat near the coast. Obviously Dan wouldn't accept the decision and neither did Enea. Despite everything that his dad had put the children through, Enea still wanted to stay near him.

Their voices were raised in anger and offensive words were said, but the decision wasn't up for discussion. It was for the children's best interest, reminding him that all of this commotion was as a consequence of his action, therefore he had made his bed, so he had to lie in it.

I promised Enea that after we had moved away, he would be able to come and visit his daddy at any time. So we got the documents for the place and printed letter with directions and we left to catch the train to Bournemouth. It felt like we had been caught up in a whirlwind, but somehow I felt strong enough to walk away from it. The train to Bournemouth was due to leave in a few hours, so we had to go to the hostel to collect our things as quickly as possible and get to the train station. We left the hostel saying a quick goodbye. It was hard and upsetting for the children. Down the corridor, I saw Dan running after us.

'Wait a minute,' he murmured. 'I just want to walk with them to the bus stop.' He held their hands as we walked towards the bus stop.

We were all upset and apprehensive about our future, about another journey to another unknown place. The bus finally came, and we were all in tears. It was overwhelming for everybody. He said his goodbyes to the children and as he looked at me he said, 'One day we will get back together.'

'Not ever,' I said, turning away fiercely.

It was a sad day, not as I had anticipated when I took the most dangerous route with my children to reunite us with their father, and unfortunately not what they had dreamed or wished for either. The bus moved away and their tear-stained faces looked through the window as they waved goodbye to their daddy. It hurt. But as the shackles fell away from me, my freedom from the wickedness and the betrayal of the people around me, from those who promised me a happier life, from those who I was foolish enough to give a second chance to, left a sweet taste in my mouth.

However, I had learnt that when you give people a second chance you have to be prepared for disappointment. That's the hardest part, because you will feel alone. The given advice is that you shouldn't be afraid to fly alone. As my father used to say, 'Eagles fly alone, whereas magpies fly together.'

I learnt that I must love and respect myself enough never to let a man stamp on me again. If I did, then my soul would be broken, never again to be made whole.

CHAPTER 17

Leaving the scourge behind (Bournemouth)

An ear-shattering noise signalled that the train was pulling into the station. Here we were with plastic bags in our hands, waiting to board the train, stepping carefully over the gap, to take the first step towards our future and hopefully a better life. Hope was holding tight this big doll in the little pram that we had found in a charity shop in London, and Enea was helping me, holding one of the bags with some of his clothes.

Once we had found our seats, the train slowly jerked away from the platform, allowing us to leave behind the fears, horrors, life or death scenarios and to look forward to the journey to our new life in the city of Bournemouth. I sighed with relief and scooped my children into my arms, kissing their heads and promising them that everything was going to be all right. Looking out of the window, questions were running through my mind. What was our life going to be like? A single mother in a strange country, speaking little English and with no job to support my children? I hoped that I could find the strength for them and that our suffering would end at this point forever.

One thing I knew was that I was going to do the best I could to protect and look after them and to be as good a mum as I could be until the day I died. As I grew up without *my* mum, I wanted to make sure that my kids were growing up with their mum's love and devotion.

'Mum, you promised me you were going to let me go back to London to stay with my dad,' Enea said, looking at me for answers.

'Let's just get settled and then we'll talk later,' I said.

'No, I want to know now. If I'm not going back to see my dad, I'm jumping out the train now,' he insisted as he stood up, agitated.

I looked at him, shocked at hearing him say such a dreadful thing.

'Shhhhhh, sit-down, sweetheart, don't make a scene. You will, I promise, when we are settled,' I said quickly, almost in a whisper.

He relaxed and eventually sat down, looking out through the window.

I looked at my boy with pity and sadness. His dad didn't deserve a son like him. He loved his dad unconditionally, but unfortunately his dad's love for him wasn't in the same league. He was just such an innocent and naïve little boy who didn't understand anything.

When we arrived in Bournemouth it was late – around 10 pm – and the city looked forbidding and overwhelming. I had the address that had been given to us, on a piece of paper but we didn't know exactly where to go. We approached the first taxi driver outside the station and showed him the letter with the address, wondering if it was near enough to walk to it. He shook his head and said loudly, 'It's too far to walk; you need a taxi.'

However, with not enough money to pay for a taxi, we decided to walk anyway and follow the directions on the paper. Except for a few passing vehicles, the roads seemed very quiet. The street lamps were bowed like a swan's neck, lighting the roads slightly because of old overgrown trees whose branches arched to create a beautiful panorama that almost hinted at woodlands.

We had walked for more than half an hour when we spotted a very tall Asian man walking behind us. Overloaded with bags, holding Hope's hand and the piece of paper with directions in the other, we were confused as to whether we were going in the right direction. It didn't take him long to realise we were looking for an address and with a great gesture of kindness that was definitely needed at that time, he asked, 'Can I help, sister? You seem lost. Where are you going?'

'I'm looking for this place. Could you tell me where it is, please?' I said in halting English, as I handed him the piece of paper, so grateful that he had approached us.

'Oh, I work at the restaurant just next door to it!' He smiled surprisingly. I was flabbergasted, I felt as if luck was finally edging over my way. We all smiled, and he kindly took hold of one of the bags and starting walking with us.

'Too dangerous,' he said, 'for a woman alone with two kids to be walking at this time of night.'

'Our train just arrived from London,' I replied.

After walking for a while we finally arrived at the building where our apartment was. We thanked the kind man who had shown us the way and started walking towards the two-floor building where we were greeted by the manager who was expecting us. He showed us around the basically furnished one-bedroomed flat. I couldn't have been more thankful that in a very short time we were secure with a place well away from Dan and the terrible London life. It had been such a long day that the children fell asleep almost instantly.

I carried on unpacking and exploring my new home. I opened the window and I could smell the fresh sea air and hear the waves crashing in the distance. It was a windy but clear night with a breath-taking full moon. I stood there and felt the wind of freedom rush into my soul. I sighed deeply, gradually letting out all the sorrow and sadness.

In the distance, further out to sea, my eye caught a flickering light that was disappearing and reappearing constantly in the darkness of the night. It seemed to come from a little boat that was fighting with the fierce ocean wind and through my mind passed the Jewish proverb, 'A little bit of light can push away a lot of darkness!'.

Somehow I felt there was a similarity between that boat and myself, the present and the future. An incredible strength flowed through my body. I felt strong and unassailable and thought to myself, 'Mountain girl, now is your time. Take it and never look back.' The steering wheel of my life was in my hands and I was determined to turn it in the right direction, just like that boat fighting to move forward to its journey.

Life began to be peaceful away from everyday traumas. It seemed strange as I had not experienced this tranquillity for a very long time. I had forgotten the feeling of a normal, untroubled, anxiety-free life. I felt happy and content.

However, seeing my son's sad face was painful as he unfortunately didn't share those feelings. He was struggling to get used to life without his dad and feeling unsafe and insecure without him. He became a very unhappy child and his behaviour became erratic and almost uncontrollable. Constantly he was talking about going to see his dad, with or without my permission. A few times he tried to hide and try to get on the train by himself, but fortunately was caught by staff and taken back to where we live. Every attempt to stop him going there wasn't working. After everything his father had put us through, it wasn't very healthy for a child of his age. It was heart-breaking for me, but in the end I had to let him go. I knew that he would soon regret it and would soon return. He had decided he was going to London for a while as *he* had promised his daddy.

So, we took him to the train station and sent him to London with another friend who lived in the same building as us who fortunately was going to visit his family in the capital. I missed my boy so much even though I spoke with him on the phone every day. It was like my soul was torn in two.

I don't remember exactly how long it had been since Enea left, but I do remember that several months had passed when surprisingly I received a phone call from Moka's husband. He was the last person on earth I expected a call from.

'I know it might come as a shock that I'm ringing you,' he explained, 'but I found Enea in the park on his own. He is distraught. The truth is, Moka left Dan. He would not accept it and he is not dealing with it very well. He has left the hostel and Enea is scared that his dad might do something stupid. I left a message for his siblings too, but I haven't got any replies from them yet.'

My stomach lurched. I couldn't believe what I was hearing. I went into an absolute panic, with wild thoughts whizzing through my head. Without wasting any time I got ready and made my way to the train station. The journey to London seemed to take an eternity. I was terrified that something might have happened to my son. I had to stop thinking about that and to focus on getting my son back home safely. Maybe this time he would think twice about demanding to stay with his father.

My arrival in London brought back sad and painful memories that I wanted to forget but unfortunately they were embedded in my mind and wouldn't leave. Every road I travelled down, in every café or phone box I passed, I could see Dan's aggressive face, I could hear the sound of his voice, and my anxiety took over. I tried to persuade myself that those days were well and truly behind me, and somehow my soul became stronger to overcome my demons. However, my real worry at the moment was only my boy, Enea.

I finally arrived at the hostel happy to find my boy well even though he was frightened and terrified by what could have happened to his father.

As I hold him closely, he asked, 'My dad is going to kill himself, isn't he, Mammy?' desperate for some comfort.

'Now you listen to me, Mammy's sweetheart. I can assure you that he is not going to do any such thing. By the time we pack your clothes I'm sure he will be back.' I tried to reassure him.

I knew that his dad was never going to do something to himself; he was far too much of a selfish coward. This was just another one of his games trying everything he could to keep his lover and involving his son in this game too. I was finishing packing Enea's clothes when his dad appeared with Moka.

I shook my head in disbelief, looking at him with contempt. I did not even want to be near them, never mind have a conversation with them. Any excuses were in vain. Without prolonging it further I said, 'Don't you dare come near my children again or I swear...'

'Uh-huh, and what are you going to do to stop me?' he replied fiercely and came close to my face, so close that I could feel the anger radiating from him. His eyes narrowed and the veins stood out on his neck.

'Hah,' I snorted. 'Men like you don't deserve to be a father.'

He kicked me hard in the shin. I grabbed the silver door handle so I would not fall to the floor, and I looked at him with disgust and said, 'You're not even worth it.'

I turned around at Enea and saw Moka was grinning at me as if to say, 'Loser, you are nothing.'

In that moment being kicked was not nearly as bad as being laughed at that low moment. Seeing her gloating and enjoying the satisfaction of my humiliation made it more embarrassing and hurtful. Enea quickly caught my body and embraced me. I tugged him to my chest, comforting him by stroking his head.

'Let's go, Mammy's sweethearts,' I sighed with pain. 'We are late for the train.'

By this point, his siblings had arrived at the hostel. One of them grabbed Dan and glared, saying, 'You are not a man leaving your wife and kids alone in a strange country. Do you know how lucky you are to have a wonderful family like this? What the hell are you doing?'

Dan looked at his brother's face, speechless, until he murmured, 'I don't care, I want to be with Moka.'

'She doesn't love you; none of your nonsense will make her come back to you. She just used you. All she wanted was your money. She's spent your money and that's why she doesn't want you anymore,' they scoffed. 'Can't you see that? How many times did we tell you that before? She's taken you for a ride.'

I took no interest in what they had to say anymore. I looked at my watch. I had less than one hour to catch the train back to

Bournemouth. I grabbed Enea's hands and started walking out of the room and said to his siblings, 'I don't have time to waste, I'm going to miss the train.'

'Please don't go. You can't go and live alone. A woman with two children in the middle of a strange country won't be safe,' his siblings said.

'I don't have a choice,' I replied.

'Anything we can do to help?' his other siblings asked.

'Yes, you can do one thing for me. Take him away from me and my kids. He's destroyed my life. I'm not letting him do that to my kids too. It ends here,' I replied while I was walking out of the door.

We managed to catch the train back to Bournemouth – just.

When we arrived at our apartment, mentally and physically drained, we all got into bed together and I wrapped my arms around my babies. They had gone through so much and the only person who could protect them from this horrible life was me, their mother.

Finally, after a day full of stress and trauma I was more relaxed now that I had both of my children here next to me sleeping peacefully. I rested my head on the pillow and sighed deeply, releasing the pain that came from the bottom of a suffering soul, the only soul that could give them the love and protection for their life. I was determined to turn their life around and give them the best I possibly could.

The time we stayed in Bournemouth didn't last long. After a few months, just when we had all started to become settled, we were transferred by social services to a small town in Lancashire called Morecambe. Another place, a new adventure where our lives would take its rightful course, and little by little a balance would be restored.

CHAPTER 18

The right direction
for our destiny

The 9p flour

There we were again. All three together, Enea, Hope and myself, with two large suitcases waiting for the train to take us to a small town in the Northwest called Morecambe. Another unfamiliar place, another mysterious chapter of our lives, that could hold our destiny.

It was late. On the platform passengers were eagerly waiting for the last train on a beautiful warm night. We were all sitting together on the wooden bench waiting patiently. The train's whistle in the distance seemed as if it was giving the signal of the path our life might take, and as it approached, its front lights lit up the steps we would perhaps follow into the future.

The train stopped and its doors opened. Once Enea and Hope had climbed on board with their rucksack, I struggled on with our heavy suitcases as I tried to follow them. To my right an old gentleman of around 90 years of age, who was barely able to hold himself upright, approached me and, taking hold of one of the cases, said, 'Jump in, I've got this one.'

I thanked the kind man and without hesitating, I did as I had been told. I took the other suitcase and got on the train and helped him with the other one. We settled into our seats. He sat next to us, amusing Enea and Hope while the train pulled out of the station on its way to the Northwest. I never forgot the elderly man with a kind face and especially the four medals pinned to his grey jacket. He bade us farewell when he got off at the next stop.

Hope fell asleep with her head resting on my lap, and Enea gazed through the window. I was engrossed reading a book from my favourite author; our great Albanian Ismail Kadare. His book 'Spring Flowers, Spring Frost' had just been published. It was a well told story about the troubled land of Albania, the political turmoil and the blood feuds that had returned to Albania after the fall of the communist regime. Kadare was born in my hometown and I grew up with his poetry and novels. Many of them had gained international prizes and he has always been a source of inspiration to me.

The quietness was broken by an authoritative voice: 'Tickets please.' The train inspector, a short man wearing a flat cap, smiled gently at us, looked down at our tickets and said with concern in his voice, 'This is the last train of the night and does not go to Morecambe. The last station is Preston.'

'Is there any other option?' I asked with worry on my face.

Understanding my confusion he smiled and shook his head emphatically and said, 'Leave it with me.' He took some details of where we were to stay in Morecambe and walked away.

After fifteen minutes he returned with a note in his hand and as he approached me, he sat down and said cheerfully, 'All sorted, the place you're staying in Morecambe is sending the manager called Steve to pick you up from Preston station. Relax and make yourself comfortable, you have plenty of time,' gesturing at his watch to further explain his words.

I felt so grateful and lucky enough to have met a nice person like him at the start of our crucial new beginning, restoring my faith in humans slightly and in their ability to show such compassion to a complete stranger. This act of compassion nurtured my thoughts of hope for better days and a better future.

At around 11pm, the train arrived in Preston. It was dark, which only added to the sense of unfamiliarity that we all felt. As we emerged from the train station, under the steady beam of light filtering through the car park, we saw a young plump chap in a grey tee-shirt with a big smile on his face approaching us and asking, 'Are you Yllka from Albania?'

'Yes, I am,' I replied in broken English, pointing at my children. 'This is my son Enea and my daughter Hope.'

'Beautiful kids,' he said. 'I'm Steve, the manager of the hostel and I'm a foreigner too by the way, I'm from Wales.' He chuckled at his own joke, obviously one he had chosen in order to make us feel comfortable. He took the luggage and in no time we set off to Morecambe.

Half an hour had passed when we finally arrived. I looked outside and saw an old four-storey terraced building that formed the hostel. The tall streetlamps glowed onto a long asphalt road, picking out a white sign stick that read 'Regent Road'. It was deadly quiet, with not a single person around. It was late. We parked the car and walked through the hostel's flaky green door. The place was better than we expected. You could see a large staircase and a kitchen directly opposite the front door, with a spacious living and dining room. The rooms were on the upper floors.

He led us to the second floor and to our rooms and after he had shown us around, he smiled cheerfully and said, 'Sleep well, chaps.'

Enea looked at me sadly, his eyes filled with tears. 'I don't like it here, Mum,' he whispered.

I cuddled them both and replied softly, 'Don't worry, we won't be here forever. I'm going to find a job and then we can get our own place, but for now it's late so let's get to bed and we can explore the town tomorrow.'

We ended up staying in the same room, as the children were too frightened to sleep in separate rooms. I was so grateful that we had a roof over our head once again, and were far away from the demonic life that we had endured for so many years.

Next morning I quietly got up before the children to find out what was for breakfast only to discover that the hostel didn't provide breakfast. Quickly I got my purse and checked inside, only to find it was filled with lots of coppers that we had left over from our journey, not even enough to buy a loaf of bread. I knew that I was scheduled to get some money from the few days cleaning job that I had done in Bournemouth which was delayed, and the children's tax credit, but what was I going to do right now? I took my purse with me and as I went downstairs to the front door a Sainsbury's flyer caught my eye on top of the junk mail. It immediately occurred to me that that I might find something cheap in there.

However, I had no idea where Sainsbury's was. Outside the door I saw a lady walking her dog. 'Do you know where Sainsbury's is?' I asked.

'The only one is in Lancaster,' the lady replied. 'It's about 10 minutes in the car, three miles away.'

Obviously, I had no car or any money to get a bus. So, my last and only option was walking. I was used to walking, and thought three miles walking there and three miles walking back would take me a good hour and a half. I was panicking in case my children awoke and there was nothing for breakfast. I rushed back upstairs. Enea and Hope were still fast asleep. I wrote a quick note asking them not to go out until I returned from the shop, explaining that I might be little bit late. I got my jacket, left the room quietly, and headed off. I walked quickly asking for directions, so that I could return before the children woke up.

It reminded me of the Sulkuqes fairy tale that I used to tell the kids in bed before sleep. Finally, I arrived. The store had just opened, and I guess I was the first customer.

As I walked into the store, just on my right I spotted the discount shelf. I saw a slightly torn small bag of economy flour sitting on the shelf with a bright sticker stuck on it which read '9p'. I checked my purse again. I had enough change. This can't be happening I thought. I looked at it in amazement. It was as if somebody had placed it there especially for me. I couldn't believe my eyes. To save any embarrassment, before going to the checkout I asked one of the staff who was filling the shelves, 'Is this really 9p?'

'Let me check,' she replied and she took the flour bag in her hand, scanned it and, slightly surprised, replied, 'Oh wow, yes. It is 9p.' She smiled warmly.

Instantly I rushed to pay and, overjoyed with my torn bag of economy flour in my hand, quickly made my way back to the hostel in Morecambe. A bit of luck at the right time and place. It took me less than an hour, my walking almost turning into a jog as I was so eager to make sure that I could get back to my children as soon as possible.

At the hostel Enea and Hope ran happily as they spotted me from the bedroom window. Without further ado all together we went to the kitchen where I started to make some Albanian petulla (similar to doughnuts but savoury). All I needed to make them was flour, water, and salt, and they just needed to be fried in oil. Luckily, already in the kitchen was salt and oil. I used one third of the flour for the petulla and the rest for the home-made bread with which I started to make the dough. Unfortunately, I realised I was missing one vital ingredient – yeast. A Russian lady next to me was cooking breakfast for her children as well, and kindly offered me some of her yeast to put in the baking tray to prove for later. Our make-shift breakfast was over and all three of us went out to explore the town. On the end of Regent Road we reached the promenade. Happy being near the sea once again, Enea and Hope were jumping merrily from the waves splashing into the grey rocks coming from the warm sea breeze. I hadn't seen them that happy and content for so long. It seemed like they wanted to forget the past and aim for some peace and serenity, and so did I.

It was nearly afternoon when we returned to the hostel, and as I was putting the bread dough into the oven, a soft-spoken lady with a warm smile on her face came towards us and greeted us. It was Lesley, the owner. She was a middle aged, slim and elegant lady with shoulder length brown hair and a very kind face. By her side stood a medium-sized man with glasses and dark thick hair. A black beard almost covered a big smile, her husband Rodney Black.

She kindly offered her support unreservedly, helping to find schools for the children and everything else we needed over a hot drink that she made for me and my children. I was looking at the modest lady and I marvelled at her kindness. Do people like her really exist? Well, it was a question where the answer was written right before my eyes.

-o-

Without wasting much time, the next day my first task was to find a job. We set off together with Enea and Hope, trying to knock on the door of every hotel on the promenade that had a 'Vacancy' sign displayed in the window, thinking with my poor English that this was the sign for job vacancies. After a few doors being slammed in our face, we came across a nice little lady who had colourful rollers in her hair and a beautifully made up face. She was the only one who understood our confusion and explained that the sign wasn't for jobs but for available rooms. She was even kind enough to invite us in for a drink but I kindly declined as we had to get back. That was one of the many embarrassing moments that we now laugh about when we think back to those days.

As promised, Lesley sorted out Hope's and Enea's schools in no time, and myself, I started work in a nursing home called Moss View, thanks to the Albanian couple that I met, Teuta and Miri, who also used to work there. They used to live across the road from our hostel and meeting them provided a bit of familiarity in such an unfamiliar place. Maybe a little bit of luck was about to wing my way. Could things get any better? Everything was going in the right direction. I'd got a job, my children were in school, and we were making lots of new friends and finally starting to settle into our new life. Peace at long last and a good feeling about our future life. And talking of peace that I much needed, I was surrounded not only on each day but also on Sundays when we attended the little Baptist church on Stanley Road that was 5-10 minutes' walk from the hostel. Sheila and her family were the first people I met. She was a lovely tall, slim lady with short blonde hair and a stunningly warm and welcoming smile and a soft, caring manner. Her husband Rob was a lecturer in physics at Lancaster University. He was a tall, quiet man with a kindly smile. They were blessed with two children – Phil and Ruth – who played instruments during the Sunday morning services.

At that time, Sheila was a manager of access resources for mature students as well as a mathematics lecturer at Lancaster and Morecambe College. From that moment, our friendship was forged and we were inseparable. She was one of those friends, lucky to have and hard to find. She became one of my lifelong best friends who is still there to this day, on good or bad days, to wipe away my tears and make my soul light up. Just what I need. And you know when goodness approaches, it attracts other good people who became part of my life. Just like Meg and Track and lots of other people in that small town church.

Meg was a 5 ft lady with short dark hair, an extremely friendly woman with a beautiful heart and infectious personality, and her husband, Track, was tall with blond hair and rosy cheeks. His blue eyes, jovial character and friendly smile were mirrors into his kind heart. As we came to know each other better, he became my 'English brother' and I was his 'little sis'.

These ladies were good friends and examples of great independent women that I needed around me. They were both working ladies who were able to have their own house and look after their own loving families. Their lives gave me hope that one day I would be able to live a happy and settled life, just like them. Feeling the bond that I had made with both families and the moments that we shared, I knew they would be very close friends with me and people whom I would always hold dear.

Over coffee times while talking to each other about hair and especially mine, the conversation led to the hairdressing courses at the college that Sheila suggested. At first it seemed unattainable to me as my English wasn't that good, never mind learning in a college. However, discovering that I would be allocated a support teacher to help me with everything, it sounded like a wonderful opportunity. So after considering it for some time and thinking whether I could manage everything with children and work, I decided to give it a go. During the following weeks, I registered myself at the college for a hairdressing course even though it was three months behind the start date.

I was very nervous. Learning things in Albanian was easy, but English was much harder. However, I had a feeling that this was going to be a good opportunity not only for me but for my family. That very first day is imprinted in my memory. The lesson had already started when I entered the class full of young girls. I looked like I was babysitting them. As I presented myself I sat down and prepared myself for my first lesson. The tutor was a lady called Bev Martindale, with beautiful long blonde curly hair and piercing blue eyes, who welcomed me with a surprised smile since she had not been informed about my arrival. The first lesson dealt with theory. Listening to unknown words coming out of her mouth, I couldn't help but look and feel puzzled through the whole lesson, looking like a bewildered capuchin monkey.

'What am I doing here?' I thought to myself. 'I can't even understand a word she is saying never mind learn anything. Who am I kidding?'

As soon as the lesson finished, I decided I was going to leave and never come back to the college. However, unbeknown to me, my face had told a thousand stories as the tutor noticed my confusion.

The worry was soon to be extinguished by the end of the day. Understanding my confusion, Bev told me that I would be joined by a learning support teacher who would work closely with me during every theory lesson to help me with English. While she was telling me this, her words came across as respect for another woman rather than pity, it gave me just what I needed – hope for my future. I couldn't understand why people were being so kind and understanding. I mean, could you blame me? It had only been a few months since I arrived in Morecambe and, unusually for me, good things were happening. I was meeting such considerate and caring people that sometimes it felt almost too good to be true.

The practical lessons were easier as it was more visual so I could see and understand without any words. I still made lots of mistakes, but I was determined to learn the right way. The fire had been sparked within me and my passion had begun to develop.

Fridays were the days that we had customers booked who used to pay less to have a trainee practise on their hair. I had been on the course for a couple of months and had gained a few regular clients on salon days. One of them being an elderly lady called Mrs Lee, who would come every Friday without fail. She was petite and well dressed, over 70 and every single time she would enter the salon she had a gentle smile decorating her face. She was a lovely lady who spoke to me like I was no different from anybody else.

But what happened on 'the red mousse Friday' as I called it afterwards, I thought I had lost her custom and failed to pass the practice exam that day.

This time the practice teacher was Tracey, a lady of around my age, with shoulder length dark hair, who approached you with tranquillity and a ready smile. I shampooed Mrs Lee's hair as usual and went to get the mousse from the dispenser. I took one of the mousses and after it foamed in my hand, I noticed it was red. I stopped for a second looking at the peculiar colour but dismissed it as I thought it was just a new updated version of the mousse I had used before.

To my horror as I started to massage it into her hair, it started to turn a pale shade of pink. I looked into the mirrors that were reflecting to each other throughout the salon and caught the eye of my practice tutor Tracey. My terrified eyes darted to the hair and back to her as Mrs Lee's hair started to look more and more like candy floss in my hand. The poor lady's hair floated like a pink fluffy cloud as she leaned back in the sink for it to be washed.

Tracey quickly came over from the end of the salon, and calmly handed me the cleansing shampoo, whispering, while she nudged me on my shoulder, smiling, 'Use this. It will be fine.'

Fortunately, after a few washes, there was only a slight bit of fairy pink tone. To my surprise, however, Mrs Lee really liked it.

I breathed a huge sigh of relief and continued putting her rollers in. Each time I twirled the hair into them, I was convinced that she would not come back to have the hair done with me. How wrong I was! She booked with me every Friday until I graduated, and often I used to meet her when I visited one of my other friends who lived close by. Sandra was an English and French teacher who I met through college. She was an elegant

219

dark-haired lady with a beautiful smile and the biggest heart ever. Something that we both had in common was being single mums trying to recapture our lost years after an abusive and difficult life.

The big house she lived in with her two beautiful children, Jack and Gabrielle, was on the street next to where our hostel was. She would regularly take care of Hope and Enea along with her own children most nights when I had to work late or go out. She would often take me for a barbecue on the beach with her friends to make memories and enjoy life.

I had reached the end of my training for level one hairdressing. At the end of the course, there would be an awards night to celebrate completing the course and also an opportunity to win trophies for different aspects of hairdressing. I was nominated for an award at the presentation. It was a fancy affair, and everybody talked about the nice dresses they had bought to wear from the expensive shops. I didn't have enough money to buy a dress from places like that. But luckily for me, in the window of a charity shop in Lancaster I spotted a beautiful floor-length sparkling silver sequined gown for only £3.99. To my surprise it was a size 10, just right for me, which after washing and ironing, looked as good as new.

The presentation was held in the Carlton Hotel on Morecambe Promenade. The function room was upstairs with a large window looking out over the calm bay. The room was elegantly decorated with round tables draped with white linen tablecloths and with plush chairs dotted around them.

I looked around at waitresses carrying trays of champagne threading through the crowds of ladies with expensive dresses and jewellery, accompanied by gents in black suits and ties. I walked around to join other nominated students, trying not to show concern that someone would have seen the dress I was wearing in the charity shop window. On arrival, one of my assistant teachers complimented me on my dress and asked where I had got it from. 'From a charity shop in Palermo,' I jokingly said, laughing away as I grabbed a glass of champagne.

We moved to find our seats. The ceremony began at last, with the special awards. I was happy to have completed the course and didn't expect to win any special award. The head of college presented the awards and soon my name was called out. I turned quickly to my teaching assistant and squealed in disbelief, 'Did she just call my name?'

Before she could answer, the applause exploded in the room. Against all odds, I had achieved two special awards in one evening. I was filled with joy and overwhelmed.

The party started afterwards and the atmosphere was splendid. Just over a year ago it would never have occurred to me that I would laugh wholeheartedly. I was having a fantastic time.

The end of the night came and with my two trophies and flowers in my arms, along with my balloons, I walked out of the door and called my older sister, Liljana, in Albania. Her words were so overwhelming, that they brought tears to my eyes, although, for a change they were tears of joy. What a beautiful night it had been! It looked to me like the stars were dancing with the moon. The sea breeze whispered in my ear, whilst it coated my skin and tousled my long dark hair with moisture. I could hear the waves crashing on the rocks by the promenade and could see the waters rising and falling like they were dancing, too, with me on this happy evening. Across the bay the light from the houses glittered on the water's surface.

Next morning's light had filled the room when Hope's and Enea's voice woke me up. 'Mammy! Mammy! Are these crystal trophies yours?' they asked with growing excitement.

I smiled at them and said, 'Just one of them, but the big one I keep for only one week. I have to take it back to college where my name will be engraved on it and it's going to be put in a large glass cabinet.'

Their eyes filled with pride, as they both embraced me with joy. It was nice seeing their happy smiling faces again. The next day I went to college only to see my picture on the honours wall and felt the pride and desire to go further and further and never let anyone stop me again. So, I registered for Level two of hairdressing.

CHAPTER 19

Our first home in England

The gem heart

We were on a mission to find a house and finally leave the hostel life, move forward and make our own nest. A search was organised by Lesley and Rodney as promised and it took us a few weeks looking around Morecambe, somewhere not too far from the shops and schools. We found a little flat above a fish and chip shop at Christy Park on Lancaster Road in Morecambe, almost half a mile away from the town centre. Enea's school was just 10 minutes' walk from it, but Hope's was near the college, which meant she had to walk with me or get a bus.

The flat was owned by the shop owners, respectful and hard working people. They keep that shop clean as a whistle and surprisingly never once did my flat smell of fish and chips.

I didn't usually buy the fish and chips as it wasn't my kind of food, but if I had any English friends around I would and it was nice.

As the flat was unfurnished, amazingly to me, Lesley insisted that whatever was needed to furnish the flat should be taken from the hostel as it would soon be put up for sale, and that meant that everything, furniture, bedding, electricals, kitchen utensils etc...

As for the settees, my other two good friends, husband and wife Zubida and Rob, brought their old three-piece suite that they had stored in their attic after they got a new one. They only lived around the corner.

With an old sewing machine that I had found in the hostel cellar and a few pieces of second-hand dark green suede curtain material, I set to reupholster the settee. By the time I had finished, the furniture looked as good as new.

The following morning, the removal van that was organised by Steve arrived and with everyone's help all our belongings were put in the van and in just 20 minutes we arrived at our very first home in England. I was so happy. A frisson of accomplishment ran through my body. I stood there for a second, in shock with an overwhelming feeling at the generosity and kindness that these amazing people had showered upon me. It was interrupted by a gentle tap on my shoulder.

'Yllka, one more thing,' Lesley said. 'You and I are going out to get something.'

We got into her car and after a short drive she stopped opposite the electrical goods shop. Slightly confused, I followed her in. When we got through the door, Lesley smiled and said, 'Now I know the only thing you don't have for your new home is a washing machine, so choose the one you like. This is a gift from me and Rodney to you, my present for your first home in England.'

I stared at her in shock, unable to speak or move for a few moments. I was speechless. Why was she doing all this? 'What's the catch?' I thought to myself. There was no catch. She was a one in a million lady with a gem of a heart that would give you her last penny. To meet a special lady like her was beyond all of my wildest expectations.

Without wasting too much time, the plumber had been called to fit the washing machine. He was called Stephen and was a medium-sized, middle-aged man with blue eyes and thick, slicked back hair styled like in the 80s that suited him well. He sat and had a coffee with us and promised Lesley if anything needed fixing or sorting out in the flat he would be there to help me. Different to most people I knew at that time, he would talk to me with respect without judging me on where I come from, how I spoke or how I acted, but tried to show me in his so gracious way, things that you do not know or have ever heard about without patronizing you. I learned a lot from the wise man, a very respectful gentleman, with charm and kindness – something that I had never experienced before and I was very impressed. It became a good friendship.

After a few weeks Sheila and Meg, with friends from church, gathered together for the house warming with bits and bobs filling the gaps of a few necessary things that needed it. In no time our first home in England looked complete.

-O-

I was living an overwhelmingly positive experience, an experience that offers you knowledge and nourishes your mind. My experience continued by meeting and learning daily from other good people, who became my friends.

It was less than two years since I had moved to Morecambe, but my world had changed considerably – and for the good. Everything was moving so fast and life was becoming very hectic but still enormously enjoyable.

I was standing up at the window, thinking, that a few years ago I could not have believed that good things would ever happen to me. Breathing deeply, I felt the fresh air rushing between the large trees at the front. It looked like the stars, that had been hiding behind grey clouds on those long dark nights, had been switched on like tiny lights sending me a message of hope from the sky.

Somehow, somewhere, my mum was watching over me. I felt content. I felt like I had come to life again like in those years in my youth when I dreamed for a happy life. My desire to *live* had returned, and my eyes had regained the sparkle and I felt my face smiling again. Where had I been all these years? Where did I go? It looked for a while like I was lost somewhere in the middle of the desert, hopeless, but finally I had found myself, my own course, as no one was there to find it for me.

Another chapter in my life had closed and a new chapter, the beginning of a brand-new life, had just opened. I no longer felt trapped. Instead, I felt free and independent. Now there was just me and my children. There might be hills and hollows on this itinerary, but for now I was so grateful that I was standing there. My two beautiful children and I had a bright future ahead of us, and I was sure it was going to be much better than the ugly past we had endured.

CHAPTER 20

The rusted bicycle

T he loud buzzing of the alarm clock suddenly startled and jerked me awake. I tried to focus on the time. It was 5 o'clock on a very cold winter's Saturday.

Quickly and quietly I made breakfast for my children and put it in the oven to stay warm together with the stuffed peppers that I had cooked from the night before. I made a full tray of sandwiches, covered with foil and left them on the table with some crisps and some fruits for them to have through the day. It was very important for me that I left enough food for them to eat so they didn't need to go out for anything. I always asked them to promise me they wouldn't open the door to anybody until I came home. I was terrified of leaving them on their own but had no choice. I telephoned them every half hour to make sure that they were ok. After I was sure they had everything, I wrapped myself well and made my way out. The surface of the pavements shimmered under a layer of frost. The statuesque trees stood still on the frozen earth as they showed off their dark grey skins, shivering in the bitter wind.

I did two jobs – one during the day, and another in the evenings and on Saturday and Sunday. Durings weekends I worked at Moss View nursing home at the very end of Heysham village, and I had to get there before 7 am to get the breakfast ready for the elderly. The journey took me nearly an hour on foot. I worked at another nursing home at Altham Road during the evenings. It wasn't as far, as it was nearer the flat where we lived. I used to take a short cut and got there in 20-30 minutes.

Through the day I went to college, and at night I studied for my assessment until midnight. Most of the time we would walk, saving bus fares which I put in a separate envelope to buy football shoes for Enea or ballet shoes for Hope. Being a single mum, money was always tight.

The children tried to help with what they could; especially Enea who was growing up fast and trying to do his best.

The end of the spring approached and summer was knocking on the door with warm breezes that were beginning to waft across the Bay. I finished my evening shift and quickly made my way back home, only to find Enea at the bottom of the stairs trying to fix this very old rusted bicycle that looked like it had not been used for decades. The tyres were bald, and the brake pads were heavily worn. 'Where did you find this?' I asked.

'By the canal, Mum,' he answered, excitedly.

'Are you sure that bike doesn't belong to anyone?' I asked.

'No, Mum, it doesn't. It's been thrown out for a long time because it is not in good condition, but we can try to fix it. It will save you walking to work,' he replied, overjoyed that he had found something to do to help.

Standing there, looking at him so pleased, I couldn't have been prouder. My boy was growing up. The next morning, we went to the second-hand shop to find a few parts that were missing, and in a few hours the bike was fixed.

'Yeahhh, we did it, Mum,' Enea gasped ecstatically. Then he lifted the bike up and put his foot on it. The screeching noise went through our ears. His happy face changed as qickly as it had come.

'Oh Mum, we need black oil,' he said disappointedly.

'Well,' I said, 'we can try some cooking oil for now, can't we?'

He shook his head, not sure if that was going to work. But it did! The screeching noise disappeared for the time being, and the bike was ready. At that very moment I felt so blessed. I put out my arms and embraced him with love and warmth.

Happy that finally I didn't have to walk so far because I was riding to work and saving a lot of time, which meant I could spend more time with my children. For a while, up to the autumn, the bicycle was all right and took me from A to B, even though I had to endure the loud grating noise and the clunk, clunk, when I pushed it up the hill on Heysham Road at 6 am each Sunday morning!

However, my old two-wheeled friend could not keep riding for long. It was the end of September. I finished my evening shift and started cycling back home. The heavens opened and the rain bounced off the roads and the wind howled against me. I had been riding for less than five minutes and as I started uphill, my foot lost control after the chain came off and with it some other nuts and bolts scattered in the dark. I stopped and tried to gather the bits and pieces from the road, but the cars that were driving in the dark and the heavy rain didn't make it easy. The water streamed through my hair and my clothes. It was impossible. Well, that bike's life was over. I was getting panicky as I wanted to get home to my kids as soon as possible. I wanted to throw that old bike away, but thinking that it was a big thing for Enea having done something for his mum, I couldn't. I took my pay-as-you-go phone to ring them and let them know that I was going to be late but the voice message on the phone replied, 'You don't have any credit...'

I started walking faster, dragging my useless bike along with me to get home to my kids. Out of the blue the phone rang. 'Hi sis.' It was my brother Bushi from Albania. 'Happy birthday,' he said.

Surprisingly, I only just realised that it was 30th of September; mine and my brother's birthday.

'Happy birthday to you,' I replied. The noise of the rain and wind was making it difficult to hear very well, but I could hear that there was a party going on in the background.

'We are all here, having a party,' my brother went on. 'Wish you were with us. What you doing tonight? Are you celebrating?'

'Of course,' I replied, holding back my tears and trying to put on a happy voice.

'That's good, sis; glad to know that you are celebrating too,' he said, then in no time at all I could hear lots of voices gathered together singing the birthday song to me and wishing me all the best.

That was the best present ever, hearing my brother's voice and everyone singing to me. It was just incredible. The rain and tears mingled on my face.

After an hour's walk, I arrived back at the flat. I was drenched, and my hands were black from trying to fix the bicycle. As soon as I opened the door, Hope and Enea threw themselves at me with tears in their eyes. They had been sitting and waiting at the bottom of the stairs, upset and scared that something had happened to me. With relief I scooped them up in my arms and we all went upstairs. On the nicely dressed table was a few balloons. My children had prepared beans on toast but it had gone cold because they had prepared it a few hours before.

'Happy birthday, Mum,' they said. 'We love you.'

My heart melted. I couldn't have been happier or prouder at that moment. I looked at their innocent faces, showing love and pain. Pain for the disappointments and sadness they had had to go through, and love for the only person they had left at that moment – their mum. Maybe I hadn't been so fortunate when it comes to love and marriage, but for sure I was so lucky to have these two beautiful children that life had bestowed on me. Mammy's treasure.

As for the rusty bike? Enea fixed it again and it lasted for a few more months. We took the bike to the tip and after that our friends Rob and Zubida offered me one of their bikes until I could save some money and buy a new one.

CHAPTER 21

When you don't deserve forgiveness anymore

The divorce

Y ou are doing the best you can to forget the past and move forward; and that's the best thing anyone can do. But what do you do when others try to stop you taking that step; take what belongs to you; what you deserve? Just when you thought that they were out of your life forever, they appear like a bad penny.

It had been less than four years since we had left London. Dan was keeping in contact with the children every day and he told Enea that he was no longer with Moka. It was something that I knew was inevitable. Their relationship had been born out of lies and betrayal so there was no way it could have lasted.

The words of the social work lady that day who'd said to him, 'One day you are going to be sorry about leaving this lady but it is going to be too late' had landed. But it doesn't stop here.

He invited himself to my house. Ludicrous, out of the blue, my former husband had turned up at my flat playing mind games with his own children, regardless of my strong opposition. Never! According to him, it was more than normal to come back to his wife and kids after everything he'd done, and life was going to be as it once was. How wrong he was! I had no intention of making the same mistake that had consumed me all those years when I was with him. To make matters worse, he wasn't taking No for an answer and was doing exactly the same thing he did many years ago when I was just a vulnerable young girl, demanding and imposing on me becoming his. He hasn't changed a bit. That man had so many chances to put things right and he didn't, consequently that made them twice as bad.

It was early Sunday afternoon when I received a shocking phone call at work from Hope. Frightened, in a low trembling voice, she tried to explain to me what was happening and unfolding before her eyes. Her dad was there at our flat and to make it worse he was pointing out to his children that I must take him back. If I was not willing to, he would not be responsible for his actions – he was going to kill their mummy like a dog.

And through this fracas and drama, his 14 year old son stood up to his dad, opposing him with all his might, saying that he would have to kill his son before he got to his mum.

My entire body was wracked with fear while I was asking Hope to try to stay calm and reassuring her that I'd be there in five minutes. I managed to get a lift with one of my work friends, Pam, and in less than ten minutes we had arrived at the flat. I rushed to open the door and there he was at the top of the stairs, the same arrogant man, showing no remorse. There was no love left in my heart for this man; if anything, just loathing. Hope and Enea ran past him and down to my arms. All the anxiety was now back and transformed into pure anger.

'Get out my flat,' I snapped sternly. 'The police are on their way.'

Standing at the door with my friend Pam I felt so embarrassed. He pounded down the stairs and stabbed his finger at me, screwed up his face and threatened me.

'I'm going to bury you alive. You'll see by tomorrow your place will be at the cemetery,' he snarled, while walking out of the front door.

For once in my life I felt strong and sure that I was not going to be trampled all over anymore. I looked him straight in his eyes. No tears, no sorrow, I stood high with no more fears and humility and told him what he didn't want to hear.

'Get out and never come back. I'm not scared of you anymore,' I said, although my body was shaking from the mixture of adrenaline, fear and anger. I felt I had my life under control for the first time and there was no way he was going to take that away from me.

I slammed the door behind him, and we all went upstairs. I looked at my children's faces and I saw the looks that had been seen too often in the past. They were scared, and it was plastered all over them. It shattered my heart into pieces. When was this pantomime going to end?

Since then he has never come back to Morecambe, although he did try one more last threat a few years later, when we lived in Lancaster. What was it about this man? It was like every now and then he wanted you to know that he still had control over you, he's not done with you yet.

I was working as a manager at the time in the little salon in town. That morning Dan rang Hope telling her that he was in Lancaster on the way to her mum's salon, and he would cut her mum's head off and walk through the streets with it held in his hands. These exact words that have been vivid in my head make my body tremble even to this day imagining what they can do to a little girl's soul? Threatening women gave him the pleasure of feeling a stronger man by scaring the life out of his own children, not even concerning himself with the damage he was causing.

I looked outside to the street but my ex-husband was nowhere to be seen. I don't know how I kept myself to the end of the day. The businesses of the town were closing down for the day. Most of the members of staff had gone and the last few people down Penny Street were rushing home, after a long day at work. The reception area of the salon had big glass doors and the shop window faced the main street and I was very cautious and scared that he might be waiting for everyone to go – waiting for me.

I locked the doors leaving the salon I looked up and down Penny Street, just in case he was waiting for me somewhere then set off home. I walked quickly, periodically looking over my shoulders to check I wasn't being followed. It was a quiet twenty minutes' walk home. It was dark. I was passing the Millennium Bridge, with my phone in my hand. Fear seized my body. Almost every step across that bridge I was crucified with fear, looking behind me every few steps, imagining that at any moment I could feel a heavy blow to my head. Then I imagined his face sneering while gripping my head in his hands. Shivers convulsed my body. Instinctively my hands began to cover my head like they wanted to protect it from some unseen blow. My phone slipped from my hand onto the metal walkway.

I looked down through the dim lamp light on the bridge, scrabbling to find it. Then the shadow of a human loomed over me.

I tried to let out a fearful scream, but nothing came out. Putting my hand up, trying to protect my head from the blows I was convinced were about to rain down upon it. I looked up, terror in my eyes, to see ... just another chap walking quickly home to spend the evening with his loved ones. It was clear that the fear was still embedded on my soul. It had been built up over the years like a woollen jumper that was knitted with needles by hand slowly, slowly, day by day. The thread on this jumper had to be pulled out and stripped to what it once was, just thread. This fear was my challenge and my devil to zap once and for all. Edit it and delete.

Fortunately I found my phone, grabbed it quickly, and I checked both ways. No one was there and the road was empty. I grasped the rail of the bridge and took the deepest breath of relief. It was another empty threat. They were vicious games. Another attempt at emotional blackmail from him by using his own kids to get to their mum. The lights from the quayside apartments reflected in the river Lune that rushed on rapidly towards the open sea.

A loud knock that echoed up the staircase made Hope and Enea jump up in fear. They thought their dad has come back again. Quick frightening glances towards me. I waved for them to sit down and quietly ran down the stairs. It was the postman. He passed me a large brown envelope, which I had to sign for. I tore open the envelope and started to eagerly read. The documents that I was longing for, that confirmed our separation and cut those final ties, had finally arrived. There it was in black and white, from the High Court of Justice: the Decree Absolute.

What a harrowing experience it had been! For a moment I felt a failed wife and mother, I felt defeated, and my stomach felt like an empty pit of sadness. He took twelve long years from me that were supposed to be some of the most beautiful. To my mind came those moments, years ago, when I made the wrong decision—a decision that had shaped my destiny which changed my life forever.

I had cried a thousand tears. I had been mistreated, beaten but not broken. I gave everything I could to this man; all through his lies, betrayals, and cruelty. I didn't know how strong I was until then. This was the part of my life where I found out who I was. I learned to be like water, seeping through the cracks and finding its way to the river and just keeping on moving with its flow. I had made a wrong decision during the most important chapter of my life which I had been paying for so long and maybe I always will, but for now it was over and sometimes the wrong choices do bring us to the right place. The end of that chapter was like a bad dream fading way.

I breathed a sigh of relief; a massive onerous weight had been lifted from my shoulders. Finally, he was out of my life for good. I wiped my tears away in one swipe. It was done. No more tears would fall because of that man. It had taken me a while to understand my own worth and put the pieces of my shattered life and self-confidence together again. Those years when he threatened, manipulated, scared, and abused me so easily had completely disappeared, never ever to return. Those times that gave him pleasure when he had stomped on me like a cigarette butt, domineering over me, disappeared like a puff of wind and with it the fear of abuse. Too many chances missed – there was no chance left for reconciliation.

I opened the window, watching the natural movement of the trees swaying from the breeze, looking as if they were dancing a slow waltz. Like a signal of wordless news, a single orange leaf fell from a tree near the window. It circled around at the touch of the chilly breeze, floated down, and landed lightly on the outside of my windowsill. I took the leaf in my hand and noticed that the lines on it were similar to the lines on my palm. Strangely enough I had never before considered the importance of this small detail. These lines had been created in that leaf since the beginning of their germination, just like the lines in our palms are formed whilst we are still in the womb. It was just like as if the path of life was marked in that direction before you even started your life, and there is nothing you can do to change it even if you try. It's called destiny.

The chill of the air crept into the house. I breathed in the fresh air as if it was a breath of freedom. I no longer felt trapped. Instead, I felt free and independent. Now there was just me and my children. There might be hills and hollows on this itinerary but for now I was so grateful for my two beautiful children wishing a bright future ahead of us, and I was sure it was going to be much better than the ugly past we had endured.

From that moment I made a promise to myself that I would never again allow anyone to hurt and abuse me or again stop me from living my life. I looked up into the sky; the clouds were disappearing, and the sun was coming out after a stormy night and its warmth was caressing my face. I can't undo the trauma we went through, but I can adapt and overcome.

CHAPTER 22

The winning over discrimination

As I said my final goodbyes to my last customers that month of June, the hairdressing teacher approached me and said, 'You have been invited to the presentation night, you have been nominated again.'

I must have looked so stunned by the unexpected invitation that she followed up by saying, 'Don't look so surprised. It is well deserved. Just make sure you're there.'

'I will,' I said joyously. 'I guess it's an excuse for a new dress.'

She smiled back at me and said, 'Oh, for me too. I'll see you there then.'

On that hot summer night I won two awards – a gold and a silver for different achievements. My hard work had paid off. I walked out of the event once again with two trophies. My name was engraved once again on one of the trophies and was put back in the hairdressing department glass display cabinet. My long wait had come to an end and as I was now a qualified hairdresser, I went out looking for hairdressing jobs. My passion for hairdressing was immense.

It was very difficult though, to find a job without any real-life experience and with my English at that time didn't help either. My first interview was so bad that it stripped me of my confidence in minutes and made me think that I had wasted my time for two years studying and left me with no hope that I would ever find a job in hairdressing.

The salon where I went for an interview was one of the most well-known hairdressing salons in Lancaster that had been established for 40 years. I went there with my friend Sheila who waited for me until the interview had finished. The owner of the salon was a tall man, around 65, well presented and looking very smart. He was wearing a grey suit jacket covering a well ironed light pink shirt with a blue tie that he kept stroking to keep it in line while he was talking. He welcomed me and asked me to follow him to his office. He started to ask me a few questions. Then as soon as my first words came out of my mouth the look he gave me through his black framed glasses said it all. I knew that my English wasn't perfect . I tried not to despair as I was well prepared for the interview and was able to answer the questions on hairdressing confidently. However, it took a turn for the worse when he asked me where I was from.

'From Albania,' I replied confidently.

He gazed at me over his glasses, took them off, shook his head, and placed his hands on the table.

'Oh, I'm sorry, but I cannot give you the job.' He carried on, 'You see, I don't have a problem with that, but my customers will. They can be very funny and choosy about whom they have doing their hair, and some people have especially strong feelings against Eastern Europeans.'

'What happened to equal opportunities?' I asked.

'Unfortunately that's just a fable in the real world,' he replied mockingly.

What hurtful words to say! My heart dropped to my stomach and my cheeks started to burn a scarlet colour. I couldn't have been more shocked and mortified. His words cut me like a knife.

'Well, I'm sorry I wasted your time,' I said sarcastically and then picked up my coat and rushed outside quickly to get away from that place. He obviously did not understand right from wrong, as his words were not only extremely hurtful but also very racist. I went outside in tears. I had experienced many shocking things, but I had never experienced discrimination like that.

'Well, how did it go?' Sheila asked.

I shook my head in disappointment and said, 'Apparently he doesn't have a job for foreigners like me.'

'He never said that! Did he really?' she said, shocked.

'Unfortunately he did,' I nodded.

'Do you want me to go and have a word with him?' she asked.

'Definitely not. It's not worth it. Who wants to work with people who judge your descent and your culture?' I said.

'I totally agree,' she said, nodding her head in approval. 'There will be more jobs out there to go for, so don't lose hope because of what he said.'

However, the world has a funny way of 'having a word' with people. Little did he know the tables were going to turn and in only a matter of years I would be taking over and be the owner of that business, and we would work together.

Fortunately the next day I had already arranged other interviews, so I had to forget the mishap and act professionally so I could secure a job. I found a self-employed job at a small salon in Morecambe town which I was very excited about. I knew I needed a full-time and secure job if I was to support my children, though, so, while I was working there, I was actively searching for a full-time job.

After a while I managed to get an interview for a full-time job at a little salon named Hair Flair on the back road of the promenade in Morecambe. The owner was a beautiful, tall middle-aged woman with short blonde hair and a warm smile which completely looked past my accent and made me feel so comfortable. Her name was Trish.

The interview turned out to be more like friends talking and laughing over a coffee about families and daily life. It couldn't have gone any better. Then suddenly she looked at the clock and said, 'Is that the time ? Oh it's gone fast,' then, straight to the point, she said, 'Well, Yllka, when would you like to start?'

'Really?' I replied, surprised. 'You're offering me a job?'

'Yes,' she smiled, 'the job is yours. When would you like to start?'

Still in shock, I replied, 'I can start tomorrow.'

So that's it. Finally I've got a full time job which I started the very next day, five days a week 9-5. I organized a weekly deal taxi to pick up Hope every day after school and bring her to the salon at 3pm. She was allowed to stay here in the kitchen, do her homework until I finished work.

The first day I started I was introduced for the first time to customers who would often ask lots of questions about me, which I did not mind. However, there was one question that would always make me feel slightly uncomfortable – when they would ask: Why did you leave Albania? Some of them would tread more lightly around the question and asked it tactfully. They would start with, 'You have a very nice accent, where does that come from?' And as soon as I said Albania, they would pick up the topic. 'Why did you come here?' What made you leave Albania in the first place?' I guess just out of curiosity. Sometimes I tried to tell a long story in a short way by explaining everything in a few sentences.

But there was this one time when two ladies had appointments with me one after another. While I was doing the first lady's hair she asked, 'Where you from?'

'Albania,' I answered.

'I never heard of it,' she said, rather disparagingly, waving her hand backwards.

Calmly I explained to her which countries were bordering Albania while I was styling her hair. Through the mirror I saw the sarcastic expression on her face that was rather insulting. I felt deflated. I finished her hair as quickly as I could. Happily she went downstairs to reception to pay.

Her friend then sat down on the chair and she said rather embarrassed, 'Were you offended by my friend's attitude? I want to apologise on her behalf.'

'Oh, not at all,' I replied smiling, 'because she doesn't know geography that's not my problem.' As I laughed and tried to slip away.

Sometimes I still pronounced words incorrectly or used them in the wrong context. It became clear through a funny occurrence with my next customer, a young man around 30 years old with dark blond hair and a receding hair line. I was doing the consultation and politely asked him, 'You're empty on your head, so do you want me to keep the hair on top longer to cover it?'

He stared at me in the mirror, looking stunned. 'Excuse me?' he said.

Reading his facial expression, I looked at him confused, pointed to the bald patches at either side at the top of his head and replied, 'Errrm, you're empty on your head,' not understanding why he looked so shocked.

'Oh, I think I know what you mean. The word is 'bald' if you must know.' He started laughing to ease the awkward situation.

I could feel my cheeks getting warmer and warmer and immediately apologised. 'Oh, I'm sorry, I was trying to...'

'Don't worry about it,' he chuckled. 'You do what you think is best.'

We all laughed at that point – Trish too. That was the impression I made on my very first day, not to be forgotten as the gentleman, happy with his haircut, came back to me every time. He never forgot to remind me saying jokingly, 'Don't forget to leave my hair long on the top to cover my empty head.'

While I was working at the salon, I carried on studying for my Level three qualification at college. It was difficult to study at the same time as working but I knew that I was going to get the best possible experience and another qualification. Taught by one of the most talented teachers, Shelley Rose, who helped me not just professionally but also to gain my confidence. Shelley was an eccentric and very confident woman who would always colour her short hair an array of colours. She not only stood out for the way she looked but also for her very kind heartedness.

Monday and Tuesday evenings from 6-9 on the lessons, Hope would sit and do her homework next to our training room, in the little annex, while I was training thanks to Shelley. 'Sometimes breaking the rules for a good cause won't harm anyone,' she would kindly say. Thanks to Hope's quiet personality she would sit there quietly until I finished, without bothering anyone. At the end of my qualification, I was nominated yet again for the special award. My name was called for one more last time and I got up once again to pick up the crystal trophy that was presented by an incredible lady, Helen Morton, the manager of the hairdressing department.

That was my last day at the college. I left feeling proud and grateful. My dream did not come true through magic, but with determination and courage. Life gave me the strength to believe in myself so I could accomplish something against all of the odds, and I couldn't have been more elated.

Everything finally was going smoothly and at the end of September we were gathering together all my friends and family to celebrate my 35th birthday. After talking to Meg and Sheila, we decided to have a little party in a little place on the promenade called Fred's on the Ball. It was a party to remember.

That night as I walked through the door, I couldn't have been more surprised. Unexpectedly, the long tables were full of food, and a cake with my picture prepared and made by Meg and Track. My face said it all.

Then Sheila appeared with a big dish that she placed on the end of the table. In less than half an hour the function room was full of friends offering me their best wishes. I couldn't have been happier. Track filled a glass and raised a toast for my birthday.

As I was sitting there, my mind went back to that rainy night, many years before, when my brother had rang me to wish me a happy birthday. On this day, years ago, I was completely drenched from the rain because I had been trying to fix the old bicycle. And now I was wearing a beautiful gold dress that my sister Moza bought me as a present for my birthday. This day years ago for my birthday I had beans on toast made by my children, and now here was a full buffet table of food and cakes.

I took my phone out of my bag and went into the hallway, away from the music, to call my brother and wish him happy birthday too. On this night I felt happiness and sorrow in equal measures for the most important people in my life. I took a deep breath and let out a deep sigh of relief. That sigh seemed to relieve those pains and replace them with joy. Looking around, I became overwhelmed. Now I was at my birthday celebration with my favourite people – my beautiful children and my incredible friends.

Looking at Enea's and Hope's happy faces – those glowing faces that tried so hard to smile and uplift the wounded soul; those eyes that reflected their love for their mother – they were happy because their mum was happy. They were my world, the world of love that warms my heart and soul every minute of their existence. I love them unconditionally, and indeed the influence of these beautiful people surrounding my life. It felt like the sun was coming out after the storm that not only brightened my day but warmed my heart through its rays.

CHAPTER 23

The nightmares

The troubles we went through in Albania and the horrific times in London with their father haunted not only *my* mind but also the minds of my children through vivid nightmares. The trauma that they had witnessed for so many years left them with constant anxiety and fears. It was a consequence that I could not bear to see them go through, but something that had been tattooed into their minds. Even though our flat had two bedrooms, they had to sleep in my bed as their constant nightmares wouldn't allow them to sleep solely on their own.

They both battled things that children of their age shouldn't even have to experience. I had to talk to them constantly and remind them that we were in England and nothing bad would happen if they slept on their own. A few times I tried to let Enea sleep in his bedroom but had no joy; he would come straight in screaming after yet another night terror and get into bed with me and Hope. It was always a sleepless night with the three of us in a double bed with me wedged in the middle like sardines and I had to do something about it.

It was a dilemma not only for Enea to get used to sleeping in his bedroom, but more importantly to find the key to his nightmares, insecurity and anguish, and try to alleviate as much as I could the feeling of his trepidation. So that night after a quiet and soothing conversation over dinner, Enea agreed that he would try to sleep in his room as long as I stayed there until he fell asleep.

He went to bed and I remained by the bedside until his eyes started to tire and he finally drifted off to sleep. Standing up as quietly as I could to tiptoe out of the room, I went back to my own bedroom to stay with Hope who would always sleep with me in the double bed.

Relieved, I felt we had reached a milestone that had been so difficult to achieve, but not for long as after just an hour his demons caught up with him, and his crippling nightmares woke him, screaming out, 'Mum, Mum, where are you?'

I jolted out of my sleep to run through to him. He was sitting up in bed, covered in a cold sweat. I managed to settle him down, sitting on the floor next to his bed with my hand over his chest. Between his mumbles he started to tire again, and when he started to feel as if he was in a safe space, he drifted off again. I took a blanket to cover myself and I stayed there until the morning light whilst still checking on Hope in the next bedroom. It broke my heart seeing my son in that condition. The terrifying life that we had been through was still a stalking nightmare. It was so bad that sometimes I would wonder if he would ever have a normal life again. Yet, I was determined to get him over this last hurdle. I knew that if I surrounded them with love and let time heal their deep-set wounds, then we would live a life as normally as we could.

At the start of each morning, it was often a struggle for him to get up. Although he was unwilling to set off for school following those sleepless, troubled nights, he felt he had to try to leave the terrible haunting behind him. On school days he hated wearing the uniform, especially the shirt and tie. Often, he would 'lose' the tie as he used to take it off and put it in his pocket, or not wear uniform at all, saying that it wasn't uniform day.

At this time, he was a student at High School. Just when I was thought that he was beginning to cope, he came home upset, took his tie off, threw his bag on the floor and said, 'I don't want to go to school anymore.'

'Why? What is wrong?' I asked, concerned.

'The teacher discriminated against me in front of everyone in the class today. One of the boys said that I was an Italian, and the teacher answered sharply and said, "No he is not, he is just a refugee from Albania.".'

While I was listening to him, trying to hide my feelings of pure shock, he was carrying on and telling me how he ran out the class embarrassed and didn't want to return. It was a reason why he always said that he was Italian and begged me to say the same. It wasn't about being ashamed of his identity. The past left him afraid that history would repeat itself. The blood feud, the troubles in Albania left him feeling traumatized and paranoid that he would be followed. Lying about it by hiding where he came from was just a small piece of comfort.

'I suppose the teacher was a little bit insensitive about that,' I tried to comfort him.

'But that's not all, Mum,' he replied tearfully.

'When school finished I was walking over Broadway Bridge then I heard a few boys from school shouting at me, calling me a refugee and telling me to go back to my own country,' he said, embarrassment written on his face.

'Oh sweetheart,' I sighed, 'they have no idea about your life. They're just selfish kids, and I'm sure after I speak to the teacher, they will apologise to you.'

'No, you're not coming to my school,' he spat back quickly. 'I'll beat them up myself. If my dad was here, they wouldn't dare talk to me like that.'

Unfortunately, despite everything, his dad was still his hero. He was still yearning for his father to keep him safe, feeling that he needed him by his side and that if he was there everything else would be okay. He was missing that father figure; in some way that was his safety net. It felt as if I was not fulfilling that role for him. I could see that he was suffering inside. It didn't help that his dad phoned him nearly every day, telling him that he was now living on his own. However, from Enea's perspective those awful days caused by his dad were soon forgiven, and it seemed a long way back.

So, as always that evening his dad called.

'Do you know what happened today, Dad? Some guys were calling me...' and the entire story flooded out again.

'Who the hell do they think they are?' his dad's angry voice cascaded from Enea's phone. 'I'll come there and stamp them like cigarette butts.'

It seemed that everything had to be sorted out through violence. Was that the only advice he could give his son?

'He is not coming here, and nobody is doing anything,' I said to Enea. 'We will sort it out ourselves and that's that.'

'No, Dad, I'm not scared of them. I'll face them myself,' Enea replied. Wanting that constant acceptance from a man who faked his own masculinity. In the morning with no other option he got himself ready to go to school.

'Do you want me to come with you and speak to your teacher?' I asked.

'Don't even think about it, Mum,' he said, shaking his head. 'Everybody will laugh at me saying that Enea's mum is walking him to school. I'm going on my own.'

Then he stormed out only to bump into our family friend Meg who had just appeared on the doorstep. 'Heeeey Mr Enea, what's the matter?' – She used to call him Mr Enea jokingly.

'Nothing,' he scowled as he stomped off.

Meg looked at me inquisitively.

'He is having trouble at school,' I tried to explain.

'Have you spoken to the school?' she suggested.

'That's what I wanted to do but he won't let me,' I replied. 'I'll try and get in contact with his form teacher later.'

'Let me know, love,' she said, as she turned around to Hope who was waiting with a bag in her hand ready to go. (Meg also used to work as a dinner lady at Hope's school and often used to take Hope to school with her in the morning some times.)

'Come on, get a wiggle on before we get stuck in traffic,' Meg urged.

She put her arm around Hope and they both made their way to Meg's car that was parked at the side of the road.

As they left, I got ready myself and made my way to work. All the way to work I thought constantly about how unhappy Enea was and discrimination was the last thing he needed. At lunch time I had to ring and have a long conversation with the form teacher but unfortunately, it didn't seem to make any difference. He despised anything around him that reminded him that his life had completely changed. This meant he rapidly started to lose interest in school and so would never behave. This resulted in him befriending the wrong crowd. Instead of helping to keep him out of more trouble, they encouraged the bad behaviour. He felt like he belonged in that group but for the wrong reasons, so he would carry on playing up in school. He didn't have to think about missing his dad, because he filled that void with a very negative distraction.

He often used to go and play football with one of his Kosovan friends called Dardan, who lived in Lancaster with his wonderful family (his parents, four brothers and two sisters). They were another survivor family from war-torn Kosovo who had escaped the nasty crimes, hiding in mountains and forests where the youngest boy of the family was born then was saved by a British army aircraft. Dardan was a nice quiet boy and had a positive impact on Enea, but unfortunately he wasn't a friend that Enea would have by his side in school every day. He went to a different school in Lancaster, but even so it was a good thing that the two boys had each other, to watch each other's back and they have kept their friendship to this day.

A phone call from his school made me more worried to find out that he 'was being so disruptive in class, missing lessons and his performance has changed'.

Consequently, a meeting was arranged and a few things were pointed out and we thought we were getting somewhere but back home Enea burst out annoyed and said, 'I don't like going to that school anymore, the teachers hate me.'

'They don't, they only want your best interests.' I was trying to calm him down.

'Mr English is funny though. I like him,' he said, smiling.

I knew he liked Mr English as he often used to talk about him. Often, as soon as he got home from school, Enea would tell us about Mr English's hilarious jokes that he had told that day in class. He knew exactly how to deal with negative behaviour with a positive style of humour that Enea could relate to. Enea often nicknamed him Mr Cartoon Tie as he would always wear wacky ties with different cartoon pictures on them. He was a middle-aged man of medium height with a jovial character. In fairness, there were also other good teachers who tried in one way or another to help Enea through the lessons.

We also organised a few lesson sessions sitting with Sheila but unfortunately, it didn't last long.

Meg suggested that Track might understand him better, and would have a word with him man to man. We were invited the next day for a nice fish pie dinner cooked by Meg with fresh fish that Track had just caught the day before. Enea used to get on well with Track and used to listen to him, he even started to support his favourite football team, Liverpool. Although he was getting as much help as possible, little things tended to trigger his temper. Often, he would take his worries and fears out on me or Hope, swearing and using foul language that he had never used before. This wasn't him. Even the owner of the shop next door, that was separated from our flat by a paper-thin wall, could hear Enea swearing. Next time Enea went to the shop Bryan said, 'You are banned from coming into my shop until you change your attitude and stop swearing at your mother, young man.' He stabbed his finger at him, and Enea left the shop embarrassed as he swore at him, and never went back.

That was nothing compared to when Track had to come and have words with him again. Meg and Track were always nice and calm with him, but usually had to treat him with kid gloves. But because of this behaviour, Track had reached the end of his tether. They were at our flat having coffee when they heard Enea at the bottom of the stairs as he arrived with his friends, swearing at me. Shocked, Track stormed to the top of the stairs where he could see Enea, and said, 'Who do you think you are talking to? You don't talk to your mother like that! Come here, you rascal!'

Enea rushed out in shock as he had never heard Track raise his voice at him, muttering profanities at *him* too. Enea didn't come back until after Meg and Track had left. No matter what was said, there was no improvement. My boy was changing dramatically. I felt like I was losing him. I felt like a failed mum. What's happening to my boy? In Albania everyone had nothing but nice words to say about him and I was the proudest mum at school and in the community.

In Morecambe, slowly but surely, he had become very difficult to control, both in school and at home. One of our rules was that he must be home before it got dark as he knew that I would worry, but breaking rules didn't seem to be a big thing anymore as he would start an argument and storm out anyway. Just when you thought it couldn't get any worse, the worst was yet to come. It was like the saying 'You complain about the rain, and hailstones start to fall'. Maybe that was the path with Enea.

One winter's night the rain was torrential. I put Hope to bed and tried to ring Enea. It was getting late and he hadn't been seen anywhere. His phone was switched off and none of his friends whom I contacted seemed to know where he was. Fear splintered my heart. Had something happened to my boy? Making sure that Hope was completely asleep, I decided to slip out to look for him. As soon as I opened the door, lightning flashed and an enormous clap of thunder rolled overhead, splitting the darkness. I locked the door and headed down the street to find him. Still no sign of him. I started knocking on the doors of some of his friends, but no one seemed to know where he was. After a few hours of looking and drenched to the skin from the heavy rain, I walked back home, very worried.

Once back, I ran upstairs ready to phone the police. As I took off my coat, I heard the door lock turn and then slam. The sound of his heavy feet grew louder as he came up the stairs. With the sound came a very pungent smell of cannabis. He tried to walk straight into his room, but I had to stand in front of him and ask, 'Where have you been? I've been looking everywhere for you?'

'Leave me alone. I want to go to bed,' he said as he tried to walk to his room.

'No, not until you tell me what you've been doing. Have you been smoking something you shouldn't?' I asked.

He looked at me blankly, and replied, 'No, I haven't.'

'I can smell your clothes,' I said, screwing up my nose in distaste.

'My clothes might smell from it because some of my friends have been smoking it, but not me. They told me that if I don't smoke cannabis with them then I'm not allowed to be their friend anymore. I don't even like it though, Mum, it makes me feel sick even smelling it,' he tried to reassure me.

'Who were you with?' I asked.

'No way am I telling you that, Mum, even if I have to die right now, I'm not a grass,' he replied.

I knew he was stupidly loyal towards his friends, and there was no way Enea would tell me their names. However, after a bit of digging through his friends the next morning, I found out. I knew the mum of one of the boys – I had met her a few times at school during parents' evenings. So, I decided to go and see her. On the way there, I was a little worried about how to approach her, how to find the right words and tell her, thinking that this would be shocking and upsetting for her.

As I arrived, she was waiting outside the front door in her dressing gown, enjoying a cigarette.

'What's up, love?' she asked, as soon as she saw me from a distance. 'You don't look well, come in.'

'I'm ok,' I said, shaking my head as I walked in the door. 'I think we perhaps should be concerned for our two sons.'

'Tell me,' she said while she was inhaling the cigarette smoke and slowly exhaling it through her nostrils.

'Now, I don't know how to say this, and I don't want you to freak out because I don't know how true it is, but I think your son might be smoking cannabis.' My words blurted out. I expected the same surprise and shock from her that I had experienced.

To my surprise she looked at me, confused, and let out a laugh. 'Oh, is that what this is all about?' she replied. 'You had me worried for a second there. You should try some, love. It will make you more relaxed and make you feel better.'

I looked at her in a state of shocked bemusement. 'Are you serious?' I said, absolutely flabbergasted about her answer as I got up. It infuriated me that she would think it would be okay to allow her child to start on a path to self-destruction. 'How could you let your son smoke cannabis and say it's okay?'

She was unbelievably shocked at my reaction as if it was uncalled for and said as her face dropped, 'Well, I do, and look at me. I'm fine, aren't I,' she replied with indifference.

I shook my head in disbelief. 'I'm not going to tell you how to bring up your son, but you couldn't be any more wrong. It will lead them to something dangerous.'

Disappointed, I made myself a promise that my son would never go back to that house again. But would Enea listen to his mum? I doubted it.

An appointment was booked for Enea to test whether he had been taking cannabis himself but thankfully, it came out negative.

With everything I tried I still wanted to stop him from seeing this friend and told him to remove himself from this destructive group. But no joy. Unfortunately he got expelled from the school and was transferred to a behavioural school in Lancaster hoping that things would change for the better. At first, he was settling in well and there were a few positive changes and things were looking promising. However, that didn't last long, because he soon reverted to his old ways and getting into lots of trouble. After a disagreement that led to an argument and with everything that was happening around him and to get away from his troubles, he made a decision. 'I want to go and live with my dad. He is on his own now, because he's not with Moka anymore. The drama is over,' he said.

'Sweetheart, you're not going anywhere,' I warned him, trying to put my foot down.

'I'm not a kid anymore. Everybody makes mistakes in the past, and besides, Dad has changed now and he wants me to go and live with him,' he insisted. 'And it will be good for me to get away from their troubles as well, Mum. Getting away from the negative influences will save me from getting in trouble with the law.'

My heart was shattered to see him going back to his dad. That was the last thing I could have wished for, but I was caught between a rock and a hard place. He had made up his mind to go back to London, but because he didn't get along with his dad, he didn't stay long with him. It turned out to be the best decision he could have made. He met Ina – now his fiancée – and years later they were blessed with a beautiful son, Nosh. We would never miss speaking to each other every morning to wish him a good day and every evening to wish him a good night. They would come back to spend time with us, and still do to this day. He is a grown up, wonderful, caring, handsome man with determination to take care of his family. Unfortunately the past has left a scar on him. To this day he has to fight the depression and anxiety often followed by continuous therapy. However, as the years go by, the wounds of the past are healing and fading away, hopefully until one day they will disappear forever and enable him to move on to the right life that he deserves so much.

On the other hand Hope was doing well at school and she was extremely mature for her age. She was very happy and hardworking but still a very shy girl due to still developing her English. She was attending a school near the college where I would drop her off then go on to college. She was the complete polar opposite of Enea. When I attended her parents' evenings, I was astonished at the amazing feedback that I would get from her teachers. Nothing but good things would be said about her. It was strange having two children that on the outside looked exactly alike but had different personalities and attitudes towards education and life.

As with Enea, the past had also left its mark on Hope. The noise of the gunfire outside had stuck in her mind and triggered anxiety in her when she heard something that sounded similar. And I didn't realise that until the Morecambe Water and Light festival that took place on the jetty on the promenade in Morecambe on a beautiful night and the atmosphere in town was fantastic. The children loved it and so did Hope... until the fireworks started. The explosion went off and, in an instant, the first colourful firework stretched itself across the sky in a spectacular shape. I felt Hope's little hand shaking in mine. She was the sort of child who would never complain or make it clear she was uncomfortable. I looked at her, concerned, and asked, 'What's wrong?' She started to tug at my hand in desperation.

Feeling her fear, and seeing the frightened expression on her face, made me realise at that moment that we had to walk away and make our way back home as soon as we could. It was heartbreaking seeing her so apprehensive about the fireworks where other children around her were jumping with excitement. It seemed clear that she was deeply affected by the tumultuous past even though we were far away from where it had all happened. The deep scars had been left in her mind. That night was traumatised by fireworks – she woke up every couple of hours from nightmares and terrible trembles. The time for High School approached. She tried to get along with the other pupils in her class. However, as ever, bullies were very much in evidence, ready to pick on a shy girl like her, especially as she was over-weight at that time and that triggered some more. She was holding it all together for a while and often hid in her bedroom, upset.

I didn't know until the next day when she came home from school really upset. She was trying to tell me everything that had been happening though her words were getting flustered from panicking. As I tried to comfort and calm her down, finally I found out that someone was writing a letter and passing it round the whole class saying that Hope looked like a boy and everybody was laughing. And as if that wasn't enough, to make her day worse, when school finished, while she was waiting by the bus stop, a boy just slapped her across her face without any provocation using foul swear words towards her and calling her even worse swear words. It was more the humiliation in front of everyone rather than the pain of the slap. That was the last thing she needed.

The very next morning I went to school to speak to the form teacher and after a series of events between the teacher and the pupil involved, an apologetic letter was written. But bullies are bullies; you stop one and another starts. Even the letters that school sent to the parents had no effect this time. She just carried on insulting and bullying Hope in front of everyone without giving it a second thought.

That night, when she was home from school, she decided she never wanted to go back again. By this time, I had had enough. Left with no other option, I had to do something about matters before she trod the same path as Enea. My girl had gone through enough. So, I sat her down and said, 'Right, you have to stand up for yourself and fight back.'

'I can't, Mum,' she said, frightened.

'Well, you are going to school tomorrow and if she calls you names again, you go near her, face to face, look her straight in the eyes and say confidently, "What did you just say? Say it again please". Then if she repeats and calls you a name again and touches you, you fight back. You will only need to do it once and she won't come back. You will have to stand up to her. No-one will do it for you.'

'I can't *do* that, Mum,' she explained. 'I will get expelled.'

'You won't,' I tried to reassure her. 'That's the only way you will get free from bullies.'

The next morning she did exactly what her mother had told her. She slapped her back. Hard though it was, she was never bullied again. Although it was extremely difficult for me to give such advice, it turned out to be the only way to stop the bullies in their tracks.

She went on to do tremendously well in school, getting involved in shows and dancing, surrounded by a good crowd of friends and putting her life in perspective. I couldn't have been prouder. My girl was growing up to be a beautiful, smart young lady, enjoying every minute of her life, and I couldn't have been happier.

CHAPTER 24

Accepted

Visiting the homeland after seven years

'**M**rs Sinani?' I heard the voice behind me as I was about to open my flat door. I turned around immediately.

'Yes, that's me,' I said clearly.

It was the postman offering me a large brown envelope. He said, 'This is for you. Would you sign for me please?'

I took it from him, wondering what it held, with its underlined capital letters across the front. I signed for it and quickly opened the door to get inside. I had been waiting for a few years for the documents to tell me I could stay in the UK, so quickly I shot up the stairs. A mixture of excitement and nerves caused my hands to shake as impatiently I tore open the envelope and slid the letter out.

There it was, in black and white, just what I had been waiting for. The long-awaited decision had finally been made. It said baldly: 'You have been granted indefinite leave to remain in the

United Kingdom.' I let out a squeal of happiness. It took a very long time and effort, with Sheila, Meg and Track having to drive back and forth to court hearings in Manchester or Liverpool, battling for my documents. If there was anyone to call first and spread the good news, they were the first.

We celebrated with a few drinks relieved as we reflected on the turmoil that had engulfed my life over the last few years. I felt very fortunate; maybe after such a rocky start my life in England had jumped onto the right tracks. Now I was able to make my plans for our future.

So, now the time had come for us to apply for our first Albanian passports before applying for British citizenship. After getting the Albanian passport and to be awarded British citizenship, I had to take an exam where the questions were based on official material taken from the *Life in the UK Test Book*. Later in the year I passed my exam and I got my first British passport.

Finally, we had everything we needed. I could not wait to go back to my homeland after seven years of waiting to see my family and being apart from them for such a long time. It would be the first time in a long time that I would finally be able to go back to Albania and feel the strength of my upbringing, putting this strong woman back in control of her own destiny again. I knew I didn't associate Albania with fear or hostility anymore, instead I felt thrilled and free.

The tickets were booked and we were ready for our first trip back to Albania. We arrived at a bustling Heathrow airport. In my hands I held our passports with our real names. It felt good. It was our real identity. No pretending to be someone else, no fear of rejection and certainly no one would take them from us. No sitting in the dark forest dictated to by the traffickers or threats to jump on the back of lorries fearing for our life in the middle of the English Channel. There was just only one plane straight to Albania. I looked at Enea and Hope's faces. They looked anxious. They had not been in an airport since we made the horrific journey to England. All they ever knew about travelling overseas was scary and fearful, and it was so evident in their facial expression – the same ones that I saw when we left Albania – sheer panic of the unknown. I asked them to sit down for a minute and I opened their passport and said, 'You see here, it's your real name. Hope and Enea. Your own passports. No need to be frightened or concerned. Once in that plane we are arriving in Albania in three hours as safe as houses.' A joyful smile crossed their innocent faces and together we made our way to the gate.

The plane landed and as soon as the doors opened, I breathed in deeply with the smell of my homeland filling my nostrils. It felt so nostalgic. We collected the baggage and made our way out. The white doors opened, and I saw my emotional father standing in the middle, surrounded by my family's smiling faces and, surprisingly, some of my ex-husband's family too. I was completely overwhelmed, emotionally greeting everyone, with a special embrace for my father who rushed towards me, beaming. Outside it was almost as if I was surrounded by an entourage. We were ushered into my brother's car and everybody else got into their own cars.

We drove back through Tirana. Everything was so different. The old, damaged roads and the half-burnt down houses had been replaced with new ones. The homes had been transformed beyond belief. There were new roads under construction, and brand new buildings. It was a new way of life now. It was safe, and people were walking around with no fear. My country had been reborn and transformed again into the beautiful place it once was.

We arrived at the house that I built, where my ex-mother-in-law still lived. I could hardly see the front of the house as it was surrounded by the green, tall trees that had grown so much since I first planted them all those years ago. The palms had reached the roof of the house and they created a beautiful shadow that cascaded over its eaves. The lemon and orange trees were fully grown and the branches entwined together, creating a beautiful sight.

Our dogs, Lassie and Gina, ran and jumped straight up to us with their wagging tails, followed by my ex-mother-in-law who tearfully came forward and embraced us. We had an emotional chat reflecting on the past that left irreparable consequences in my children's life and mine too, the past that sadly left so many scars never to be healed. We didn't stay too long as we had a long journey ahead to my childhood city of Gjirokastra. We drove through the mountains and refreshed ourselves by the natural waterfall, I felt at home and fully complete, content and relaxed.

A big party with all the family was organized at my father's house. It was so special as I listened to my father's honourable words towards me, together with his blessings.

I was so grateful that once again we were all there together, holding each other and dancing together like old times. The party carried on until the morning light peeped from behind the mountain. There was so much love in that house that night, with so many things to celebrate. We had a fantastic time with all our family and friends, and before we knew it the two weeks had passed so fast, and our time to return to England had arrived.

But before we came back to England, I wanted to see face to face the man who had once shaken our hands and pledged us the safe journey that we nearly paid for with our lives. The man who took advantage of our situation, and others', and took millions and deceived us with his false promises. But he no longer lived. They had killed him in revenge barbarically after a family of five tragically lost their lives, drowned in the Adriatic Sea on their clandestine journey to Italy.

A shiver went through my body reminding me how lucky we were to be alive. After so many tragedies that had happened to so many families, I hoped people would think twice before they fell prey to fraudsters and false promises.

CHAPTER 25

Nice men don't come around too often

Unforgettable proposal

I woke up to steady rain splashing across my window that early Sunday morning in July. I sat there sipping my espresso until the last drops of rain had fallen. The clouds started to dissipate and the sky began to show its blue colours. I opened the window and could detect that the air was perfumed by the beautiful aroma of the rose gardens mixed with a scent of lilies that created the most vibrant blooms. The fresh air started to clear my head which was heavy from too many brandies I had had the night before. We'd been out for Linda's birthday – Hope's dancing teacher who had very quickly become one of my closest friends. She was a tall lady with a lovely figure, short dark hair, and a quiet personality. We would often joke and call her Miss Linda – the name all the kids would call her.

We gelled as soon as we met as we both liked going out sometimes for a glass or two, but mostly dancing. Once we had a chance to be on the dance floor that was it, we never left until our feet hurt like we'd been walking on fire. It was a special friendship which led to me meeting my future husband, Neil. Linda's partner, Paul, had been best friends with Neil for donkey's years, and on a night out we would often see them and sometimes have a glass of wine and exchange a few words. He was a medium-sized, very handsome man, with brown hair and hazel-coloured eyes.

That particular Saturday night Lancaster was busy and so was our favourite place, The Litten Tree, a two-storey pub at the bottom end of the town that was packed to the rafters. People of our age would often go in there to sounds of a mashup of 80s and 90s music where the sound and rhythm would made it impossible for us to keep away from the dance floor. Over the thumping music that dominated the hall we laughed and chatted like friends that had known each other for an age, but I found myself unprepared when, out of the blue, Neil asked to take me on a date. 'Now, where did that come from?' I said, laughing. As I was nervous, I spluttered out the first thing that came to my mind. 'We've both had a lot to drink. Maybe another time, perhaps,' and embarrassed, quickly turned around, pretending to meet one of my friends. Indeed I was now free to decide about my future but after everything that had happened I had to be very cautious – setting myself a reminder of the past, that would never get repeated. Yet, the thing was that I really liked him. Almost as soon as our eyes crossed for the first time on the stairs in that same place, I had found it hard to get him out of my mind. Was this the start of something special? Now that life was becoming more settled and everything else was going smoothly, why shouldn't I? I deserved someone to make me feel special and love me unconditionally. As my grandma used to say, 'Nice men don't come around too often'. After saying our goodbyes at the end of that night, we never stopped texting each other. Finally, we decided to have a date. It was a walking date.

Monday morning, we both had trainers and jeans on and went for a walk on the beach. It was my idea as I thought it a good way to see exactly what he was like without alcohol interfering with our minds and to have a proper grownups talk.

I gathered my hair in a ponytail and poped it through the back of the baseball cap and as I put my rucksack over my shoulders I made my way across the road where Neil was waiting in his car.

It was late morning on a beautiful, warm, sunny day – a perfect day to drive to the Middleton Sands beach. Walking in the sunlight, accompanied by a nice man and with great conversation, I didn't realise the passing hours. Surprisingly, we didn't even feel our faces getting burnt from the hot sun of that beautiful Monday 11th July 2005. As we walked and talked along the beach it was like we had known each other for a very long time and we discovered many things about our lives. However, being from a different country and a different culture, there were a few things that I thought were important and that I wanted to lay on the line before we could go any further. Call me old fashioned, but as an Albanian woman and at a mature age, I wasn't going on a date with someone just for fun, but a serious relationship that hopefully, one day, would lead to commitment and marriage. I have children to look after too, and I wouldn't settle for anything less than a person who treats me and my children right. I stated clearly that my daughter, who was only nine at the time, should never be shouted at or reprimanded angrily.

So, after listening patiently, Neil smiled and said, 'I wouldn't settle for anything less, I have two precious sons, Neil and Lee, but I never had a daughter and it would be a privilege to have one.'

I couldn't have wished for a better answer. The more I listened to him, the more I thought about how fortunate I was to have found someone like him. He seemed to be a nice man, talking with a slow voice that could calm even a ferocious animal and that's what I needed above all else in my turbulent life – tranquillity and peace.

You would think that is way too much to ask on the first date. I agree. But that was me then.

By the late afternoon we drove to 'The Globe' in Overton for much-needed refreshment, sitting outside under the shade of the ancient trees. There and then we made a pact. If this relationship was going to work, then we would get married on the beach! Even though it was just our first day together, somehow we both knew and felt that special connection. The sense of mutual love was the first step onto the platform to take the train of our life together.

-o-

A few months passed and it was now time for Neil to meet my daughter. He had met her once before when he gave us a lift as we were walking back home from Hope's school, but that was about it. So, that weekend brought the three of us together for the first time with the pleasant company of each other and the wounderful smell of Albanian cooking when Neil and Hope talked comfortably together. It was very important to me that

Hope and Neil got along. If they hadn't, there could never be any sort of relationship between me and him. My daughter needed to feel comfortable and happy around him.

'So, what do you think? Do you like him?' I asked Hope sheepishly after he left.

'He is ok,' she replied, smiling.

'Does that mean he can come around again?' I asked eagerly.

'Yes,' she replied.

Neil came around a lot more often, building a great relationship with my daughter as she was growing up.

He often helped with her education, always speaking truthfully about life, what she did wrong without raising his voice at her, dealing with her teenage years calmly without trying to be too demanding and directing her to the right path for her in life. He took care of her as he had promised without forgetting my important precept about Hope – never to be shouted at or reprimanded angrily. This came back to bite me years later when I really wanted him to step up and say something to my stubborn teenage daughter when she wanted to go out in a short skirt. His answer? 'Rememeber those precept words on our first date on Middleton Beach?' I looked at him shocked. How had he remembered those words that I had already forgotten? It was a question that needed no answer. Without saying another word, shaking my head in frustration, I walked out of the bedroom as we say – like a horse without a saddle. It suited me well that he didn't want to spoil the relationship that he had built with Hope over the years. However, I often thought about what Enea's attitude towards him might be. He was living in London with his girlfriend Ina. She was a London girl, a pretty brunette with a beautiful smile and hazel eyes. With her gentle nature she was bringing to Enea exactly what was needed.

Often they would tell me to find someone, get married and be happy. But it felt different the way Enea vacillated backwards and forwards undecided in what he truly felt. Something deep inside him wanted his mum to be happy, but without involving another man, making me feel it was more what he felt he had to say to make me happy.

The best idea was to sit down with him and talk, but I was unsure how he would react. Reasonably anxiously, I sat down beside him and told him about Neil. As the words tumbled out of my mouth, I could see Enea's face almost crumble, at a loss, as if someone was taking his mother away from him. He was always very protective of me and I knew he was going to be cautious of anybody that was replacing his father.

Impatiently he went to meet the man who had won his mum's heart and have a few beers together. Surprisingly they seemed to be getting on reasonably well with each other. So, I was a little relieved. Enea warmed to him as he felt that Neil would not only look out for me but also my children. It felt fantastic to know that Neil was getting involved with my children in a positive way. It felt like he was helping me to take down the destructive wall that had been built.

But it was a different feeling meeting Neil's mum Ilonia. I was apprehensive of her reaction and possible rejection, being the opposite of what his mother might have wanted for her son. I was an Albanian, immigrant, single mother saving the pennies to pay for her children's shoes and clothes. That morning as our car pulled into the driveway, I saw an elderly woman with short grey hair and a tall frame. She rushed to open the front door and I was greeted by one of the warmest smiles I have ever seen. Her eyes were full of love as she embraced me and said, 'Hello dear, what's your name?'

'Yllka,' I replied nervously.

'Neil has told me all about you,' she replied cheerfully.

'Oh, I can explain,' I jokingly said as the words escaped out of my mouth nervously.

She smiled at my joke as she ushered me into the living room. There was something about this lovely lady that attracted my attention as soon as I met her. The reflection of her sincere smile, her simplicity and acceptance said it all from the very first moment I met her. Maybe it was that feeling of a warm motherly figure that had been missing my entire life. Perhaps right there in front of me, without me truly knowing it, I had found the mother I had always wanted and needed. It was the beginning of an unconditional friendship between her and myself which grew into a deep mother and daughter love.

'You have to meet the whole family,' she said. 'Maybe we can gather together for dinner, perhaps at the Lancaster House, they do a good roast over there.'

And without wasting any time the table was booked and on Saturday night they were all there. As we walked in, a middle-aged man at the table got up as soon as he saw us, started walking towards me, arms wide open, and said with a bright smile, 'Hi, I'm Paul, and this is my wife, Janet.'

Neil's brother Paul looked completely different to him. Paul was a man of medium height with lovely blue eyes, a beautiful smile, and a rich deep voice and very welcoming. His wife, Janet, was a medium-sized lady with beautiful wavy blonde hair and dark eyes, who was wearing a beautiful flowery dress with pearly jewellery. She had an extensive knowledge of life.

They were very understanding about our relationship as they were both on their second marriage. Paul had a daughter, Lisa, from his previous marriage, who was now married to Wayne, and Janet had a daughter, Sharon, who was married to Alex, and her son Alan was married to Hannah.

It was a wonderful time meeting them all and sitting at a table surrounded by another family that soon would be mine too. Years ago, who would have thought.

Paul and Janet would be able to go some way to filling the emptiness that my brothers' and sisters' absence had caused, allowing me to become their new 'sister'.

They made me feel that others viewed my life with intrigue, and certainly never judged me. It was a mutual respect, without prejudice and resentment. I never felt like a foreign girl around them, it never occurred to me that I didn't belong to the family. We were – The Thompsons.

I met Neil's two sons Neil and Lee after a while. They'd grown into lovely young men and they were not so different from their father's personality, calm and friendly. It has always been a sincere and respectful relationship between us all.

-o-

It was all happening so quickly.

It was around two years later when Neil and I bought our first house together in Lancaster. The house was on the other side of the beautiful River Lune, which divides the city in two, built on the very bottom of the steep road named Beaumont Street. Hope was carrying on studying at high school and I found a new job in a hairdressing salon in Lancaster. It was a small salon in the heart of the city in a very busy area. In the meantime, we were getting ready to go back to Albania, this time with Neil to meet my family for the first time.

A few days before travelling to Albania, we went to see Neil's mum.

Unfortunately Mum was in the early stages of dementia, and things weren't the same as before. As we got there, Mum approached me with a smile, and without waiting for me to sit down she took me to her bedroom. She opened her jewellery box, as she always did, and asked me to pick up any piece of jewellery I liked, and I always used to say, 'I'm not a jewellery person really. Maybe I'll choose one next time.'

This night, when she took me to her bedroom, she opened her jewellery box and surprisingly she picked this ring herself – a beautiful gold diamond and sapphire cluster ring and said, 'This is a very special family ring, and I want you to have it. Try it on.'

I looked at her hesitantly and said, 'But Mum, I'm not...'

'You have to try on this one,' she insisted. 'It means a lot to me.'

Without a second thought, I picked up the ring, and I put it on my middle finger.

'Oh no, not that one. This one,' she said, pointing at the wedding ring finger on the left hand.

I looked at her, confused, not understanding what she was trying to say. I took the ring off the middle finger and passed it on back to her.

Out of the blue she then asked, 'Do you not want to marry my son?'

With no time to say anything, Neil walked into the room, only to see Mum with the ring in her hand as if she was proposing.

'Oh Mum,' he said, embarrassed, 'I was going to—'

Confused, she interrupted him, 'Oh dear, I was supposed to give it to you, wasn't I?' She remembered and her face took on the appearance of the chid who has just been caught doing something wrong. I quickly hugged her, comforting that it was fine. For the first time we realized how much her dementia had deteriorated. The plan that they had made the week before, mother and son, was now all out in the open. It was her wish that her family engagement ring be passed to me when Neil proposed. But now she thought that she had spoiled this very special surprise.

A quick glance at each other and we burst into laugher to displace the embarrassment and make Mum feel at ease. She laughed too.

'May I finish the proposal?' Neil said cheerfully.

'Oh, you must, my dear son,' Mum replied while she passed the ring to him.

He looked at me, laughed, and shrugged his shoulders and with the ring in his hand he asked, 'Do you think that you could spend the rest of your life with me?'

'I'll try and see where that takes me,' I replied with a giggle.

'Ah,' he sighed with relief. 'In that case, this belongs to you.'

I felt like this wasn't real. In front of me was the man who loved and accepted me for who I was, asking me to spend the rest of my life with him without demands or preconditions.

The cork of the champagne bottle was popped, the glasses were raised and the words of this special lady whom I was proud to have called her mum remain in my memory to this day. 'I'm blessed to finally have a daughter that I never had,' she said happily.

'And I'm blessed with a mother that I always wanted,' I replied.

She had no idea how much those special words meant to me. I was so happy. I was lucky enough to get two birds with one stone as they say. I was getting a great fiancé as well as the mother that I had always longed for. I felt a range of emotions, every single one of them laced with feelings of joy. I was one lucky girl. I felt loved and wanted.

My whole life was changing, and I was going in a direction that I never thought I would ever be going in again. I was living those moments of happiness.

CHAPTER 26

The blessing

We had just taken our suitcases out the front when the taxi arrived.

'Just in time,' Neil said. The taxi driver greeted us and helped Neil to place the luggage in the boot and we were ready to set off for the airport. We were going to Albania!

Not only was this the first time for Neil to visit Albania but by chance he was also going to be introduced to my whole family who luckily were going to be gathered together at the wedding of my niece Enkelejda. Excitement mixed together with nervousness seemed apparent on Neil's face as he was visiting the country that I had told him about and the troubles and stigma of the past communist regime. But that wasn't his main worry. His main concern was facing my father, the man whom he had heard so much about and especially of his opinion about Englishmen.

Growing up as a communist, my father always believed his culture ruled and he had no good opinion about marriage in the West, which he believed was different from marriage in *his* culture.

We took the British Airways flight which arrived in Tirana in under four hours and we were picked up by my brother Bushi .

Longing hugs and joy, introducing for the first time, the brothers-in-law-to-be, overjoyed at their presence, we made our way towards the car. Bushi insisted that Neil sat in the front seat as a sign of respect. Removing his jacket, Bushi suddenly revealed his gun that was holstered around his waist. He took it out of the holster and placed it in a compartment between the passenger and driver's seat. He worked as a bodyguard and chauffeur for the Mayor of the city and he was always armed.

Neil looked at him shocked, moving back.

'Don't worry,' Bushi said while patting Neil on his shoulder, immediately realising his reaction. 'I'm just taking the gun out my body holster because otherwise I can't get my seatbelt on,' he carried on.

'Okay,' Neil replied, letting out a sigh of relief as he laughed. That laughter continued throughout the whole journey which made Neil feel more comfortable and relaxed. Within no time we arrived at my sister Lindita's house where all the family were gathered together for the pre-wedding party. Not long after greeting everyone my father asked Neil and I to sit on the veranda and asked me to translate as he spoke, asking him questions. This time he was going to make sure that he had done all the checks about Neil and his family. It was like we were at the police station being interrogated for hours. I looked at Neil, who had sweat droplets forming on his forehead, and he appeared to be very flustered. Finally it was over when my sister interrupted, bringing us some cold drinks.

I sighed with relief.

'We need a raki to celebrate, not lemonade,' Dad said quickly. Then he poured the raki into two little shot glasses, showing

Neil how to link hands with each other and how to drink it in one gulp and said, 'You have my blessing, and I wish you a wonderful future together.'

Neil took it all in, and then his face said it all as he downed the raki.

'Uhhhh!' he gasped, taking a deep breath. 'It's certainly strong!'

'Actually, the Englishman's OK,' my dad said with a wink. 'I like him.'

He beckoned Neil to follow him into the garden. As they sat there, he pointed out the direction of other countries that bordered Albania.

'To the north is Montenegro; north-east Kosovo; east is Macedonia; to the south-east-south is Greece and to the other side is Italy, across the water.'

Neil shook his head slowly, astonished at everything my dad was saying. I looked at them, amazed at how they were getting along, having a conversation together without speaking each other's language.

The day of Enkelejda's and Ardian's wedding came which was grand and spectacular with over 100 people invited. That's the perk of being a big close-knit family. It was well planned, well designed and set up wonderfully. *This* was the perfect moment for Neil to meet the whole family.

It was very hot so as soon as we took our seats at the beautifully dressed round tables, Neil took one of the cold beers from the table and drank it in one go. Then he asked the waitress, 'Can I have another please?' pointing at his empty bottle while he was trying to get the money out of his pocket.

'What are you doing?' I asked.

'Getting the money to pay for the beer,' he said.

'You don't pay for your beer at Albanian weddings. It is free,' I said with an indulgent smile.

'In that case, two beers then please, boy !' he said with a glint in his eye.

It was obvious that he was getting on so well with my whole family and enjoying every moment. It was a wonderful evening. Seeing Neil and Hope side by side with arms linked, dancing in the Albanian tradition along with my siblings, filled my heart with joy. It couldn't get any better. What a great feeling – he'd got the blessing from my dad, met my family, and now had the time to relax and perhaps travel through the mountains to the seaside.

It was late morning when we set off driving towards the south, to my town of Gjirokastra. We had been travelling for a few hours now when we made our first stop at the side of a little restaurant. It was built on the top of a naturally clear waterfall that passed through huge rocky outcrops under a bridge until it cascaded into the green water of the stunning and beautifully wild Vjosa River which then hurried through wonderful canyons and drained into the Adriatic Sea.

As we were having a drink on the restaurant's veranda under the shade of an old tree, we heard a whistle. We turned around and saw a middle-aged chap waving at Bushi.

'Wait here,' Bushi said. 'I won't be long.'

We watched him as he walked to the other side of the road where there was a pond full of live fish. He chatted to the fisherman for a while and chose some fish. The man scooped them up in a net, struck them, cleaned them, and handed them over to my brother.

'*You* are going to enjoy this, this is right up your street,' Bushi said, pointing at Neil.

'I don't eat fish,' Neil replied.

'What do you mean, you don't eat fish?' Bushi said, trying to hide his surprise behind a smile. 'You're English. Is it not the English's favourite food, fish and chips?'

'Yes, it is, but we put it in batter and then fry it. We don't just barbecue the fish,' Neil replied.

'What about chicken?' Bushi asked.

'I'm fine with that,' Neil replied.

'Chicken it is then,' and without wasting any time Bushi called one of his acquaintances who kept chickens, on the outskirts of the city, and ordered one of them to be slaughtered and roasted just for Neil.

In less than an hour we arrived. As soon as I could see the castle peeking through the mountains in the distance, I knew I was home – my city Gjirokaster. The fish was put out for barbecue and Neil's little chicken arrived and in no time at all everything else was ready for another great evening under the warm breeze that wafted down to us from the mountains.

The next morning, the first thing on my agenda was to visit my mother's grave. I put my mum's favourite flowers on the marble white gravestone – beautiful fresh lilies – and I knelt next to the rosemary plants growing around the head of her grave, feeling spiritual, at peace and a calmness in my heart. Getting older didn't stop my old habit of taking a few sprigs of rosemary that always gave me a feeling of her presence.

As was planned the next day we set off with my brother Bushi and his family to the coast where our beach holiday was booked in the little village of Borsh near Saranda. It was another long drive through the mountains before we reached the beach. The beauty of the Albanian countryside has no limits. On the way we had taken a pit stop at the Blue Eye, a deep blue lake that looks like a sapphire-blue eye fed by an underground spring and shaded by centuries-old oak trees. We then drove through the southern coast and we left behind the beautiful little town of Saranda, reaching the Ionian Sea looking over to the Island of Corfu. It was a city with 2000 years of history, rich in cultural and archaeological heritage, that was covered by the bunkers that looked like giant mushrooms on the seashore built in communist times. We reached the top of a steep hill, turned a corner, and suddenly a magical vista opened up to us. An endless azure blue sea drew our eyes to the beautiful little village where we were going to stay. By the side of the road, we were captivated by another gloriously cascading waterfall, and under the shade of the old trees we found a bar made from curved wood from where we could see water running under the restaurant. What a magnificent sight.

We stopped, relaxed, and had a drink at the bar. The owner of the bar, an old man of around 80 years of age, approached us and we started to chat together. He spoke good English.

'Where do you come from?' he asked.

'From England,' Neil replied.

'Have you been here before?' the old man asked again.

'No, this is my first time,' Neil said.

'Do you know about the village legend?' the old man offered as he brought his chair forward, without invitation, shook his head slightly, and with whispered words he muttered mysteriously: 'The legend has been passed by word of mouth from the elders of the village. A very long time ago, a boat docked out of the blue and dropped off an English boy. The village at the time only had one house. The only family that lived in the village took care of and raised the English boy and eventually married him to one of their daughters. They had six sons. The boys grew up, created their families, and built their own houses.

'As time passed, the village population multiplied and there were more families, and more houses were built. The six neighbourhoods of the village were named after the six sons. I'm from the same origin as them, so that means I have English blood in my veins,' he said, smiling proudly while putting his hand around Neil's shoulder.

'You never know,' Neil replied, laughing as we said our goodbyes to the friendly man, 'we might be related.'

Finally, we arrived and in less than an hour we were resting on the marvellous sandy and rocky beach beside the crystal blue water, under reed umbrellas. The slight breeze wafted the aroma of oregano from the mountains to caress our senses. And on the horizon, just a few miles away, we could see the sun was setting behind the Island of Corfu.

CHAPTER 27

The Beach Wedding

Tying the Knot

Happy, and blessed by both families, back home in England we had to choose a date and get married somewhere near the seaside – since the day we met we had promised each other that if the relationship worked out, we would get married on a beach. Yet, we couldn't take any chances with the English weather. So we decided to get married somewhere abroad in a hot country.

As luck would have it, my sister's husband's nephew, Niko, who lived on the beautiful Island of Zante in Greece, was working as a chef in one of the hotels in Tsilivi. I had known him from a very young age when I used to stay at my sister's house. My brother-in-law's siblings had their houses built near each other and their children were of similar age to mine. We used to play together and sometimes share meals and eat together.

Niko told us that lots of people got married on the island and suggested that it would be a great venue for us. So, we decided we would get married on the island and after talking to the wedding organizer in Tsilivi, we set the date for 2nd June 2008.

It was the second wedding for the both of us so we didn't want anything big, just a small ceremony, as long as it was on the beach. Niko and his wife, Moza, who lived there already, were going to be our witnesses, and one of his daughters, Nertila, would be a bridesmaid with Hope, and his younger daughter, Marina, would be a flower girl. We had a small budget so before we set off to Greece I hit the sales. With great luck, I found a champagne-coloured long evening gown on sale which I had to adjust. Then I found two dresses, one light blue and one lilac, for the bridesmaids. I was elated with my purchases, because I had always believed that you didn't have to buy an expensive dress to look nice. They were perfect dresses for a beach wedding – simple, floaty, and elegant. Then to enhance the look of the beach wedding, we were to put flowers in our hair to match the theme.

Linda's mum, Pauline, was very good at craft making and as a wedding present she made all the flowers for our hair and the bouquet to match our dresses. My best friend, Sheila, made us a two-tier wedding cake, and everything had come together for the big day. After excitedly and patiently waiting, the day finally came to fly out to Zante for our special day.

The flights took less than four hours and from there we were transferred by bus to the hotel where Niko was waiting. As always, a smiling and welcoming chap as he is, he greeted us with open arms and joy and he showed us to our apartment on the first floor of the hotel building.

-o-

In the hot summer of 2008, the morning of 2nd June had finally arrived. I opened the sliding balcony door of our apartment that looked out to the distance. The sparkling blue Ionian sea stretched out to the distant horizon and the golden light of the sun glistened on the perfectly calm water. The warmth of its brilliant rays mixing with the scent of the pink bougainvillea growing in abundance and vitality, spreading itself and climbing up the wall to the balcony and forming a luscious arched crown. The magical birdsong relaxed my soul and mind, calmly painting smiles upon my face and heart. A little caramel coloured butterfly with black spots on its wings, flitted up and down the bougainvillea like it was dancing a classy old waltz, changing from one arm to another.

It was so serene and tranquil. I could have stayed there and relaxed all day, but I had to get myself ready for our big day, do my hair and make-up and make myself beautiful. That morning there was a power cut, with no electricity from the main power station and it would not be on till late afternoon we were informed by the receptionist. With less than two hours to get ready I quickly towel-dried my hair and rushed to the balcony, trying to dry under the hot sun. Being a sunny hot day had its advantages.

For the beach wedding, my aim was to look as natural as possible. Hope and Nertila, Niko's daughter, were trying to take care of each other whilst getting ready.

Marina, Niko's little daughter, with his wife Moza had just walked in with a little white basket full of petals.

'Are you ready to go?' Moza asked. 'Niko is waiting in the car outside.'

A quick glance at each other making sure of our appearance and we made our way out to the car. In less than five minutes we had arrived at the Alexandra Hotel, a beautiful white building at the top of a hill, with arched windows looking down onto the stunning view of Tsilivi beach where our wedding was going to take place. It was a perfect spot under a beautiful arch of fresh flowers.

As I took my place on the grand staircase leading down to the breath-taking beach, I breathed in deeply – the sea air touching my soul. The stairs had a long red carpet laid on them all the way to the bottom. Ready to walk down the aisle, I looked over at the stunning view of the Ionian Sea which was perfectly calm and reflecting like a mirror; the bright blue sky overhead seemed to stretch forever. A beautiful Greek-inspired melody was played by a violinist and pianist.

I started walking down the stairs, my long champagne dress floating in the sea breeze. I was followed by my two beautiful bridesmaids Hope and Nertila and the flower girl Martina. I looked down at the beach and saw my husband-to-be, Neil, standing up waiting under the colourful arch of flowers. He looked so handsome in his classic blue pinstripe suit and white shirt with a pink rose clipped to it, and a champagne tie to match my dress. I reached the last step and walked towards him.

Our hands entwined as we began our vows in front of the man who had been ordained to marry us, and Niko's family. We were just seven ordinary people on that endless, beautiful Tsilivi beach where happiness caressed us all. The rings exchanged and finally we became Mr and Mrs Thompson.

The noise of popping champagne corks and the chinking of raised champagne flutes was mixed with the lapping waves that gently washed up on the rocky shoreline.

We moved away from the shore, splashed by the sea waves breaking on the rocks and caressed by the breeze. The sun started to dip behind the sea, creating a beautifully bronzed horizon. It was the most perfect romantic day.

The wonderful celebration with just the seven of us lasted into the late hours as we sat on the terrace and listened to the melody of the Greek Suzuki mixed with the soft noise of the waves lapping at the beach. Back to the hotel as a married couple.

It was 5 am when the light, shining through the window onto my face, woke us up.

We were both awake, so decided to walk and explore the island. We sneaked out, laughing quietly, trying not to disturb anyone, especially the receptionist who was asleep in his chair.

We walked along the sandy beach and followed the track towards the hill surrounded by olive and lemon trees, and then walked to the few houses at the very top. It looked very quiet, as if nobody lived there.

Untouched apricots and other fruits were hanging heavily, nearly touching the floor in the tree branches outside the garden wall.

We started to collect them, putting them inside our tee-shirts like little naughty kids stealing the fruits from a neighbour's garden; as we laughed excitedly. Eventually, we sat down under the olive tree on the top of the hill, and, taking a big palm leaf and laying it on the floor with all the fruits on top of it, we took our first breakfast as a married couple surrounded by the beauty of the Island of Zakynthos.

The sun rose slowly above the horizon and its rays started to awaken the glorious azure sky. The sea breeze caressed our faces, whispering and filling our hearts with contentment and happiness.

At around 9 o'clock, we made our away back to the hotel. By this time the receptionist was in place and was trying to organize the schedules of the day ahead. He looked at us, surprised and said, 'Have you been sleeping outside?'

'Yeah, we were locked out of our room and nobody was at reception to help us,' Neil replied with a grin.

He looked at Neil shocked, guilt crossed his face.

'Relax, I'm only joking,' Neil laughed.

'Ah!' the receptionist gasped in relief, stabbing a finger at us as he laughed cheerfully. 'You got me there for a second.'

-o-

After a fantastic holiday, we went back home to England and gathered family and friends in our house to celebrate our marriage. It was a new beginning, a fresh new chapter in my life.

I was incredibly happy, looking forward to my new life as Mrs Thompson. I looked at Neil and thought about all the twists and turns that had got me to this wonderful and magical moment. I felt lucky despite what may have happened in the past. I was ready to embark on a lifelong journey with a better future, this time with a man whom I really loved and adored. This marriage was not a forced marriage and neither was it a marriage through tears and pain. It was a marriage of pure love that anchored two hearts together. I felt a spiritual serenity, without fear of the darkness, without worry of the unknown, without drama and boredom. It was a deep love where no clouds could block the warmth as the sun shone through to the heart. It was eternal.

My heart was full at the thought of being part of a wonderful new family.

My life was complete. I had my beautiful children, a husband who loved me, the warmth of a mother that I had always craved and a family that treated me with respect and dignity. That's what I had envisioned for my life; not money, not posh cars or big houses, just the love and normality that had slowly unfolded into my life at last.

CHAPTER 28

Mum

Dementia

I used to wait impatiently and excitedly for Tuesdays, not just because it was my long-awaited day off but because I had the chance to spend it with Neil's mum – *my* mum. That's what I would call her both to her and to my friends. Every time I would talk about her I would beam with pride and it filled my heart with joy that finally I had found someone I could again love enough to call Mum. It was something I did not take lightly as the last time the word passed darkly through my lips was in January 1972. The feeling of closeness and love that I longed for for years; those hugs, that warmth and a smile that only mothers can give – I finally had it. And to make it even better, she was the best mother-in-law that anyone could wish for. Since the first day that we had met there was an instant, special connection. There was something about this lady that resonated in me as soon as I met her, welcoming me with love and simplicity as if we had known each other forever. It led up to very special friendship, something that you can't buy or sell, friendship that will be part of our onward lives, something real.

It was an early afternoon on a cold autumn day towards the end of October, when the golden-brown leaves were cascading from the half-naked trees onto the frost-bitten ground, creating a colourful mosaic carpet. Even though it was sunny, the cool air was blowing from the North. I wrapped myself up warm, took the bouquet of fresh carnations (Mum's favourite flower) and made my way to the bus station. It was three or four bus stops to Mum's house, so I got there in no time.

As always, she was waiting patiently by the window, ready as usual with her beige coat on. Her happy face glowed as she saw me, and she waved eagerly, rushing to the main door in a warm embrace.

She took the carnations to put them in water and we made our away out.

We used to go and have lunch at the William Mitchell pub that was only 200-300 yards away from her house. While I was walking arm in arm with her she patted my hand gently, often reminding me to keep my posture perfectly straight as she always did, walking like a soldier on parade. Her back would be so straight that if you looked at her from behind, you would never have guessed that she was an eighty-year-old lady. She stood tall and slim with her immaculate iron-grey hair that was set and blow-dried every week at the hairdresser's.

As soon as we arrived at the pub, we would sit down at the same table by the front window. As usual she pulled the chair out for me and took my coat. Then I did the same for her, as we teasingly laughed together. We ordered our shandies as usual and the food that we always used to choose from the chef's daily specials written on the chalk blackboard. 'It might be fresher than the rest,' she used to say with a wink.

Over the meal and drink, we would chat for hours, tell each other all the gossip of the previous week and try not to laugh too loudly. The time had gone so fast, she would call the waiters for the bill. This was something that she categorically refused to allow me to do, even though I always tried to insist.

'Be a good girl and accept that I will always pay, and that's the end of it,' she ordered, suggesting that it would always be so. 'When all is said and done, I'm your mum and mothers always pay for their daughters.'

Now how could you argue with that? It wasn't about paying the bill or the money, but it was the way she would address me and say my name; the way she talked to me so gently and treated me without pretending or trying too hard. It truly made me feel like I was accepted as if I was her real daughter.

After dinner we would get back to the house when she used to take me to her drawer full of glamorous jewellery. Every time without fail, she would ask me to take anything I liked. I would tell her time and again that I wasn't a person that would often wear jewellery and that it would just be wasted on me (except for the engagement ring) and she would say, 'Well, they are always here if you change your mind. They're all yours.'

I would smile and hug her as a gesture of utmost appreciation. Then she would point to the top of her wardrobe that was full of tins of biscuits and chocolates and ask me to choose some. You didn't have to ask me twice! I wouldn't say no to chocolates or biscuits, stretching my neck upwards, and looking eagerly at which one to choose; just like a little kid with a Cheshire Cat grin when they see chocolates.

To top off a wonderful day we would look over the family album with a cup of hot tea in our hands. Her husband (Neil's dad) who appeared in so many of the images always had a warm and charming smile. She used to say, 'Oh, I miss him,' while caressing the photos with her fingers as tears filled her eyes. You could see she loved him dearly. Then she would look at me and raise a wrinkled hand to my hair to stroke it softly and say, 'He would have loved to meet you, sweetheart.'

She would talk endlessly about him and the family's story over and over again due to her dementia that was getting worse every day. Before dark I would say my goodbyes over her special hugs and promise her that Sunday would come soon, and it would be a family day at our house for Sunday lunch that was deliciously prepared and made by Neil. But she wouldn't stay too long. Soon after dinner she used to have a cup of tea quickly and say, 'I'm off. It's your only day off to spend together and you need some time for yourselves.' Even though we would reassure her that we spent lots of time together so she could stay as long as she wanted, she wouldn't hear of it. Instead she would get up, put her coat on and wait for Neil to get his car keys.

So, I would see her two days per week and Neil would see her every morning without fail. He would get her the newspaper, make her a cup of tea and spend an hour or two with her before he set off for work. Then Paul and Janet would visit her most late afternoons. Between these times she would go to the hairdresser for a blow dry on Fridays only as soon as she got home, she would forget that she had just had her hair done and go back there again. It was the same when she used to call in at the local butcher's to buy fresh slices of ham. Not even one hour had passed and she would go back and they would sell the ham again to her without giving it too much thought. When Neil used to visit her in the morning, he used to find packs of ham in the fridge to feed a family of ten. This situation forced him to have a word with the butcher's. Worse than that, however, was when she forgot the gas fire was on. If Neil hadn't gone to visit her that particular evening, the house with her inside would have been set alight. Consequently, we all used to try to pay careful attention on each visit because her dementia was getting worse to the point that it was causing things to happen that were a risk to her life.

The sons took her to see the doctor, and we decided she needed more care, perhaps a daily visit from the carers who would help her and spend time with her. It would put everybody's mind at ease knowing that she was safe. But Mum didn't like the carers, they invaded her privacy, as she used to say. It wasn't surprising and certainly wasn't easy for an independent woman like her.

The summer approached and we were going on holiday to Albania that was booked from the previous year. Leaving Mum with just a carer wasn't an option so we decided to move her to a private home for two weeks until we returned.

'I don't want to go,' she demanded.

'It's just for two weeks, Mum,' Neil replied. 'We can't leave you alone in the house. It's for your own good.'

She looked at me and asked, 'Do you promise me that you will bring me back home after you come back from your holidays?'

'I promise, Mum,' I replied. We said our goodbyes the next morning before we set off to the airport.

Only one week had passed before Neil got a phone call from the doctor in England. We were sunbathing at the seaside in Borsh, Albania.

'Your mum is getting worse and it is far too dangerous for her to return home,' the doctor advised. Under Neil's sunglasses the tears cascaded down his face. I had never seen him like that before.

'This can't be allowed to happen,' I insisted. 'I will leave my job and take care of her – I promised her that we would bring her back home when we returned to England and I'm keeping my promise. We can't do that to Mum.'

'I know you did, but we have to do what the doctor said is best for our mum.'

It felt like the end of the world for me. Her pleading look that morning we left stayed before my eyes. Travelling back to England, worried by the decision taken by the doctors, I could not help thinking how I was going to face her, to tell her that we could not take her back home. How could I? What was I supposed to say? Would she understand me? I was just enjoying having a mum around and what happens? As soon as we arrived home we eagerly rushed to see Mum at the private home. She was waiting at the window with her handbag in her hands. As soon as she saw us her face brightened with a smile, and she opened her arms and embraced us longingly. 'Oh, I thought you were going to leave me here,' she said, relief etched on her face. 'I'm so glad you've came back. Let's go.'

'Let's just sit-down first and have a drink, Mum,' Neil said.

She sat down edgily, not letting go of her handbag, impatient to get out of there. As we sat next to her, our minds clouded with worry. 'Well, come on, finish your drink and let's get out of here,' she said impatiently.

Neil moved close to her, holding her trembling hands and looking at her with pain and said, 'I'm sorry, Mum, the doctor won't let us take you back home.'

'What? Why? You promised me. How could you?' she said softly through trembling lips, as tears rolled down her wrinkled face. She got up, shocked.

I embraced her tightly. 'I know we did, Mum. I'm sorry, but the doctors have the power over us. They won't let us bring you home. I would if I could – I swear.'

Suddenly she stopped talking, tearfully she looked at me again, rested her hand, bowed and kissed my forehead. We stayed there for a while but she never said another word. It was heartbreaking. Walking away from her that day was painful. Her sad face at the window waving to us while the car slid away, never left my memory. It was like a vivid nightmare.

We visited her every Sunday and I couldn't wait for her hugs and the love she so effortlessly gave me. But most of the time she couldn't remember our names or who we were, while she was sitting on the blue chair, confused and fatigued. Due to her progressive dementia getting worse, she was transferred to another nursing home, then cancer spread and she began to deteriorate more from day to day. Her arms and legs became skin and bone, and there was nothing left on her anymore. It was painful seeing her in that state; so frail, so not her.

-o-

May came and with it, her last few days. She lay helplessly in the nursing home bed with her hazy, discoloured eyes staring, confused, at the white ceiling. She was too far gone to understand who was coming in and out of her room as if she was in another world. I kept wondering what she might be thinking, what she could be feeling, but I couldn't understand it. But I knew she felt our presence coming into the room when suddenly she rolled her eyes randomly towards me. The left side of her mouth curved up a little almost like a soft half-smile. She looked at me; her eyes spoke more than a thousand words. I shuffled to her bedside. Her face had shrivelled, her skin looked so fragile. The red cheeks, that once made her glow from inside, had turned a pale grey colour and her beautiful chestnut coloured eyes had diminished into a ghostly white and her soft warm smile was nowhere to be seen.

Her breathing had deteriorated as her lungs could no longer support her fragile life. Her chest struggled to rise beneath the sheets as her tired heartbeats stubbornly started to slow down. Her once rosy and soft lips were now dry and chapped from her constant temperature. I took the little pink sponge from the box that was on her bedside, put it in water and wet her lips. She held out her gnarled, powerless hand and held onto mine as if to say thank you. Then her eyes glazed over again, staring at the ceiling once more.

On one early morning in May 2012, she came into my dream. Suddenly I saw her in our bedroom, sitting on the end of our bed, smiling. Shocked, I nudged Neil next to me in bed. 'Look, Mum is here,' I said, surprised.

Before Neil could awake properly from his sleep and was able to turn his head, my dream was interrupted by the piercing ring of the telephone.

'You have to come urgently now,' the nurse at the nursing home said. 'Your mum is fading fast.'

We got up and sped along Morecambe's back roads just so we could find her alive. Unfortunately, it wasn't to be. She had passed away before we could get there. It felt like a piece of my heart was taken away never to be replaced. Death had claimed her. I held onto her still warm but lifeless body, to see if she could even smile at me just for one more time, but her gentle smile was gone forever.

I held her hand in mine, but her hand didn't squeeze mine back as it used to. I stroked her silver hair and slid my arm around her neck but, of course, that drew no response. She looked like she was in a beautiful deep sleep, finally at blissful peace from the pain. That's why she approached me in my dream that morning – to say her last goodbye and to tell me she was no longer in pain. It was as if she knew that we wouldn't be able to make it in time.

Those special times that I treasured with her were now just a memory; a memory that I will keep in my heart forever. Unforgettable lady.

CHAPTER 29

Full Circle

I had just had a meeting with the city's Bay Radio who had come to finalise the details of the promotion for our new business that late morning. As I sat in my office designing some new posters, my gaze wandered over Lancaster Castle where the morning sunshine had thrown its first rays in the spring of 2010. Suddenly, the words of Maddie, a wise lady who I had met a year ago, leapt into my mind. The very first time I spoke to her, I was working as a manager at another hairdressing salon on Peddy Street. She was a lady of medium height with short dark hair and a warm smile.

'In less than a year you will be leaving this place,' she explained. 'I can see you standing in a three-floor building, and this time you will manage your very own business.'

'Ha! Yes, right. Of course, like that's going to happen to me!' I scoffed, not believing a word she had said and commenting to my friend how people are so naïve, wasting time with this psychic stuff. Yet, here I was, not quite a year later, sitting exactly where she said I would be, in the three-storey building, managing my own business, in partnership.

Goosebumps crawled over my body. What could I say! Quickly I stood up as if someone had pinched me, looking around to see if I could see or feel something strange. I don't know why. I was in shock. How could she possibly have known? I would never have believed it if someone had told me. Is this what they call a message from the universe? Maybe I unknowingly realised this in my dreams or it was already written? Did I need to go down this winding path to fulfil my destiny? Or maybe it is my ambition and focus, my hard work that I never gave myself credit for. Instead I dismissed it as being something that had to be done. Either that or it was the direction that was given to me as a little girl by my father: 'Mountain girl, you should not settle for something inferior that you might feel destiny has to offer. You should fight until you accomplish your dreams.' That is what I lived my life by.

And this three floor building is a hair and beauty business that's been here for over 40 years, before we took it over a month ago.

Believe it or not, I'm in the same building, the same place where I went for a hairdressing job interview a long time ago, where the owner of that company at that time told me that his clients wouldn't be happy to have their hair done by an Eastern European woman such as me. *That* had me in tears.

It was something that had followed me for so many years and had led me to believe that it would be hard for me to have a good future in this country. Now to my surprise I'm standing there as the owner of a business. What a turn-around!

Even though he had sold the hairdressing business to us, the previous owner still had a business in cosmetics at the other side of the building and he also spent time in his part of the shop as he had a few clients left who were still loyal to him.

I looked around again and a shiver passed through my body. I needed a drink. I left the office and made my way down to the cellar where the kitchen and laundry room were. The previous owner D was sitting down for a break, drinking coffee with a few staff in the staffroom. I greeted them, and as I put the kettle on to boil, I went to the tumble dryer in the next room. Just as I was trying to fold the towels back into the basket, I overheard him saying, 'Do you know, girls, that people from Eastern European countries are very hard-working – even more so than us.'

An ironic smile crossed my lips. Quickly I took the basket full of towels and returned to the staffroom. 'You've changed your tune, D,' I said.

'What do you mean?' he asked.

'Well, do you remember a few years ago, you had this Eastern European lady come for an interview?' I smiled.

He shook his head and looked confused, as he said, 'Erm, I'm not with you. What do you mean?'

'You didn't give her a job because you thought that your customers wouldn't want to have their hair done by a foreigner and especially one from Albania,' I carried on, trying to give him a clue to jog his memory.

His face dropped. The shock of that memory had suddenly hit him. Sarah, one of the girls, got straight up from the green chair, amazed, turned around, and asked, 'What? You never! Did you really, D?'

'Oh,' he said, with his posh voice. 'It must have been a misunderstanding. I would never say such a thing.'

'Well, sadly, you did,' I replied with a wry smile.

He shrugged his shoulders, as he squirmed. 'I can't remember,' he said, sipping the last of his coffee, as he made his way slowly upstairs.

After a few hours, as the day came to an end, I went upstairs to switch off the electricity and make sure that everything was left ready for the next day. Through the mirrors I saw him coming down the stairs from his office with his grey jacket on and a local newspaper under his arm, approaching slowly towards me.

'I must say, I do apologise if I offended you in any way,' he said quietly. Straight words in one sentence, no buts or excuses, it was genuine with positive intent.

Unprepared, I turned around and looking at him I smiled, quite surprised at his sudden words. 'No worries,' I replied, trying to make him feel at ease. 'Is in the past, it cannot be changed but can be accepted. Thank you.'

'That is very nice of you to say,' he replied as he started to make his way home. 'Many thanks and goodbye for now.'

For a second, I stood there in disbelief. Did he really just apologise to me? One of the most successful businessmen in town said those words to me and had apologised after he had said something that had haunted me for a long time? If I thought longer I would have asked as I wanted to know, what was the real reason that made him change his views regarding this topic. I guess people learn and do change, not just for the sake of humanity, to adapt to the world, but change their course, their beliefs and their mentality. Life goes on. I never mentioned those words again. I drew a line under it as we carried on working together and I learnt some valuable things from him. He was a hard-working man, you have to give him credit for that, and in some ways he reminded me of my father. I knew that he wouldn't have asked for me to be any different.

Due to D's serious diabetes, in the past he had been found collapsed from his low sugar levels. Since then very often I would check on him, taking him some biscuits and coffee to his office which was next door to ours. His second wife had passed away of cancer and later on he passed away too. One of the hairdressers that also cleaned his house, had found him in the morning in bed lifeless with his clothes all ironed on the chair next to his bed for the next day.

I went back to the office to take home my bag containing paperwork. Looking over at the window, I noticed that dark clouds were over the castle, moving and changing their shape and forms rapidly.

'Who knows what lies ahead in this new business adventure, eh?' I asked myself. It was too early to know. Like the river that runs its course, it would no doubt carry lots of rotten tree trunks, rocks and other obstacles that could not be controlled. So, for now, I had to grasp the present moment and follow the path that life had laid before me. And that was just the start.

This was the start of an unknown and unplanned chapter of my life whose path I couldn't foresee, drawing me carefully forward, and feeling the hope of a genuine future ahead, hope of a pure journey just like the purity of my soul.

Life has taught me many lessons that have helped me to become stronger, courageous, and the self-assured woman I am now. I haven't accomplished anything phenomenal but I have achieved something worthwhile that made me believe for the first time in my life, in my own worth and my own abilities. I never believed that anything good would happen to women like me who have gone through a traumatic childhood and abusive marriage, but I had survived because I refused to be defeated. I had fought for it, worked for it, and brought it to fruition by overcoming anything or anyone that had put obstacles in my way. And here I am, still standing. I am not rich and I do not live a luxurious life but I have my own home, I have a husband that adores me and loves me without prejudice. I have two beautiful children who have overcome their horrible past, built their own family and are blessed with the love and laughter of a child, and finally for me some peace. That's all I ever wanted. Was that too much to ask?

It was the year of 2010... To be continued...

ACKNOWLEDGEMENTS

I would never have thought of writing a book.

There was never a day missed when the conversation between friends didn't turn to my upbringing under the Albanian communist regime. Their curiosity led to questions that I often answered with my real life stories. They encouraged me to put pen to paper and turn it into a book. And that's how it all started. I'm not an academic writer, but the story has been written from my heart.

Writing this memoir was like a very long return journey to the dark path that I passed. It was like therapy. I found my strength. This gave me opportunity to reflect and revaluate the past and have a clear vision for the future.

I want to express my sincere appreciation to my best friend Sheila Henderson for being with me all along the journey of this book, unofficial editing, her great advice and her incredible support all the way.

My siblings who supplied their memories as well as their support. My sister-in-law Janet Thompson for her help and giving me the confidence to write this memoir.

I owe an incredible amount to my daughter for her patience, understanding and helping with structural editing of my book. The support of my son who provided some unforgettable moments and his fiancée for her prompt help when I needed it.

I would like to thank my editor Ruth Lunn for her incredible work and the entire staff at UK Book Publishing for their fantastic service.

Also, special thanks to my unofficial editor Frank English for his encouragement and wealth of knowledge.

And Edith Newby and Krystina Kellingley for their time and help.

Last but certainly not least my husband, Neil Thompson. Immensely the credit not just for this book but also the happy life I lead belongs to him.

Printed in Great Britain
by Amazon

23861913R00172